Christmas Cantata, Bringing True Happiness and Joy

It has already been 10 years since we first started the Christmas Cantata. The beautiful performances of the Gracias Choir which make the world more radiant and warm through music have now become our close friends. Countless people have through the Gracias Christmas Cantata shed their darkness and rejoiced.

The Gracias Choir went to the people in Kenya, where the people had been through terrible riots, to Haiti, with the devastation of the earthquake, and to the people of New Orleans who had lost their families through Hurricane Katrina. The Gracias Choir also reached the people of Las Vegas who were grieving from the 2017 shootings. The many people there were able to come out from the long tunnel of sadness through the pure and beautiful music of the Gracias Choir.

All of this joy and happiness shared all over the world was only possible through you, through your care and your support. Therefore, with a heart of appreciation we have prepared the book, *How I Became Free from Sin*, as a Christmas gift for you. I hope that you will be greatly blessed through this book.

Author of *How I Became Free from Sin*
Founder of Gracias Choir

Rev. Ock Soo Park

Published on July 10th, 2019

Author	Ock Soo Park
Chief Editor	Hyun Joo Cho, Min Hee Park
Book Editing	Sung Mi Jeong, Yang Mi Kim
Book Design	Hyun Jeong Kim
Cover Design	Ka Hee Lee
Production & Distribution	Tae Woo Lee
English Translation	Yeong Kook Park, Joseph Park, Terry Henderson

Publication	Good News Publications, Inc.
Publication Report	No. 2006-44
Address	Sinwol-ro 24-gil 8, Yangcheon-gu, Seoul, Republic of Korea
Tel	82-2-2690-8860
Email	edit@goodnews.kr

ISBN 978-89-6443-016-3   Printed in Republic of Korea

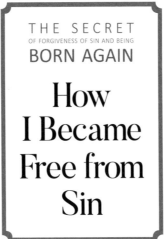

THE SECRET
OF FORGIVENESS OF SIN AND BEING
BORN AGAIN

How I Became Free from Sin

Rev. Ock Soo Park

In 1988, *The Secret of Forgiveness of Sin and Being Born Again*, was first introduced to the world by editing sermons from a Bible Crusade that was held at the Mugunghwa Hall in the Isabelle Girl's High School in Busan from October 6th to 10th in 1986. Beginning with 8,000 copies in its first edition, the book has now been published 119 times, and has acted as a messenger by spreading the gospel to countless people all over the world. After 30 years, *The Secret of Forgiveness of Sin and Being Born Again*, has been re-edited with a new name for a new generation as a 2017 revised edition.

There Was One Day That I Could Not Forget

I have been in church ever since I was young, but I was not free from sin. The longer I lived spiritual life the heavier my sins became, because I spent more time committing sin compared to realizing my sins before God and asking for forgiveness.

As I began to slowly read the Bible amidst such suffering, I was surprised to discover that the heart of God and the heart of Man were flowing in the Bible. God's heart and Man's heart were so different. Man belonged to sin and so he could not escape from the sin he had committed, but God sent Jesus to this world to die for Man's sin and thus preparing a way for us to be free from our sin. However, I discovered that people trusted their own thoughts and so they were still in sin.

The Bible tells us the path; the man with an infirmity for 38 years, the Samaritan woman, and Captain Naaman walked on when they were healed. The path was to break free from their thoughts and enter into the heart of God. Their lives then changed. In 1962, my life completely failed and I realized that I would perish if I lived conceding to my thoughts. While reading the Bible I learned that I needed to forsake my thoughts, and so I decided to throw away my feelings and experiences, and instead follow the Word of God.

From that point I began to see the Word of God. Before, I used to think I was a sinner because I had committed numerous sins. But in the Bible it was recorded, "The just shall live by faith." There is just people. In Genesis chapter 6 verse 9 it is written that Noah was a just man. Hosea chapter 14 verse 9 reads, "For the ways of the Lord are right, and the just shall walk in them: but the transgressors shall fall therein."

Reading these Words I responded, "If that is so how does one become righteous?" and began reading the Bible again, and amazingly God had already spoken that we were righteous. In Romans chapter 3 verse 24 and 1 Corinthians chapter 6 verse 11, I found that although we sinned, God called us righteous. "That's right, if God says I am righteous then I am righteous!" I moved from having a sinner's heart to having a righteous man's heart. It was an amazing feat. From then on Jesus entered my heart and the secrets hidden in the Bible began to unravel and I saw God working in my life.

God cannot work in sinners so He sent Jesus to this world to free us from our sins. God works for those who have met Jesus and have been cleansed of sin and justified. As a result of reading my sermons from the Bible Crusade in Busan that were made into a book, I hope that the hearts of the readers will not remain with the thought that "I am a sinner because

I sinned," but that they will discover the truth that, "Although I have sinned, I have been justified by the blood of Jesus." While reading this book I believe that God will be working and that the readers will be bestowed grace.

I hope that this book will allow readers to abandon their thoughts and relocate to the heart of God, so that each one of them will reach the holiness, righteousness and perfection of God to live a holy and glorious life.

October 10th, 2017
Good News Gangnam Church

Rev. **Ock Soo Park**

The Secret of the Forgiveness of Sin

Just as the rope that had once bound Samson broke free when the Almighty God empowered him, the chain of sin that had once restrained me broke free one day. On October 7th, 1962, the torturous days of struggle with sins finally ended by the power of the gospel of Jesus Christ our Lord. On that day when my sins became as white as snow and I was eternally liberated from the enslavement of sins, I could at last sing the hymn, "Happy day, happy day, When Jesus washed my sins away!"

After becoming a born again Christian, my life of unbearable misery began to change. The changes occurred first in my heart, then in my mode of life, then in my surroundings.

The greatest gift of God is the forgiveness of sin. We were separated from God because of sin. Subsequently, we had to wander in darkness suffering from guilt, pain, and fear, instead of relishing true satisfaction, happiness, and blessings of God. Now all these can revert with forgiveness of sins.

The unmistakable truth about the forgiveness of sin is hidden as secrets in the Bible. The story of Captain Naaman whose leprosy was cured was recorded specifically to teach us how our sins as vile as leprosy can be cleansed. Furthermore, the story of King David committing adultery with the wife of Uriah was recorded for the same purpose.

"Who is wise, and he shall understand these things? Prudent, and he shall know them? For the ways of the Lord are right, and the just shall walk in them: but the transgressors shall fall therein." (Hosea 14:9)

In 1986, I preached about the forgiveness of sin at a conference that was held at Mugunghwa auditorium in Busan. As always, I had felt the pain of many souls who were suffering from the problem of their unresolved sins and were earnestly longing for a solution. Through the conference, countless number of people received forgiveness of their sins and became born again Christians.

Just as the powerful work of the Holy Spirit had prevailed throughout the conference, inspiring and causing the lost souls to receive the forgiveness of sin in their hearts, I sincerely pray that the same great miracles can occur in the hearts of the readers of this book.

I give thanks to our God who has given my country and me the precious gospel of salvation.

March 25th, 1988
Good News Gangnam Church
Rev. Ock Soo Park

Contents

1

The Four Lepers

The Way of Salvation
Is Beyond Our Thoughts

There are many parts of the Word of God that do not fit our thoughts. When we accept the Word, we accept the parts that fit our thoughts and can be understood but have the heart that does not want to accept parts that are different from our thoughts. Even when listening to sermons, we filter the words by thinking, "That seems correct, but that doesn't make sense." Consequently, we are unable to see the work of God or receive salvation.

1

The Four Lepers

We will read from 2 Kings chapter 7, verses 1 to 9 in the Old Testament of the Bible.

Then Elisha said, Hear ye the word of the LORD; Thus saith the LORD, Tomorrow about this time shall a measure of fine flour be sold for a shekel, and two measures of barley for a shekel, in the gate of Samaria. Then a lord on whose hand the king leaned answered the man of God, and said, Behold, if the LORD would make windows in heaven, might this thing be? And he said, Behold, thou shalt see it with thine eyes, but shalt not eat thereof. And there were four leprous men at the entering in of the gate: and they said one to another, Why sit we here until we die? If we say, We will enter into the city, then the famine is in the city, and we shall die there: and if we sit still here, we die also. Now therefore come, and let us fall unto the host of the Syrians: if they save us alive, we shall live; and if they kill us, we shall but die. And they rose up in the twilight, to go unto the camp of the Syrians: and when they were come to the uttermost part of the camp of Syria, behold, there was no man there. For the LORD had made the host of the Syrians to hear a noise of chariots, and a noise of horses, even the noise of a great host: and they said one to another, Lo, the king of Israel hath hired against us the kings of the Hittites, and the kings of the Egyptians, to come upon us. Wherefore they arose and fled in the twilight, and left their tents, and their horses, and their asses, even the camp as it was, and fled for their life. And when these lepers came to the uttermost part of the camp, they went into one tent, and did eat and drink, and carried thence silver, and gold, and raiment, and went and hid it; and came again, and entered into another tent, and carried thence also, and went and hid it. Then they said one to another, We do not well: this day is a day of good tidings, and we hold our peace: if we tarry till the morning light, some mischief will come upon us: now therefore come, that we may go and tell the king's household.

How are you, dear citizens and beloved Christians of Busan? I'd like to tell you about how through this conference your sins can be washed as clean as snow. That which you've heard so much about; "Happy day, happy day, when Jesus washed my sins away! Though your sins be as scarlet, they shall be as white as snow." I would like to talk to you this week about this important matter, and exactly how it can happen to you. It is important that you listen with an open heart.

How, then, are you supposed to open your heart? A long time ago, I led a conference at Yeachun Airforce Base. I had preached the gospel to the airmen at that base. One evening, there was a reception. I was sitting down, having some refreshments, when a pilot's wife asked me, "Pastor, how do you open the door to your heart?" Ever since she asked me that question, it became harder for me to say, "Open the door to your hearts." Harder because people are unaware of how to open the door to their hearts.

In fact, this week, I want to have a conversation with you. There are a lot of you and only one of me, so we won't be able to have individual conversations. However, I hope that you'll ask me the questions that are in your heart. I will be asking you questions from time to time, as I speak to you, so please answer me quietly, in your heart. I cannot hear the voice in your heart, but I think I will know your response, just by looking at your faces.

I think it'll be difficult to have a heart to heart conversation with God tonight. Can we hear the voice of God? We cannot. So, please just open your hearts. Let's begin by having a conversation. Come forth with all the questions you have in your heart. All the frustrations in your heart that you've had during your spiritual life, all the things you don't know about, how to wash your sins away, how to become born again, and how you resolve the problems in your heart. Who doesn't know that praying is good for you? Who doesn't know that reading the Bible is good for you? Who sins because they don't know that sinning is bad? Nobody, but we cannot control ourselves the way we would like to.

For years, I've gone into prisons to preach the gospel. I never once told prisoners not to sin. No one commits sin because he doesn't know that committing sin is bad. I wanted to have them understand how to conquer sin through the Bible.

Loving folks, I'm not asking for any sort of determination from you. I am not asking you for a commitment. If you simply open your heart tonight, and if the Word of God comes in, if Jesus Christ takes dominion in your heart, you will no longer have to fight against sin. There will be no need for you to have to try to quit drinking and smoking. There will be no need for you to have to try not to steal and live a riotous life. Jesus Christ, who is in your heart, will help you overcome all of the sinfulness of your heart. He will free you from your lustful and filthy thoughts, from your loathing of others and from hatred. That is why I have come here, to introduce Jesus Christ to you.

People know and call out the name of Jesus Christ, but there are many whose heart is far from Jesus. Jesus Christ is close to you. No, He is right there at the door to your heart. Perhaps He is right there with His love for you, telling you to open the door to your heart. When you hear the Word, and if you receive these words into your heart, and say "Amen," I believe that Jesus Christ will work through those words.

Let me tell you a story. In Spain, there was a certain captain of a ship. This captain sailed from harbor to harbor and would come home only about once a month, or maybe once every three, or perhaps every sixth months. He had a son who he loved very much. Whenever he returned from a voyage, he would hug his son, kiss him, and give him presents. And when it was time for him to set sail again, the captain would be so sad that he had to leave his son behind.

He would leave, telling his son, "Just wait a while, I'll be back soon. Take care and be good to your mom." It became time for him to set sail again, after having returned home and having spent a short time with his son. This time, however, the son did not want to let his father go. So the father promised to take his son with him on his next trip out to sea.

Several months passed and the captain returned home. The son was so happy, he didn't know what to do because he was now finally allowed to go with his father. The father could not disappoint his son's expectation and decided to take him along. By then, the son was around 15 years old. The captain's wife was worried, but he comforted her saying, "Don't worry. It's okay. We're not going far this time, so I'll take him along." The night before going on the trip, the son was so filled with excitement and anticipation about sailing with his father that he could not sleep.

The father said to his son, "If we go out to sea, it's really lonely. All you see out there is the ocean and the sky. So bring all the toys you want to play with." The child brought drawing books and toys, and he also brought his pet monkey, which he played with like a friend. The ship blew its horn and set sail.

While the child was busy watching the waves and the seagulls, the ship was soon out at sea and there were no seagulls in sight, just the lonely sky and the sea. The captain and the sailors were busy and the child was playing in the cabin with his monkey. One day, the monkey stole the child's hat and ran away. The child chased after the monkey to get his hat back. The monkey sprinted to the cabin and onto the deck, running all over the place. Finally, the monkey climbed up the mast.

The boy thought, "Now I've got you!" and hurried up the mast after him. He would climb up a little, then the monkey would climb up a little more. He would climb a little more, and the monkey would go up a little higher. The child didn't realize how high he was climbing. He simply followed the monkey, looking up. Now, the monkey sat on the top of the mast. The boy climbed after the monkey, saying, "Ha ha! You have nowhere to go," when immediately the monkey jumped off.

Only after the monkey jumped down did the child look down from the top of the mast he had unknowingly climbed. When he looked down, everything was distant. The people looked like little ants. As soon as he saw that, he began to lose strength in his hands and started to panic. He was too scared to climb down from the mast. His legs grew weaker and weaker. . . Right then, a sailor who was working on deck looked up and saw him.

"Oh! That's the captain's son! Oh, no! Oh, no! What are we going to do?"

Now, who can bring the child down from the top of the

mast? A commotion arose among the sailors. The child was losing his strength. If he let go of the mast, he would fall and die, so he held on tightly, barely clinging to it. One sailor said, "Captain! We have a problem! A serious problem!"

"Yes? What's wrong?"

"Come out! Come out, quickly! We have a big problem!"

When he came out, his son was trembling on the mast.

"What happened?" asked the captain.

Upon hearing from a sailor the details of what had happened, the father closed his eyes for a second to think. Then, all of a sudden, he pulled out the gun he had on his side. Everyone became nervous. People were thinking, "What's the use of shooting and killing the monkey now?" Holding his pistol, the father looked up at his son and said, "Son! Can you hear me?"

"Yes, Father!"

"Jump into the sea or I'll shoot you! I will count to five! Then I'll shoot!"

The son knew that his father was a man of his word. He thought, "If I'm going to get shot and die anyway, I'd rather jump into the sea." Although it was frightening to let go of the mast, the son got ready to jump off.

"One!"

"Two!"

"Three!"

At the count he let go and at the same time kicked off from the mast as hard as he could, jumping into the sea. The sailors watched and pulled him out of the sea.

Loving folks, I am not trying to disturb your hearts.

I hope that you will have an opportunity to sincerely, for once, think about your spiritual lives. To live good spiritual lives people fast, pray all night, and make New Year's resolutions at the beginning of each year. Yet, spiritual life remains extremely difficult. Ask a taxi driver, "Sir, do you believe in Jesus?"

"Don't talk to me about those things. I'm busy enough, just trying to make a living."

Speak to a police officer, "Sir, do you believe in Jesus?"

"I'm so busy, I don't have time to go to church."

Ask a doctor, "Do you believe in Jesus?"

He answers, "I don't know why I went to medical school. On such a nice, clear spring day as this, everyone else goes out to enjoy the weather, while I'm stuck here surrounded by these frowning patients. I want to believe in Jesus, but for me, it just doesn't work."

Ask a soldier, "Do you believe in Jesus?"

"I'm too busy with my duties. I can't."

Ask a salesman, "Do you believe in Jesus?"

"Oh, I have to run my business and make money to educate my children and marry them off. Later I'll believe in Jesus. Pastor, you may not know this, but if you want to do business, you have to lie. If you say you got something for one dollar, you cannot sell it for a dollar. Even though it cost only one dollar, you have to say you got it for two. Then they'll buy it for a dollar. I have to lie. Then they'll buy it. So how am I supposed to believe in Jesus like this? I'll believe in Jesus after I've finished with my business."

"Because I can't quit drinking." "Because I can't quit

smoking." Because of one excuse or another, most people think they cannot believe in Jesus. One time, I spoke to a military unit in the front lines. I had a conversation with the soldiers. I said, "Raise your hands, if you think believing in Jesus is difficult."

Most of the soldiers raised their hands. Then I said, "The battalion commander is here next to me. Major Park, please stand up. Everyone, this is, Major Park, your battalion commander right? Raise your hands if it is difficult for you to believe that he is your battalion commander."

No one raised their hand.

"It's easy to believe he is the battalion commander, but why is it so difficult to believe in Jesus? Is Jesus not as good as the battalion commander?"

Because we are not familiar with the concept of believing in Jesus, believing in Jesus becomes difficult. I am so happy that I can believe and trust in my wife, I do not trust in my wife because she is pretty or good-hearted. I'm so happy that I can believe in my loving children. If I doubted my children, I would suffer so much that I couldn't bear it. Believing in Jesus is easy and peaceful.

Jesus said, "Come unto me, all ye that labour and are heavy laden, and I will give you rest" (Matthew 11:28).

They believe in Jesus, but they do not have peace in their hearts. Jesus clearly said, "I will give you rest," but although you believe, you have no rest. "Rejoice evermore. Pray without ceasing." If you are always worried and stressed, although you believe in Jesus, shouldn't you think about this? I am saying that you should take an opportunity to reconsider your spiritual lives. I ask this question from time to time.

"If you pray according to the words of the Bible, if you tithe, if you attend Sunday services, and do not sin within the faith and believe in the Lord, then you will go to heaven, right?"

"Sure, everybody knows that."

But is that really possible for us? Raise your hand, if there's anyone among you who obeys every law. Raise your hand, if you have never skipped a Sunday service. Raise your hand, if you've never hated anyone. Raise your hand, if you've never once thought about committing adultery. Folks, we are people who cannot reach the level of God. We are like the child on top of the mast, struggling and holding on for dear life, only to fall off at any moment. God is opening a new pathway of the gospel for us. That pathway is hidden deep within the Bible.

Equally as much as you want to have a true spiritual life, Jesus, God, and the Holy Spirit sincerely want to speak to your heart. The way of God, which is different from your thoughts, is hidden within the Bible. If you come to discover this secret hidden in the Bible, it's so easy to have your sins washed clean. It's hard for you to wash away your own sins, but it's easy to come out to God and have Him wash them away. It's difficult for us to defeat sin, but defeating sin through Jesus is so easy. I will speak to you about this in detail.

Let's continue by reading from 2 Kings, chapter 7, from verse 1.

Then Elisha said, Hear ye the word of the LORD; Thus saith the LORD, Tomorrow about this time shall a measure of fine flour be sold for a shekel, and two measures of barley for a shekel, in the gate of Samaria.

A long time ago, in the Old Testament, Syria attacked Israel. Just as in China where they built the Great Wall, Israel surrounded the city of Samaria with walls. When the Israelites thought they would lose to the Syrians, they closed off their city gates. They didn't have any missiles or artillery like today. Thus when the city gates were closed, there was no way to enter. Syrian soldiers surrounded the city and were waiting for the Israelite soldiers to become exhausted and surrender.

Because the walls went around the city and not around the farmland, the Israelites could not go out to farm. And so, after one year, they had a famine. After two years had passed and as the third year was approaching, there was mass starvation. How severe was the famine? There are horrific stories in the Bible of young mothers who boiled and ate their own children because of the unbearable hunger. One woman talked with her neighbor, saying, "Let's boil and eat my child today, and tomorrow we will eat yours," because she felt she would not be able to finish one child by herself. So they ate her child, and when the woman went to her neighbor's house to eat the neighbor's child the next day, the other woman hid her child to eat it by herself. Samaria was in this kind of extreme situation.

Then one day, the prophet of God, Elisha, said, "Tomorrow about this time shall a measure of fine flour be sold for a shekel, and two measures of barley for a shekel, in the gate of Samaria." That meant the food prices in the city would be greatly reduced.

A long time ago, when there were famines in our country, they would say, "If you give me one bowl of red bean porridge, I'll give you all my farmland," or "If you give me a bowl of white porridge, I'll give you all of my farmland," because people were starving. I think it was as bad as it was at that time. It was heard in the city of Samaria, which was in an atrocious famine, that a measure of fine flour would be sold for a shekel. When the man on whose hand the king leaned heard this, he could not believe it and said, "Behold, if the LORD would make windows in heaven, might this thing be?" Then the man of God said, "Behold, thou shalt see it with thine eyes, but shalt not eat thereof."

At that time lepers banished from the city were living outside the city walls. Previously, they had families to bring them food, meat, and clothes each morning, but now even the families inside the city were starving, and the lepers, too, began to die of starvation. They were all dying, in that pitiful situation and only four of them remained. The lepers discussed amongst themselves.

"Look, my loving friend, so and so has already died. My nephew has died of starvation. So who's going to die next? You and I, we will die soon. How can we just sit here like this, waiting to die?"

"They are starving even in the city. Who can give us food?"

"That's right. If we stay here like this, we will starve. I say we might as well go and surrender to the Syrians. If we surrender and they kill us, we die, and if they let us live, we live. It's do or die, so let's go."

The four lepers set out for the Syrian camp. With their lacerated legs, fingers falling off, and disfigured bodies, these lepers began to walk towards the Syrian camp, step by step, in the twilight. I think God made great sound effects with this miserable march. The sounds of the lepers tripping and falling down were made into sounds of winds, chariots, and the galloping of soldiers on horseback. To the Syrians, it sounded like the approach of a great army. The Syrian soldiers thought that the Israelites had hired soldiers from another country. The Syrians were in such a rush to run away, they didn't even have time to jump on their horses or donkeys. They just ran away.

When the lepers arrived, the Syrian camp was completely empty. Things to eat, things to wear and treasures were scattered everywhere. They were in severe starvation, on the brink of death. How do you think they felt when, all of a sudden, they saw all that food?

This story tells the spiritual secret of how God supplies us with the living, new, abundant food of life. We need to eat spiritual food and be strengthened, but for some reason, we are not strengthened, even though we are eating. Our spiritual lives continue to be diseased, die, and wither away. The Bible clearly expresses these spiritual conditions of the heart. God wrote these words to teach us how to survive these conditions.

I grew up near the banks of the Nakdong River, in North

Gyeongsang Province. My father had a big peanut farm, so in the fall, we ate a lot of peanuts. We would fry the peanuts, boil the peanuts, eat them fresh, or make peanut rice. Sometimes I would go to school with my lunchbox full of peanuts. I had a lot of friends because of the peanuts.

Peanuts are delicious. If you pick peanuts and eat them right away, they're not so good. You have to peel them. If you peel the shell and eat the nut inside, that's the good part. Not only peanuts but gingko nuts and walnuts as well. Folks, I'm sure you have picked and eaten walnuts. Walnuts have a terrible stench when you first pick them, but when you crack them open with a hammer and eat the nut inside, it's really tasty.

Children grab long sticks and stand under chestnut trees in the fall to pick the chestnuts. If the chestnut cluster falls they prick the children's heads and hands. But, why do the children continue to do it? It is because they've tasted the delicious nut inside the shell. The nut inside is delicious, but the shell is completely covered with burrs. What would happen if you unknowingly chewed on the burr-covered shell? You wouldn't be able to eat for the rest of that day.

All of you know chestnuts are very good, but it is the nut that is good, not the shell. The Word of God is like that. The Word of God, too, has an inside nut and an outside shell. If you don't taste the nut and if you just continually chew on the shell, you say, "They say the Word is good, but how come I'm getting so sleepy?" Long ago, when I would read the Bible, I used to fall asleep all the time. People say, "The more Bibles are sold, the fewer sleeping pills pharmacies sell." Usually, I would be wide-awake, but as soon as I opened the Bible, I would fall asleep. After reading for a while, I couldn't tell whether I was reading in Greek or Hebrew. You laugh, but I'm sure there are a lot of people like that. I may not know all of you, but isn't this true? Why do you get sleepy when you read the Bible? The Bible is a love letter from God. It shows His love. People become sleepy because they do not know the taste of the "nut" of the word, but only the shell. Because you don't know the spiritual meaning, you get sleepy and you believe with the Bible closed. People say, "Believing without knowing is blissful," but let's not believe the Word closed. Let's open it up and believe.

Pastor Byung Seok Woo, of South Busan Church, invited me here and I'd like to thank him. Suppose I was to go to Seoul after this conference was over. From Seoul, I write Pastor Woo a letter:

"Dear Pastor Woo, thank you for providing all the accommodations during our conference. Is everything peaceful at your church? How are your church members doing? Is your family doing well? We are doing fine. The fall winds are blowing in Seoul right now. The cosmos flowers are blooming, and the blue sky is beautiful. We are reading the Bible. October 30th is my wife's birthday. Please come and we will have a wonderful dinner together. I hope you can make it."

I write the letter and Pastor Woo receives it. His wife, next to him, says, "Who's the letter from?"

"Oh, it's from Pastor Park, in Seoul."

"What did he say?"

"He says, in Seoul, the cosmos flowers are blooming."

Is that what the letter is about? Is that right? Then, the church members ask: "What did he say?"

"Oh, he says that the fall winds are blowing gently in Seoul." That, too, is not what the letter says. Of course, that's included, but the fall winds blowing and the cosmos flowers and the blue skies. . . . These are not the "nut" I'm trying to deliver. What is the "nut" in the letter? It is the invitation to come to my house on October 30th.

Even if you memorize the letter, if you don't know its point, you don't know the letter. If you don't know the content of what God is trying to tell you, it's exactly the same as not knowing the Bible at all, even though you may have memorized it word-for-word and mastered all doctrines of the Old and New Testaments and structural theology. The Bible is composed of stories, but it records His confession of love for us.

Suppose I went to your house one day. I had been traveling for many days, and I was very tired and hungry. Just then, you were digging up potatoes. I wanted to have some potatoes, but I couldn't bring myself to say, "Give me some potatoes." So I just said, "Wow, your potato crops did well."

"Oh, really Pastor? Yes, it did do well."

"I think it'd be so nice if we could boil some potatoes and eat them."

"Yes, that would be nice."

"You know, when I was young I used to really like potatoes."

"Oh, really? Me too! Our potatoes are really great, aren't they? Why don't you go inside and rest, and I'll take care of this?"

This person does not know my heart. Even though I don't directly say, "Boil some potatoes and give me," when I say, "Wow, it would be so tasty to boil and eat these potatoes. I really like potatoes. They look really good," then shouldn't he get the picture? Don't you agree? Even though I'm not saying, "Please boil some potatoes and give me," am I not delivering the thought of wanting to have some boiled potatoes? A young man in love for the first time was too shy to say, "I love you," to a girl. It's so embarrassing for him to say it, so he just hangs around her timidly. She should get the picture, shouldn't she? When God wants to show His love for us, because we cannot understand the great, broad will of God, He speaks to us through our circumstances. It should be easy for us to understand. If we do not discover what God is trying to tell us in the Word, we do not know the will of God, no matter how much we memorize the Bible. Tell me, why did God record these words? It is important to discover what God is trying to tell us.

What is God trying to tell us through the verses we read tonight? It is the process of the gospel being spread to the people of Israel, surrounded by Syrians in the city of Samaria, who could only die, if left alone. Suppose this was not the Israelites' problem, but your problem. Is there a person here, who could only die tonight? On the outside, you are healthy, young and smart. Your business is doing well, you're well educated, and you're doing great. But is there anybody who cannot stand before God because of sin? You go to church, read the Bible, and pray, but is there anyone here who is suffering because of the unresolved sins in your heart? That person is the person who could do nothing but die.

No matter how much you go to church, tithe, attend Sunday services and do good things, you cannot go to heaven with sin. God created this world. He created the heavens and the earth. He created the beautiful Garden of Eden, but once sin came in, this world became corrupt and fell into sin. God will not tolerate sin in the newly created heaven.

When I came to Busan today, I came on an airplane. When I arrived at the airport, the police asked for my cooperation for an inspection.

"Please open your bag."

I opened the bag, and they saw the Bible and said, "Please, go ahead." When I went to the gate, they inspected me again.

"What's in your bag?"

"I have some books."

"Go ahead."

When I was getting on the airplane, they inspected me again. Folks, why would they do that, if we were all good people? Why do they have to labor and toil like this? A little while ago, somebody did something very bad at the Gimpo Airport. They don't know who exactly might carry out such an act. That's why they must hold extensive inspections, and we have no choice but to cooperate. Just as they inspect you when you board an airplane at the Gimpo Airport, there is an inspection point in heaven. It's not a gate where they search people for hand grenades or bombs. It's a gate where they seize people with sin. When a sinner tries to pass through, the alarm goes off.

"Beep! Beep! Beep!"

"You may not enter."

"God, I tithed."

"Still, you may not enter."

"Oh, God, I helped many poor people."

"No!"

"I prayed for a hundred days."

"I told you, no!"

"But I've done a lot of volunteer work."

"Well, still no!"

Bribes don't work there, and who you are doesn't matter. Your greatness, your intelligence, your good family name, none of these things matter. You will not be able to pass if you have sin. Some people are being deceived.

"Because I believe in Jesus, even though I may have sinned a little, they will let me in. God's a God of love, you know. I believe in Jesus, so zealously. He's not going to keep me out, just because I have some sin. He wouldn't do that."

Please do not misunderstand. God is a fair God. He cannot let in some sinners and leave other sinners out. To get over the problem, God simply does not allow in any sinners. That is why He sent His Son to wash our sins clean.

The reason I often go to prisons to preach the gospel is because, if it weren't for Jesus, I could easily be one of them. When I am with them, I always say, "I'm not here before you because I'm a better person than you. I do not think I've sinned less than you. I too was an evil and filthy person. And I have many evil, filthy thoughts in my heart, even now. There is only one reason that I am standing here before you this evening, and that is Jesus."

At one point in my life, I fell deep into sin. I gritted my teeth, trying not to sin. I was very determined, but it didn't work. On the outside, I was a member of the youth group, a member of the choir, and a Sunday School teacher. I went to many pastors and asked about the sins in my heart that no one knew about.

"Pastor, how can I have my sins washed clean?"

"Repent," was the answer. So I repented, but my sin was not resolved. In 1 John, chapter 1, verse 9 it says, "If we confess our sins, he is faithful and just to forgive us our sins, and to cleanse us from all unrighteousness." I didn't understand what this meant. I thought that if I confessed, one by one, all the sins I had committed, I thought my sins would be washed clean. Then, later on, I saw that it was not so.

It says, "If we confess," right? Then, what is sin? Stealing, lying, murdering, and committing adultery, is that what sin is? No. That is not sin. What is sin? Folks, what is leprosy? If your fingers fall off, if your eyebrows fall out, and if your nose collapses, is that leprosy? No. These are only the symptoms and effects of leprosy. They are not leprosy itself. They are the effects of leprosy. What is typhoid? Is it a fever and your hair falling out? No, that is not typhoid. That is what happens when you have the typhoid virus in your body.

Likewise, sin and crime are different by nature. When you catch a cold, you cough and you have a runny nose. The runny nose and the coughing are not the cold, but rather they are symptoms of the cold. Sin and symptoms of sin are different. Lying, stealing, hating others, murdering and committing adultery are symptoms of sin. These symptoms arise when you have sin. Folks, those people who do not steal or commit adultery, are they sinless? No, they are sinners too. Those people have sins; it's just that no one has seen the symptoms.

Sin is compared to leprosy in many places in the Bible. They say, "You can have leprosy for 3 years without even knowing it. It takes 3 years for you to know it and another 3 years for others to know it." One day, if symptoms of leprosy appear on someone's body, is it then that person has become a leper? No. He was already a leper, only now it has been revealed. Even before it was revealed, he was already a leper. Likewise, even though you may not steal or commit murder, even though you may not commit adultery or hate others, the Bible says that you are a sinner. One person said, "Pastor, stop saying sinner so much. Don't be like that." Some of you may say that.

A person called me one night. "Pastor, I would like to meet you."

"Sure, come over." I told him where I lived and he came over. Then he said to me, "Pastor I've just been released from prison. This was my ninth time. That's the kind of person I am, so Pastor, give me some money." He was subtly threatening me and asking me for money.

I asked him, "Do you know who I am?"

"Aren't you a pastor?"

"What does a pastor do? Does he give out money? Does he give out food?"

"No."

"A pastor is a person who gives food for your soul. Please, sit down. Of course it's important that I give you money, but food for your spirit is much more important. A pastor is a person who gives you the food of life. Please sit down and listen." And I began to talk about the gospel.

"Pastor I know all of that already. Stop saying sinner, sinner."

"Well, I don't want to say that you're a sinner, but you have to become freed from sin."

All people are tied to sin. Stealing, lying, committing adultery and murdering are not the problem. The characteristic, which leads you to steal, is the problem. That little pleasure you feel when you hear words of hate for other people. That excitement you feel when you hear of other people's shortcomings. That jealous heart you feel when your cousin buys some land. Don't you have these feelings? If you have them, it means you have the disease of sin.

Your eyebrows fall off and your fingers fall off, if you have leprosy. Your hair falls out and you get a fever when you have typhoid. Likewise, people who have the disease of sin end up hating others, committing murder, committing adultery, and stealing. Would it be okay to reduce the fever and not treat the disease, when you have typhoid? If a leper patient were to just bandage his fingers, so they would not fall off, would that do? No. The disease itself must be cured. Folks, do you understand? I'm sorry, but those of you who do not understand, please buy the recorded sermon tapes on your way home. Listen to them one more time at home, and you will understand.

Folks, sin and the acts of sin are different. You may have

stolen, lied and committed murder, but those are not sins, they are crimes. The Bible has clearly explained about sin and crime.

If we confess our sins. . .

These words are not about confessing your acts of sin, saying, "I committed theft." It means to confess your sin.

Let me ask you a question. If a spy turns himself in, does he become your fellow countryman, your brother? Do you not know about these things? If a spy turns himself into the Korean government, they provide him with the basics for living. For example, suppose I am a spy. I go to turn myself in. How do I turn myself in?

I go to the police station, and do I say, "Police Officer, I'm sorry, but, I tried to blow up the railroads, I tried to assassinate prominent people, and I tried to steal secret military information. I hope that you will forgive me?"

That is not the way to turn yourself in for being a spy. Those are things you do as a result of being a spy. If you want to turn yourself in, you don't say those things, but you say, "I'm a spy." You confess that first. First you have to have the sin of being a spy forgiven. Then, the results of being a spy are automatically forgiven. A spy must go to turn himself in, saying, "I'm a spy. I have been sent here on a mission." Likewise, when we confess before the Lord, we should not confess the symptoms of sin, but confessing that we are by nature a mass of sin. That is the correct confession.

In the Old Testament, it tells about King David. One day

King David committed adultery with his servant's wife. He was in so much pain because of his sin that he confessed before God. Do you know how he confessed?

"Our Father God, one evening I was walking on the roof of the palace, and there was a woman, and she was so pretty. I lost my mind so I brought her over and slept with her. She became pregnant. Oh, God, she's pregnant. . ."

Was that how David confessed? Look at Psalms 51, verse 5. That is not how David confessed. "Behold, I was shapen in iniquity; and in sin did my mother conceive me." It was not about what sin he had committed. He confessed of his nature, the fact itself that he was a human who could only commit sin, saying that he was a mass of sin, completely enveloped in sin. There is a big difference between confessing the result of sin and confessing sin.

If someone asks me, "Do you know how to drive?" I say, "Yes, but I'm not good at signaling with the blinkers. Also, I don't know how to turn on the ignition. I don't know how to change lanes. I don't know how to turn the steering wheel. I'm not good at merging on the freeway. That's it." That's not what I would say. People who don't know how to drive say, "No, I cannot drive." Isn't that so? If you are good at everything else, but cannot use the blinkers, you would say, "I can't use the blinkers." If you say, "I'm not good at stepping on the brake," it means you are good at everything else. That's how it is with sin. When you have committed no other sin except for telling one lie, then you can say "I told a lie," and that would be correct. If you commit no other sin and are otherwise clean, and you have only that one sin of hating someone, then you can say, "I hate someone," and that would be correct.

Because we are full of sin, by nature we are trees of sin, children of sin, and seeds of sin. No matter how we try to cleanse ourselves, no matter how hard we try not to sin, it does not work. A heart that does not sin must come inside of us. People who try to live a spiritual life sincerely, try not to sin, but they know that they cannot do it. People who do not live a spiritual life sincerely, those who only do it outwardly, think, "I can keep from sinning, if I try." When people who truly try to serve the Lord, try hard not to sin, they say, "Oh, I can't do it," as they are falling back down. That is exactly the condition referred to in 1 John 1:9.

Because we are born in sin, if we become freed from the nature of sin, then all of our sins are automatically forgiven. When the sins of a spy who has turned himself in is forgiven, would the officials say to him, "You are forgiven of the sin of being a spy, but your sin of stealing military information is not forgiven"? Would they say that? "Your sin of being a spy is forgiven, but your sin of trying to assassinate important people is not forgiven." Would they say that? When your sin of being a spy is forgiven, then all acts of sin belonging to that sin are automatically taken care of.

That is why in 1 John 1:9, it says, "If we confess our sins. . ." It's not about confessing crimes you have committed, but it's confessing that, "I am a sinner by nature. I cannot do it, so You, Lord, come and save me," and leaving yourself to the Lord. Then He will take care of all your problems. Many people misunderstand these words. They close their Bible and simply repent. Some people don't know how to take care of their problem of sin, so they write their sins out on a piece of paper and burn it in a fire. Where in the 66 books of the Bible does it say that to be cleansed from your sins, write them on a piece of paper and burn it in the fire?

Because people are suppressed by sin, they listen with interest when they hear how sins can be forgiven. Many religious leaders make fools out of believers today over having their sins cleansed. That's how it was with the Roman Catholic Church a long time ago. They'd take advantage of the believers' sincere hearts of wanting to have their sins washed clean. They made fools out of them by saying that if they bought indulgences, their sins would be washed clean. People were laboring to believe with the Bible closed, without knowing for sure how to wash away their sins.

Loving folks, I don't know how long you've been going to church, but do you know precisely how to wash your sins away? Do you know how to have your sins cleansed as white as snow? Do you know how? "Oh, I guess I believe in Jesus, so my sins are probably washed clean." That is not it. Your sins must be washed away.

"Happy day! Happy day! When Jesus washed my sins away!"

You need that particular day, the day you received forgiveness of sin. Without that day, folks, there is always a dark shadow blocking the way between you and God, so the power of the Holy Spirit cannot be upon you. You are trying hard on your own, in your spiritual life because you do not have the Holy Spirit of God.

I struggled inside of sin and received forgiveness of sin in 1962, through the grace of Jesus. From that day on, Jesus has always been with me. I used to try to change and would always waver. But as days went by, after my redemption, I continued in a blessed, joyful spiritual life because Jesus does not waver. Now Jesus is living inside of me. I am a human who can only sin, but because I have given myself up to the Lord, He takes care of me.

I have a son in 6th grade. He always wants to do everything I do. Last winter, it snowed heavily, and I had to put snow tires on my car. I told my son, "Why don't you go put on the snow tires?" He answered, "Sure!" He ran out and put on the tires. I had to tighten them later, but he did a good job. Then, because he had changed the tires, I guess he thought he could drive.

"Dad, can I drive, just once?"

"No."

"Dad, just once, please. . ."

It would have been nice, if I could have taken him to a big field and let him drive. He thinks driving is easy because he sees how easily I drive. He thinks he can drive well, but I cannot let him drive because he does not know how.

We think we will not sin, if we try not to because we do not know ourselves. The way to overcome sin is for you to lose to sin. That is how you defeat sin. Why? The Lord helps you when you confess that you can only sin, that you cannot overcome sin. The Lord cannot help those trying desperately to defeat sin. You must be defeated by sin. That's why it says, "He who wins, loses, and he who loses, wins. It is more blessed to give than to receive. He that findeth his life shall lose it: and he that loseth his life for my sake shall find it."

I still have so much to talk about, even though so much time has passed, but let's continue.

There was a certain chief in an African village. One day he was walking about in the village and some children were playing with a little leopard.

"Hey, children. What's that?"

"It's a baby leopard. My dad went to the jungle and caught it."

"You rascals, you can't be playing with a leopard."

"Yes, it's a leopard, but this leopard is different."

"How is it different?"

"Ever since we got it, we've been feeding it porridge. It's never tasted meat, so this leopard is really kind and gentle."

And the chief shouted, "No! It may be like that now, but when it grows up, a leopard is a leopard! It must be killed!"

"No, no. Chief, look! It's kind and gentle, really!"

The chief finally allowed it because the children had pleaded so much. It was very gentle, even when it was fully grown because it had grown up eating only porridge and had never tasted meat. When the children went to the jungle by themselves, it was scary, but when they went with the leopard, they were not afraid. It would run and play with the children, the children would ride on its back, and they would all go into the jungle together. The children were not afraid in the jungle because they were with the leopard.

"Our leopard is so good. I don't know why the chief is afraid of it. There's no problem with our gentle leopard. All we have to do is avoid giving it any meat."

Now the leopard was fully grown, and one day the children went with the leopard into the jungle to play. Three children were with the leopard in the jungle when one child slipped on a cliff. When the child fell off the cliff screaming, the two other kids followed to help him. The leopard quickly ran ahead.

When the leopard ran down, the child's knee was injured and was bleeding. The leopard licked the knee with his tongue to wipe away the blood. It licked him once, twice, and then the leopard began sucking the blood. The look in the leopard's eyes changed. It tore open the child's chest with its sharp claws and devoured him. It then ate the other two children. A leopard is a leopard. It may appear tame on the outside, but its true nature, on the inside, cannot be cast off. It is hidden, but it will eventually reveal itself.

Though you may appear to be nice, though you may look holy and beautiful, we humans all have the nature of sin inside of us. Rather than the sins that are revealed on the outside, such as stealing and lying, the Lord is saying that the hidden nature of sin itself must be taken care of. That is what you must be freed from. Jesus not only forgives the sins you commit, but He came to free you from the nature of sin itself. Jesus came and was crucified on the cross to free us from sin. He hung on the cross and shed His blood to liberate us from sin.

If you are not freed from sin, you are still servants of sin, even though you believe. You still have to fight against sin. You still have to suffer because of sin. The servant of God testified, "Tomorrow about this time shall a measure of fine flour be sold for a shekel, and two measures of barley for a shekel, in the gate of Samaria." Then the lord, on whom the king's hand leaned, said, "Hey! That makes no sense at all. Even if God makes windows in heaven, how can that happen? Everyone is starving and dying now, how can we get that much food in just one day?"

The servant of God said, "...thou shalt see it with thine eyes, but shalt not eat thereof."

Folks, this is what I want to tell you tonight. I hope that you will incline your ear and listen. There is a mindset you need in order to be changed in your spiritual life, to receive forgiveness of sin and to be born again. When we hear the Word of God, how do we hear the words? "Tomorrow about this time there shall be a lot of food in the city of Samaria." When the lord, on whose hand the king leaned heard these words, they were beyond his logic. These words were complete nonsense. These words were beyond his comprehension, words he could not understand.

We cannot understand everything about God because He is greater, wiser, and more able than we are. Jesus said not only things that were pleasing to our ears when He gave sermons in this world. I am ashamed, as a pastor, that you can listen to my sermons and be so at ease. Some people couldn't bear listening to the sermons of Jesus, and they screamed, saying they must kill Him. One time Jesus was preaching the Word at Capernaum. While listening to His words, people stood up all of a sudden, grabbed Jesus' collar and dragged Him to a cliff to push Him off and kill Him. One time when the servant of God, Stephen, was giving a sermon, the listeners could not bear it. They covered their ears, kicked the dust and said, "A person like him has to be killed." Then they stoned him and killed him.

There are many aspects that do not fit our thoughts in the true Word of God. When we receive the Word of God, we accept those aspects that we understand and that fit our thinking. However we do not accept the Word, when it does not fit our thoughts and opinions. So even if we listen to a sermon, we say, "Oh, yeah. That's right, that's good!" "Hey, that makes no sense!" This is how we filter everything with our hearts. Because of that, the work of God cannot come into our heart. The wisdom of God is beyond our wisdom. The thoughts of God are beyond our thoughts. That is because the things that come from God are not the things that come from this world. Because that is too great for us to accept and to understand, we say things like, "Even if God were to make windows in heaven, how could this be?" I'm giving the sermon, and if I say things that fit and are correct, according to your thinking you would say, "Ah, that's right, Pastor Park. He's right. How graceful!" That is what you would say. But when I say something that does not fit your heart, "Yeah, I know. It is the Word of God, but still. . ." "But still. . ." There are people who feel that way, right? God cannot work because you do not receive words that do not fit your thinking.

There were four lepers at the gate of the city. Even the lord, on whose hand the king leaned, didn't believe in God. So, who will God use for the work of delivering the good news saying tomorrow about this time, there will be a lot of good food in the city of Samaria? God chose the four lepers.

Why? Because they were people who had no hope. Jesus is the hope of us all. Better put, He is the hope of those who have no hope. Jesus cannot become hope to people who have hope in themselves. Jesus is hope to those who have no hope. He is comfort to those who cry. He is the Lord of power that gives freedom to the afflicted.

Why did God use the four lepers to save the city of Samaria? These four lepers had no hope in the worldly sense. I believe that salvation will be accomplished, not for those who think they are good at spiritual life, but for those of you who are not confident in your spiritual life, saying, "I have not received forgiveness of sin," "I'm not born again," and "Now, I really cannot do it."

If the child on top of the mast could come down all by himself, the father would not have provided him the way of salvation. When the young child ran out of his own methods, his own strength, and when his own wisdom became useless, the father became his salvation. Now, the child will be saved, through the father's method and not by his own devices.

"Now, throw your methods away and jump off!"

That was the father's way. The child's method was to hang on. The father's method was to let go. They were complete opposites. The father's method and the son's cannot both be applied at the same time. Throw your ways away! And accept the ways of Jesus. Then tonight you will be filled with the Holy Spirit.

Long ago, I led a conference at a leper colony at Aeyangwon in Yeosu. It was the church at which Pastor Yang Won Son used to minister. The communists killed Pastor Son's son during the Korean War, but he rescued the person who had killed his son from death, and took him in as his adopted son. Pastor Son, who was like a saint, made a colony for the lepers, sucked the pus of the lepers with his own mouth and treated them like human beings. At that time, a lot of people were gathered at a conference, like tonight, and I talked about the forgiveness of sin. The sad thing was, they not only had leprosy in their bodies, but also had the deep disease of sin in their hearts. After the sermon, I invited them, saying, "Those who want to receive forgiveness of sin, come forward." Hundreds of people raised their hands and came forward. That evening, many people received forgiveness of sin and rejoiced tearfully. When I saw that, I couldn't describe how my heart glowed.

Jesus came to free us from sin. Jesus did not come to make us into baptized church members. Jesus did not come here to make us into deacons or elders. Jesus Christ came to this earth to free us from sin.

The four lepers had no way to live. They thought, "Even if we just sit here, we will soon starve to death. We can't get food from the city."

"They are starving to death even in the city. Let's not put our hopes in it. They're even boiling and eating children. How do you expect them to give us any food?"

"How many days has it been since we last ate?"

"I don't know, I can't even remember, it's been so long."

"A long time ago, before I had leprosy, when we were farming our fields, we used to dig up sweet potatoes and boil them and eat. And in the fall, we would harvest and have rice. It was so good. . . Those were the good old days."

"Hey, stop talking about food. It's making me even hungrier."

The lepers were lamenting their situation and were waiting for death. Then one of them said, "Hey, we can't just sit here waiting to die. Let's look for a way to live. Let's find a way, no matter what."

"What should we do?"

"Is there any other way? There is none."

"If we go into the city, we'll die. If we sit here, we'll die. So, should we go and surrender to the Syrians?"

"No, that's not going to work. How can we surrender to the enemy?" But folks, surrendering to the enemy means they are changing their way of thinking.

They are changing their methods. Although it was dangerous, they made up their mind to go, step-by-step in a new direction because their old ways were useless. Folks, God is looking for such a person. It means that if you seek God, you must go forward with a new way of thinking, when your way does not work.

The lepers confronted the new way. They thought about approaches they had never used. If they remain, they will die, but if they go there, they just might live. Amazingly, God blesses that path. Folks, it's not just waiting for good luck to roll in, but saying, "God, I'm a sinner who can only be destroyed. Open a way for me."

Folks, I am telling you about the attitude of a person's heart who can receive forgiveness of sin. Throwing away your ways, throwing away your methods, you must turn your heart around and move your footsteps in the new way God has opened. Many people change their thinking when they come forth to Jesus Christ. It was so with Zacchaeus. It was so with the woman caught in adultery. It was so with the Samaritan woman. The people who did not change their thinking, even when they came forth to Jesus, changed into people who denounced and opposed Jesus. Folks, do not try to become good people as you attend church. You must change your thinking. If you do not break your heart and change your thinking, and if you go forward as you are, you will be nothing more than a churchgoer. Captain Naaman went to Elisha to have his leprosy healed. "You must go to the River Jordan and wash yourself seven times." Elisha said. "But I'm a military captain. I thought Elisha would surely come out to me and stand and call on the name of the Lord, strike his hand on the place and make me recover. What? Wash myself seven times in the River Jordan?" Captain Naaman said. He was angry and wanted to go back. That is how it always is when you do not throw your thinking away.

Among the people who came out to Jesus, there were many who returned troubled. Some people came to Jesus and received forgiveness of sin. But some people, even though they followed Jesus around, returned troubled. Some people returned complaining, and some people returned, going against Jesus. It was because they did not throw away their thinking.

These four lepers threw away their thinking and the ways they had followed, and began to set their footsteps in a new direction. The four lepers had been starving, exhausted, and diseased for a long time. Their toes and their fingers were falling off, and their bodies were disfigured. They would trip over stones and fall over bushes.

"Oh, no. I can't do this. Hey, my leg hurts, I can't go on. Please, you guys just go ahead. I wish I could eat at least in my dreams. Please, you guys, go, and even if you die at the Syrian camp, eat all you can beforehand."

"No, we're friends. Let's go together. Get up."

"Look, if you carry me, it will be more tiring."

"No. Even if we die, we die together. If we live, we live together. Come with us, we go together. Get up!"

"No, there's no chance for me."

"Even if we die, let's go. Let's at least see the food before we die."

As they would pass out and fall over, step by step, they went toward the Syrian camp. God did not forsake their footsteps. God worked in the sounds of their steps: the sound of them falling, the sound of them passing out, the sound of their exhaustion, the sound of dragging their fatigued bodies. God amplified and converted these sounds into great sound effects, like the special effects from a studio. The Syrians heard these sounds as the sounds of Israelites with masses of soldiers, coming toward their camp on horses and in chariots, swinging swords and spears. That's how it is. Folks, in your footsteps of coming to the Lord as you throw away your thoughts, throw away your methods and throw away your will. You may be fatigued and staggering as you step, but God surely works inside of those steps. God's amazing power is at work in those steps.

I truly believe that if you throw away your thoughts and move your footsteps toward God tonight, the overflowing works of the Holy Spirit of God will be yours. Throw your opinions away. Throw your thoughts away. You must deny yourself before Jesus, no matter who you are. Throw away what it is you do well. Do not say, "I'm a pastor," "I'm a baptized Christian." "I've been going to church since I was born." Say, "I am a sinner, who could only die. Please save me."

I hope that you do not act as if you are not a sinner, even though you have sin. It does not mean you are not a sinner, just because you have not sinned. Sin will reveal itself one day when the opportunity presents itself. Like Minister Duk Man Yang testified a little while ago, he thought he was a good person when he went to the seminary, but when he went to the military, his sin was revealed. That's how it is. Sin can only reveal itself when the circumstances are ripe. Folks, I hope that you will take new footsteps toward Jesus Christ.

You may be in a situation where your footsteps are tired, fallen and worn out, but when you move your footsteps, life is waiting for you, abundant food is waiting for you, and the spiritual wedding garment is waiting for you. When people have tasted this, they cannot keep still. They change into people who go and testify the gospel to those who cast them out, who called them lepers, who despised and insulted them, to give them life.

Loving citizens of Busan, it was very difficult when I first began my ministry. My ministry began when I established a church in Daegu. At the time, I was poor, hungry and I went through many hardships. Do you know how I overcame those hardships? I did not know anything else back then. I asked the people of my church one by one, "Have you really received forgiveness of your sin? Isn't there sin blocking the way between you and God? The Bible says, "Behold, the LORD's hand is not shortened, that it cannot save; neither his ear heavy, that it cannot hear: But your iniquities have separated between you and your God. . ." but have you broken down the wall of sin that is blocking the path between you and your God?" Of course, the church members did not like this. There were some negative responses, saying, "Why does that pastor ask so many questions?"

But some people sincerely accepted those words and said, "I have not had my sins forgiven. I have so many sins." So I preached the gospel and explained to them the pathway of forgiveness of sin. David washed his sins away like this when he sinned with Uriah's wife, and Daniel washed the sins of the people of Israel away like this. I explained to them, from the Bible, how to have their sins washed clean, step by step.

I searched throughout the Bible, from Genesis to Revelation, concerning receiving forgiveness of sin. The words about being healed from leprosy are words about receiving forgiveness of sin. God taught us about Captain Naaman being healed of his leprosy to teach us about how to receive forgiveness of sin. When I tell people, one by one, about the ways of forgiveness of sin that appear throughout the Bible, some people truly humble their hearts and receive forgiveness of sin. Folks, even though I was hungry and in difficulty, it was such a great joy seeing our church members receiving forgiveness of sin, one by one. With that joy, I could more than overcome my difficulties.

If you are a patient at my hospital tonight and if you have appendicitis, I don't want to just put some iodine on your stomach or give you some anesthesia or pain killer and send you home. I have to surgically remove the appendix. In the same way, I don't want to leave your sins there as they are. I think it is a rare opportunity in your lifetime to hear about how to receive forgiveness of sin.

I have gone to many conferences and have testified about the methods of forgiveness of sin found in the Bible. I do not want you to just return home like this tonight. Are you a baptized church member? A deacon? An elder? A choir member? A Sunday School teacher? Even so, if you have not had your sins forgiven, if you are not freed from sin, everything else has nothing to do with God. On that day, many will come before the Lord and say, "Lord, Lord, we prophesied in thy name. And in thy name have cast out devils and in thy name done many wonderful works." Then the Lord will say, "I never knew you."

The good deeds you have done do not last long. But all things change if you receive forgiveness of sin and Jesus comes inside of you. A person at my church for a long time lived with a gambling addiction. Because he was addicted, he could not quit, even when he tried. But he came to church, listened to the Word, received forgiveness of sin, and became freed from gambling. How could that be? The heart of the gambler and the heart of Jesus, who came inside of him, could not both survive because Jesus is not a gambler. The gambling heart was automatically cast out because

Jesus came in. Do you think that Jesus could be cast out by a gambling heart? The gambling heart is the one that gets kicked out.

A certain daughter-in-law was suffering because she hated her mother-in-law. But that heart of hatred left her after receiving forgiveness of sin. Why is that so? The hateful heart must leave because there is no hatred in the heart of Jesus. If you receive forgiveness of sin and Jesus comes into your heart, such things inside of you will depart from you. You will be changed. If Jesus comes inside of you, you cannot help but change, not by your will not to sin, but by Him. So, I hope that you will receive forgiveness of sin. If you truly receive forgiveness of sin, Jesus comes upon your heart, so you don't need to cry and pray saying, "Let the Holy Spirit be upon me!" Even though the Holy Spirit wants to come inside of your heart, He cannot enter because of sin. Only if your sin is taken care of, today, will you be filled with the Holy Spirit.

During the morning Bible study time tomorrow, I will tell you in detail about the words of forgiveness of sin.

Loving folks, I hope every one of you will receive forgiveness of sin during this conference.

2

Jacob and Esau

The Reason Why
We Are Distant from God

There are two paths to spiritual life. The path in which you try to live according to the Word of God, and the path in which you completely allow and trust that Jesus will do it for you.

Esau was cursed for going before God with trust in his own ability, while Jacob was blessed for trusting only in his mother Rebekah's words; between these two paths which should we follow? People who trust in the results of their own works are distant from God, and they are evil.

2

Jacob and Esau

I will read from Genesis chapter 27, from verse 1 to 23 in the Old Testament of the Bible.

And it came to pass, that when Isaac was old, and his eyes were dim, so that he could not see, he called Esau his eldest son, and said unto him, My son: and he said unto him, Behold, here am I. And he said, Behold now, I am old, I know not the day of my death: Now therefore take, I pray thee, thy weapons, thy quiver and thy bow, and go out to the field, and take me some venison; And make me savoury meat, such as I love, and bring it to me, that I may eat; that my soul may bless thee before I die. And Rebekah heard when Isaac spake to Esau his son. And Esau went to the field to hunt for venison, and to bring it. And Rebekah spake unto Jacob her son, saying, Behold, I heard thy father speak unto Esau thy brother, saying, Bring me venison, and make me savoury meat, that I may eat, and bless thee before the LORD before my death. Now therefore, my son, obey my voice according to that which I command thee. Go now to the flock, and fetch me from thence two good kids of the goats; and I will make them savoury meat for thy father, such as he loveth: And thou shalt bring it to thy father, that he may eat, and that he may bless thee before his death. And Jacob said to Rebekah his mother, Behold, Esau my brother is a hairy man, and I am a smooth man: My father peradventure will feel me, and I shall seem to him as a deceiver; and I shall bring a curse upon me, and not a blessing. And his mother said unto him, Upon me be thy curse, my son: only obey my voice, and go fetch me them. And he went, and fetched, and brought them to his mother: and his mother made savoury meat, such as his father loved. And Rebekah took goodly raiment of her eldest son Esau, which were with her in the house, and put them upon Jacob her younger son: And she put the skins of the kids of the goats upon his hands, and upon the smooth of his neck: And she gave the savoury meat and the bread, which she had prepared, into the hand of her son Jacob. And he came unto his father, and said, My father: and he said, Here am I; who art thou, my son? And Jacob said unto his father, I am Esau thy first born; I have done according as thou badest me: arise,

I pray thee, sit and eat of my venison, that thy soul may bless me. And Isaac said unto his son, How is it that thou hast found it so quickly, my son? And he said, Because the LORD thy God brought it to me. And Isaac said unto Jacob, Come near, I pray thee, that I may feel thee, my son, whether thou be my very son Esau or not. And Jacob went near unto Isaac his father; and he felt him, and said, The voice is Jacob's voice, but the hands are the hands of Esau. And he discerned him not, because his hands were hairy, as his brother Esau's hands: so he blessed him.

Loving folks, after finishing the sermon yesterday, I sat around and spoke with the pastors here. A certain pastor said to me, "Pastor Park, we couldn't understand you because you were talking so fast." Because I'm from Gyeongsang Province, when I go to Seoul, people in Seoul often say they can't understand me. It makes me nervous when I'm preaching. So this morning, I will try to speak more slowly and calmly, step by step, but I don't know if it will work. I hope that you will help me. There's a Korean proverb that says, "Even though I may say wormwood cake, understand me to say rice cake." Since this is Busan, and I'm also from Gyeongsang Province, I know that you will be able to understand me well.

Today, I want to continue talking about forgiveness of sin. I heard that after someone listened to the sermon last night, he said that I didn't talk about forgiveness of sin, but rambled on about other things. I guess you can say that. When you farm, you don't sow your seed right away. First you plow the field. Likewise, because there is a difference between God's thoughts and my thoughts, the heart must be plowed first, in order to receive the Word exactly as it is.

One day, a sister who lives far away from the church, said to me, "Pastor, please come over to my house tonight." I promised to go. Because I didn't know where the sister lived, we decided to meet at Gaebong Station. I was very busy that day, so I barely got to Gaebong Station on time at 5 o'clock. I thought the sister would be there, but no matter how long I waited, she did not show up. Even though I waited for five, 10, and even 20 minutes, she did not come, and I grew frustrated. I thought, "I'd better leave," and I was about to get into my car when the sister came running toward me from the other side.

I asked her, "Why are you so late?" She said, "I was here 20 minutes ago. I thought that you would come on the Seoul-Incheon Highway, so I waited for you over there." Since the sister always took the bus, she must have thought that I'd come the same way as her bus route. As a matter of fact, I took the Namboo Belt Parkway because traffic was so backed up on the Seoul-Incheon Highway. The place we promised to meet was Gaebong Station, but she added a little of her own thinking to that promise and had been waiting for me at the Seoul-Incheon Highway. How much trouble she must have gone through, watching as so many cars passed through by the Seoul-Incheon Highway for almost an hour? Can we blame the sister, saying she was wrong? Can we say that she was mistaken?

In our spiritual life, if we don't take the Word exactly as it is, but add a bit of our own thinking, we will be waiting for God at a place completely opposite from where God actually is.

What is there for pastors to do? We wake up early in the morning, pray, read the Bible after breakfast, visit people's houses after lunch, lead a conference after dinner and then go to sleep. There isn't much for me to do, so I often read the Bible. Once, I was reading the Bible and it was not interesting. I thought, "If I want to meet God, what am I supposed to do?"

I have searched in the Bible for where a person must go to meet God. Where can I see God? Can I see Him at the prayer house? In the mountains? Once, a missionary from the Netherlands, whom I knew well, said that Koreans seem to think they can meet God only when they go to the mountains. He said, "We Dutch have a big problem."

"Why?" I asked.

"There are no mountains in the Netherlands, so we Dutch can never go to the mountains to pray."

He made a joke about the fact that they had the problem of not being able to pray in the mountains because much of the land is below sea level. When I read Exodus chapter 25, I find that God made a place where He would meet us. That place is the mercy seat. From Genesis to Revelation, no matter how much I searched for the place where we could meet God, I could find nothing. However, when I read Exodus 25, I saw that God had promised to meet us on top of the mercy seat. The mercy seat is the place where sin is forgiven. It is important for us to find out what God is trying to tell us with these words.

Now, it is important to know what story God is attempting to tell through the verses we read today. There was a man named Isaac. Who was Isaac? Isaac was the son of Abraham, right? Isaac had two sons, Jacob and Esau. The elder son, Esau, was a hunter. He was covered from head to toe with hair. His brother, Jacob, however, was a smooth skinned man. When Isaac had become old and it came time for him to die, his eyes became weak and he could not see. He then called his beloved elder son, Esau and said, "I am old and I don't know the day of my death. Therefore, take your quiver and bow and go out to the field. Hunt some beasts and make me delicious food. Then I may eat it and freely bless you."

Upon hearing this, Esau immediately ran out to the hunting grounds. But, there is a saying that goes, "History is made during the night, and at the center of it all is always a woman." Isaac's wife, Rebekah, Jacob and Esau's mother, heard everything. When Rebekah overheard what Isaac had said to Esau, she said to her loving son Jacob, "Son, your father wants to bless your older brother and told him to go hunting. How can you lose your father's blessings to your older brother? Hurry, and bring me a goat. I will cook it and make a delicious dish, and you can take it to your father. Act as if you are your older brother and receive the blessing instead of him." When Jacob heard this, he said, "Oh, no, Mother. Esau is a hairy man, but I have no hair and I'm smooth skinned. Father will find out if he just touches me. Then, I won't be blessed; I will be cursed."

"Do not worry. If you get cursed, let that curse be upon me. Don't say anything else. Just do what I tell you." His mother,

Rebekah, said.

Jacob quickly brought over a kid goat. His mother killed it and made it into his father's favorite dish. She then placed the skin of the goat upon his smooth hands and neck. Then Jacob went forward to his father and said, "Father, I am Esau. I went hunting and have brought you a delicious dish. Please eat this and bless me."

The father's eyes were weak, and he could not see well, but the voice he heard was strange. "Really? How did you catch it so quickly?"

"Oh, Father, when I went out, God allowed me to find it quickly. The beast fell in only one shot."

"Okay! Let me touch you to see if you really are my son." When Isaac touched him, there was hair. The father ate the food and believed his son, Jacob, to be Esau and blessed him. That is the story we read this morning.

A friend of mine is a missionary in the jungles of Brazil. The Amazon River is located near there with a mouth width that opens out for 25 miles. One day, a small sailboat entered the river from the ocean. The boat had been sailing for many days, and by that time, they had completely run out of drinking water. Everyone on the boat was so thirsty that they were on the brink of death. Soon, they saw a boat coming toward them. Surely, it was a boat coming from a harbor, so don't you think it had a lot of water? The tiny boat approached the oncoming boat and asked for water.

"We are all dying of thirst. We'll give you as much money as you ask. Please, sell us 50 gallons of water." The sailors of that boat laughed and said, "Why don't you just draw some water up from under your boat and drink it?" and passed them by. The thirsty sailors had their hopes up, but when the other boat passed them by, they became disappointed and resentful. Then one young sailor, who couldn't take it anymore, dropped a bucket into the water and began to draw it up. An older sailor, next to him, stopped him, saying, "Hey, you can't drink salt water, just because you're thirsty. You're going to become even thirstier. Don't do it." Nevertheless, the young sailor drew up the water. Gulp, gulp, gulp, he drank it down. Then he suddenly threw the bucket and cried out, "This is river water!" In fact, the boat had already entered the river, but everyone thought that they were still in the ocean because the river was so vast. These people were on a river full of river water, but they almost died of thirst.

Folks, the gospel is exactly like this. We are not far from the blessings of God today. I am sure that many of you here are just like the sailor on the river, who almost died of thirst. Although we have come before Jesus who has forgiven our sins and blessed us, there is a certain level that our thoughts have not reached. Although God gave us His amazing blessings, we can't receive them because we are adding our own thoughts to the Word of God, as if we were waiting at the Seoul-Incheon Highway when we should be waiting in front of the Gaebong Station.

We wind up very far from God's intentions because we add our own thoughts. Just like the people who were suffering and struggling from thirst, although they were floating on a river, the reason we can't meet God is because even though He is close, we have different thoughts from God.

God knows that, so He wants to show us His will through the Bible.

Let's talk about what God is trying to teach us through Genesis chapter 27. This morning, for your better understanding, I want to use some actors. I need four actors. To play the Father, please come forward. I need an actress to play the Mother. You two young men, in the front, come forward as Jacob and Esau. Now, what is God trying to teach us through these four actors?

In the Scriptures that we have just read, Isaac had two sons; the older son was Esau and the younger Jacob. Esau was a hunter, while Jacob stayed home, holding onto his mother's skirt. Does this situation have anything to do with you? This story is clearly related to you. Sometimes, when I used to read certain parts of the Bible, I knew that they had something to do with me, but I was often confused because I did not know what the story was about. When we read the Bible carefully, we come to understand the secret of God that is hidden within. You don't know how much of a blessing it is, when we realize the secret He has for us.

In this story, Isaac said to Esau, "Esau, go hunting and make some delicious food. Then after I eat it, I will freely bless you." When Esau heard his father's words because his heart truly wanted to receive the blessing from his father, he immediately went out to do as he was told. His mother overheard everything, however. When she saw that Isaac wanted to bless only his elder son, she thought, "No, this can't happen. I need my younger son, whom I love, to receive the blessing." For the second son to receive the blessing, she said, "Jacob, your father is going to bless your brother. You shouldn't lose out on his blessing. Get a kid of the goats from the flock. I'll kill it, quickly make a dish, and you take it to your father. Your father will eat it and bless you. That'd be great."

Jacob's eyes lit up. "Wow, Mother is really great. She truly loves me," he thought. "But Mother, my brother is a hairy man. I'm a smooth skinned man. No matter how weak my father's eyes are, wouldn't he touch me? What if he touches me and finds out that I'm Jacob? He won't bless me. He'll end up cursing me."

"Don't worry. I'll take all of the curses you receive. Don't worry about a thing, just bring the kid."

So Jacob went and brought a kid. Meanwhile, what did Esau do? He was sweating and running around trying to catch a boar, a deer, or a rabbit, right? How much suffering must he have gone through, crossing hills and running around in the mountains? Jacob calmly brought over a kid. His mother, Rebekah, rolled up her sleeves and started to cook. She sliced and diced, fried and steamed, put in this and that and prepared a delicious meal. She placed the food that Jacob's father liked the most in Jacob's hands, put Esau's clothes on him and put goat fur all over his smooth skin. Then she made him stand in front of his father.

"Father!"

"Who are you?"

"I am your eldest son, Esau."

"Oh? You've already come back from hunting?"

"Yes. God has given me a deer. I was able to catch it

quickly. Now please eat and bless me."

"Let me touch you."

When he touched him, there was hair. Therefore, he didn't notice anything and blessed him. After Jacob received all the blessings, Esau returned from his hunting. Esau quickly made his father's favorite dish, took it to him and said, "Father! I have returned from hunting and brought the food that you asked for. Now, come and bless me."

"What? Who are you?"

"Father, I'm Esau."

"What? Esau was just here. You are Esau? How can there be two Esaus?" His father was completely shocked. "Ah, your brother, Jacob did this!"

"Father, don't you have any blessings left for me?"

"No."

"Father, bless me as well!" Esau cried bitterly. Isaac said, "Behold, your dwelling shall be the fatness of the earth, and of the dew of heaven from above and you shall live by your sword and serve your brother. . ." He did not bless Esau, but rather cursed him.

Let's put aside the deeper, hidden will of God for just a moment. People who are playing the roles of the two sons, please stand here. Both sons wanted to be blessed, but one was blessed and the other was cursed. Even though all of you may give tithes and keep the Sabbath Day diligently, some are filled with grace and receive a blessing, but there are others who receive a curse. What, then, must we do to be blessed, and how do we come to be cursed? I believe that God gave us this Bible to teach us the difference. If we don't know the spiritual meaning of the Bible, no matter what we do or how hard we try, nothing works.

It has been a little over a hundred years since the gospel came to Korea. Long ago, our nation did not believe in God. People served the dragon kings, the earth gods, and the village guardian gods. They would go and bow down at village shrines or at piles of stone, living a life of serving demons and following superstitions. They could do such things only because they did not know the one true God.

Through the blood and tears of many missionaries, the gospel came to our land. Finally, people came to know Jesus and came to know God. "Ah! God is the One who created the heavens and the earth. He is the Almighty One. Jesus loves us." But while they had come to know about this, they did not know how to serve Him.

Like the old saying, even demons listen if you beg them; they would go to church and show unconditional zeal. They would pray and cry all night, fast, make offerings and do volunteer work. However, whenever God sees that, He wants to say, "Your sincerity is admirable, but those are not my ways." Then how should we come to God? Because men don't know the way to go out to God, they go before Him according to what they know. If God tells the story of how one was blessed and the other cursed between two people who came to be blessed, He knows that people will realize through the story, "Ah, this is how God wants us to come forth to Him." That is why God recorded these words in the Bible.

Folks, there is a reason why He wrote this Bible. The father in the story is depicted as the image of God. The mother is the image of Jesus Christ. The older brother, Esau, is the image of a man who tries to receive blessings by working hard. The younger brother, Jacob, is the image of a man who receives blessing by the help of Jesus, although he doesn't do anything himself. Do you understand? This is the "nut" of the Bible. Chewing on the "shell" of the Bible, without eating the "nut," is like chewing on the shell of a peanut or chestnut; only your mouth gets pricked. Is it delicious to taste only the "shell" of the Bible? No, that's not good at all. The "nut" in the Bible is what you call spiritual secrets. Esau did what his father had told him to do, right? He worked hard, right? He labored, right? But was he blessed or cursed?

And by thy sword shalt thou live. . . (Genesis 27:40)

Folks, how frightening a curse that is. Where else can you find a curse that says because of his enemies, unless he has a sword with him at all times, he will feel insecure and will not be able to sleep. The dew of heaven will not come upon him, and even though he plows a field, it will not bring forth fruit. That was the curse that was put upon him.

A long time ago, when I didn't know the spiritual secrets of God, I thought, "This is so strange. If he didn't have a blessing to give his son, couldn't he at least say, 'Have a lot of children,' 'become wealthy,' or 'stay healthy,' or something?" Isaac didn't bless him in that manner. His son went out to hunt and obeyed his words, but what did the father do? He cursed him. This means that although I try to keep and obey the Word of God, I can only end up being cursed before

God. It's because we cannot obey or keep the Word of God.

Maybe everything that Jacob had ever done was bad. There is the story of a man named Nolbu, who would go around putting stakes in pumpkins in other people's pumpkin patches and tripping ladies who were carrying pots of water. Jacob was a problem child and a sinner. That's why the father loved the elder son, and the mother loved the younger son. Esau is a person who tries to go to God with his own efforts, but God does not like people who come to Him with their own efforts. You must come to God through Jesus.

Now, let's continue with our story. The second son received a tremendous blessing from the father. He received every blessing there was to receive. The father had no more blessings to give. What did this son do to be blessed? Did he zealously go out hunting? No, he didn't. He didn't do anything. His mother prepared everything for this son to receive the blessings. Spiritually speaking, he brought forth only what Jesus prepared for him in order to be blessed by God. When he asked his mother, "What happens if I get cursed?" She said, "I will receive the curse instead of you." Jesus promised that He would receive every curse that we should receive.

There is a reason I chose to talk to you about this today. As a pastor, I have been to many churches and have preached the Word of God in many places. I don't know if they know about these words, but countless people have tried to come to God with their own zealous efforts in witnessing, tithing and trying not to sin.

Five or six years ago, I led a conference at Mt. Jiri. At that time, many people had gathered. One day, after finishing the morning sermon, I said, "If there are those among you who want to receive forgiveness of sin, please come to my tent." Many people came. Four or five people would come in at a time. I would explain step by step how to receive forgiveness of sin and many received forgiveness. It was nearly dinner time and I was about to wrap things up, thinking, "Should I take a break now?" when a young lady came in. I asked her a few things, and after I listened to her for a while, I spoke to her about how our sins are forgiven. I explained how our sins were transferred to Jesus, how our sins were washed away by Jesus being crucified, how the sins in our heart become taken care of and what to do when we break the law. I also spoke to her about how sins were forgiven, referring to the stories of Captain Naaman and King David in the Old Testament.

After I finished talking, I read her Hebrews chapter 10, verse 17, "And their sins and iniquities will I remember no more." When the young lady heard these words, she began to weep. It was summer, so the door was open, and this young lady wouldn't stop crying. I was afraid that people might misunderstand and think that I had beaten her, but no matter what I said to her, she must have sat there and cried for nearly an hour. It was driving me mad. I urged her to calm down. Finally, she stopped crying and spoke about her past.

"Pastor, my mother passed away when I was in middle school. Then my stepmother moved in. I could not get along with her, so one day, I packed my bags, took the tuition my father had given me and ran away."

She went into the city, but wound up at the wrong place.

She was then caught up in a brothel and spent several years there. She gave up on her life, thinking, "I'm rubbish," but one day, she met a certain man. That man loved a lowly, filthy woman like her, not just for some fleshy pleasure, but he loved her with all his heart. Because he loved her so much, she came to love him as well. This woman was so touched and moved, thinking, "Wow, how could he love a woman like me? Is this a dream?"

One day, the man came to her and said, "Don't say anything. Just follow me." She followed him and he took her to his house. Although they didn't have a formal wedding ceremony, she lived there as his wife. This young woman told me that those were the happiest days of her life. Although they were poor and lived in the countryside, they were so happy.

Two years passed, but this woman did not have any children. Her in-laws were waiting, asking, "Any news? No news of a baby?" No one knows through whose lips it came, but the family found out that in the past this woman had been a prostitute. Her father-in-law found out, her mother-in-law found out, her sister-in-law, and her brother-in-law found out. From then on, whenever she would serve dinner, her father-in-law would turn his face away from her. Her mother-in-law, who used to speak so kindly to her, saying, "Hey sweetie," would not look at her face. Her sister-in-law and brother-in-law would not speak to her.

Although it was the same house, that house had turned into hell for this woman. She could not live there because she felt so insecure. Even when she went to church, she was afraid to look at people, so she would sit in the back and would leave before the service ended, without anybody knowing. She lived a very lonely life, and when she heard that there was a conference in Mt. Jiri, she made up her mind and came.

Her heart was filled with the thought, "If only I could forget my past." Jesus had washed away all of this woman's sins just as it is written in Hebrews chapter 10. Because God had promised not to remember this woman's sins, she was so joyful she could not bear it. That was why she cried the way she did. Later on, I was invited by the pastor of the church that she attended and led a week-long conference there.

It was a church with about 600-700 in the congregation. One day, as I was leaving, after finishing the sermon, somebody pulled on my sleeve. When I looked to see who it was, I saw it was that woman. "Pastor, my husband came to church today for the first time." I have not seen her since. I don't even know her name.

Folks, that woman had never done anything good. However, all of her sins were forgiven by Jesus, and now she is living a bright, shining and blessed life before the Lord. When Jesus was on this earth, it was the same with the Samaritan woman, it was the same with the woman caught in adultery, and it was the same with the publican. People with many sins do not need to wash away their own sins. Jesus came and did everything for them.

What kind of a heart do we humans have today? "That's how it is in the Bible, but is it okay if we do nothing? Is it okay to just lie down and nap all day, waiting for luck to roll in?" That's not what this means.

This morning, I hope you will throw your thoughts away and listen carefully. Why was Esau cursed? He tried to live according to the Word of God. He tried to do what his father had told him to do. He labored hard, but the result was to be cursed. If you try to live according to the words of the Bible, you will only be cursed. It's because we are unable to live by the words of the Bible.

If you could live by the words of the Bible, would there be a need for Jesus? No, there would be no need. That is why God sent His Son, Jesus. Jacob's mother, Rebekah, is the image of Jesus Christ. She had prepared everything for the son who had a lot of problems with sin, so he could go forth before the father and be blessed. Was there even one thing that this son did? Who devised the plan, from beginning to end, for him to be blessed? The mother did. Who proceeded with the plan? The mother did. When Jacob said, "No, I can't," she replied, "Don't say anything. Just do whatever I tell you. I see to it that you are blessed." The mother did everything. If this son had gone out to the father and something had gone wrong, the mother said that she would take all responsibility and receive the curse instead of him. Who prepared the food that Jacob took, the food his father liked the most? The mother did. The mother did everything, so her son would not lack in any way in going forth to his father.

There are two kinds of spiritual lives. In one, we try to live according to the Word of God: trying, laboring and toiling. However, on the other hand, there is the way, saying, "No matter how hard I try to live by the Word of God, I cannot. Jesus, You do it for me." And bring forth the faith of believing in what the living Jesus has done, without adding my own strength, effort, or anything of my own. There are only these two ways.

Most people say, "I do it with faith to believe in Jesus. What is there that I can do? I can do nothing. Jesus must do it for me." Right? But you try, and if it does not work, you fall, and you try again, and you fall. That is why your spiritual lives are a cycle of falling and stumbling. When you go to a revival, you feel good, as if your faith has been restored, but it soon disappears. When you pray on the mountain, it feels like your heart is filled with the Holy Spirit and when you're speaking in tongues and prophesying, it feels like your faith has gotten much better. However, because you are doing it, it does not last long and you fall down again.

Every New Year's Day, people say, "This year, I'm going to live a good spiritual life. I'm going to turn over a new leaf, start all over." Then you pray and do things with a new heart. However, people's resolutions last only a few days or weeks. Some resolutions last only a few hours. That's right. It is only natural that we fall and stumble. That's why God sent Jesus Christ to us.

Let me ask you this: Are you like Jacob or Esau? As a person, Esau appears to be much better. If, however, you have your own goodness and truthful works, you cannot accept the things of Jesus.

Look folks, the cup in my right hand is empty, but the cup in my left hand is full, right? Can I pour more water into the cup that is already full? No. But what happens, if you pour water into the empty cup? What is the difference? In other words, the grace of the Lord finally comes upon you when your heart is empty. If your heart is not empty, but full of all the good things you've done for the Lord, thinking, "I have been a Christian ever since I was in my mother's womb," "I have been going to my church since it was first established. If it had not been for me, when our church was just getting started, it would not have survived. At that time, I sold my land to build a chapel," "I ran an orphanage," and "I helped the poor," there is no room for the grace of God to enter in. Because Esau was good, and because he always pleased his father, he thought that it would be enough if he only hunted well. However, the result was the opposite of what he thought. It was a curse. On the other hand, because Jacob had never done anything right before his father, he was afraid to go to him.

"My father hates me. What good have I ever done, for my father to bless me? Mother, just leave me alone and let my brother be blessed." What did Rebekah say? "No, don't worry. I'll take the responsibility." So, Jacob went forward with what his mother had done, without having done anything himself. There are those who rely on their own efforts and labor. There are also those who rely only on the things of Jesus because they throw away all their own things because they realize that they have nothing that is good.

Should I test your hearts this morning? Why don't you examine what kind of spiritual life you have? Let's examine this today, while we have the chance. Just like a health check-up, let's receive a spiritual life check-up. Is that okay?

When I ask you a question, think carefully. One day, you went to the chapel for the service. That day, you gave a large offering, prayed and did a lot of volunteer work. If you go out to God then, how would you feel? You would feel confident, wouldn't you?

But let's say one day, you were going out to God, after having had a fight with your spouse, or you went out to Him after a fight with your neighbor. In addition, you went out to God without making an offering and without obeying the Word of God. When you go out to God like that, how do you feel in your heart? Prayer doesn't seem to come to you, does it? Isn't this how your spiritual life is? When you went out to God joyfully, why were you able to? If you don't have joy, why do you not have joy? If you are joyful, when your actions are good and not joyful because your actions are not good, then you are not relying on Jesus. Isn't that evidence that you are a person who believes and follows your own actions?

Many people say, "Pastor! What are you talking about? What works do I have that I would go out with? I go out with the grace of Jesus."

Everyone says that, with their mouth, but most people rely on their own actions when they actually go out to God. How do most people understand the Bible?

"David boldly went forth before Goliath. So, let us have boldness! Joseph did not compromise his spiritual life, even though he was in prison. Let us not compromise our spiritual lives. Mary Magdalene met the Lord in the middle of her hardships. Let us be that way as well. Let's love one another."

There are many people who speak like this. The Bible,

however, does not teach us that. Folks, the Bible does not tell us to do those things. It tells us that when we say, "God, I can't," because we are inadequate, we can succeed through the help of Jesus. A person who thinks he can do something cannot receive the help of Jesus.

One day, Jesus spoke about the prayer of the publican and the prayer of the Pharisee. Do you remember? The publican said, "Lord, have compassion upon me. I'm a sinner."

When the publican prayed, he didn't confess each sin saying, "I've committed adultery," or, "I stole something." Instead, he confessed his nature as a sinner, just like the sermon yesterday. "I am a sinner. There is no good in me whatsoever." The Pharisee, however, said, "I did this well. I did that well." That is why God did not give the Pharisee righteousness, but He gave righteousness to the publican. Because the Pharisee thought he was righteous, he did not receive the righteousness from God. The publican came as a sinner, but returned as a righteous person. The Pharisee came thinking that he was righteous, but when he returned, he went back as the sinner. That's what it says in the Bible.

This morning, I think the story has gotten a little dogmatic, but please listen. Let's continue talking about this. When Jacob went out to his father to be blessed, there were conditions to be met. First, Jacob covered himself when he went out. He covered himself completely. If Jacob had exposed even a little bit of himself, what would have happened? He would have been cursed. Jacob was blessed because he completely covered himself.

I'm here in Busan now doing this conference. It costs a lot

of money to hold this conference. I may not know how the money was gathered, but I believe that it was offered secretly by saints to prepare for all the necessities for the entire conference. Many people made offerings for us to pay for the television advertising we did. When we made fliers, placards and posters, many people took the responsibility for payment. The thankful thing is that many people offered their money to God, but not one person revealed himself or herself. Instead, they hid themselves, making their offering unto God. There is an offering box in the back. Last night, many people gave offerings, through grace and with thankfulness, although we have no idea who they were. Folks, those kinds of offerings are completely different from offerings given by people to reveal themselves.

Most people receive blessing, if they live their spiritual lives covered and hidden, but many people work to reveal themselves. Whenever they make offerings, when they donate a piano to the church, or when they build a podium, they reveal who they are. However, if we were truly to reveal what we have done, then we should reveal not only the good, but the evil as well.

My picture was on a television advertisement and on fliers that went out. When we put Pastor Ock Soo Park's picture on the flyer, would we only put the picture of his eyes because he has good-looking eyes? Or, because he has a big, good-looking mouth, do you just cut his mouth out of the picture and put that on the flier as his picture? No one would do that. If you are going to put out a picture, you put the picture of the entire face, whether it's good looking or not. Because good and bad works show up together before God, revealing everything dirty and filthy about us, you must be covered when you come forth to God. Folks, do you understand? Even if you make offerings to God, the offering in which you reveal yourself is not an offering with which God is pleased. When your church needs a piano, donate a piano. Give a podium, if it needs a podium. But do not do it in your name. Do it in the name of Jesus. Do not reveal yourself.

Today, many people in Korea have twisted spiritual lives. Some people, when they make an offering, write, "Our Father God, at this time, I would like to thank You for allowing us to open our beauty salon. This is an offering of thanks from so and so." The pastor then stands at the podium and announces, "Deacon so and so opened a beauty salon at Shinsadong, Gangnam and has made an offering of thanks." This is corruption of religion. "God, thank You for allowing my son to study in America and earn a doctorate." It is an offering, but at the same time you're showing off your son. People do not know how fake this is in the eyes of God. If there are any among you who have received grace and have a heart, glowing with thanks, and if you choose to make an offering, make the offering, hiding yourself and glorifying Jesus. That is what God wants. Today, man is revealed far too grandly in the churches of Korea. Humans are so exposed that there is no room for God to work. The first condition for Jacob to be blessed before his father was that he must be hidden.

Loving folks, even now, it's not too late. If you have

boasted or shown off, even a little, about the good things you've done before the Lord, or if you have that kind of a thought, though you may not show it, be ashamed of yourself. I hope that you will hide yourselves. You must hide all of the wrong, as well as the good you have done. It wasn't possible to tell whether the man was Jacob, even after his father touched him because Jacob was covered with goat hair. In the same way, we must cover ourselves. With what? We must be covered with the deeds of Jesus Christ. When God sees us, He should not see us. He should see only what Jesus has done.

If a person comes before God the Father and receives blessings, what would he say when he goes to heaven? "I have done no good deeds." He wouldn't just say it with his mouth, but with his heart, "There is nothing I've done."

People say, "Oh, what did I do? I haven't done anything." They say that, and that behavior looks like humility, but they are actually subtly trying to exalt themselves behind their words. This is truly abominable, it is evil and dirty, before God.

People were like this, even during the time of Jesus. If they helped the poor, they would sound the trumpets. God said that they already had their rewards. It is said that God does not receive those who pray with reverence on the streets crying, "God!" We must be completely and absolutely hidden. Before people and before God, we must have absolutely nothing to show.

Why are people given a curse? It's because they confidently think they can do well. In Esau's heart he said, "Jacob can't even hunt. Me? I'm confident." Cursed people have the heart of Esau. What is the use of being confident? It's not as good as getting something that was already there at home. Isn't that true? Jacob completely covered himself.

Second, Jacob did not go in his own name. Rather, he went forward relying upon his brother's name. Folks, when we go before the Lord, whose name should we rely upon? We must go out to God relying upon the name of Jesus Christ, who is like the elder brother in our spiritual lives, who is the first Son of God. "God, accept me because I have made offerings. I prayed well, so accept me." That's not how it is.

"God, I may have produced some offering, but there is nothing I can bring forth to you. All I have is dirtiness and filthiness. If I'm evil, even in the eyes of a dirty, filthy person like myself, how much more so would I be in Your eyes, God? God, I'm really evil and dirty. I am truly filthy. I am abominable. God, please do not look at me. Look only at Jesus and accept me. No matter how hard I try to do well, it is useless, so don't look at me. See only Jesus Christ and see the things that He has done as what I have done and accept me."

This is what true spiritual life is. Today, many people say that they believe in God, but they are so taken by themselves and have so much hope in themselves. "If I just make up my mind and become more determined, then I can please God, right?" No, wrong. "If I just try a little bit more, God will be pleased, right?" No, wrong again. Because we can only be destroyed, it does not work no matter what we do. That's what we must realize. Then we can rely upon Jesus Christ.

There's a young man who needs 10,000 dollars. If he

doesn't have 10,000 dollars, he will die. So he comes to borrow from me. I don't want to lend him any money so I say, "I'm broke." If this young man has other places where he can borrow money, other than from me, would he continue to beg me? "Forget this," he would say. "I'm going somewhere else." However, if this young man has no other place to borrow money, wouldn't he cling to me, whether he lives or dies? This is how it is for us, receiving the grace of Jesus. People who think, "If I do well, or if I do this, it will work," do not rely upon Jesus. When you come to the conclusion that there is no hope in you, you can rely upon Jesus with all your heart. This means you look up to Jesus with all your heart. That person can be saved.

As I lead conferences, sometimes, during spiritual counseling time, I gather 10 or 20 people, sit and talk with them about forgiveness of sin. After I speak to them, some people receive forgiveness of sin. They rejoice and cry out, "Hallelujah!" but they don't know what to do. Last night, I was coming down from the podium after finishing the sermon, when a young woman came to me with her baby. She said, "Pastor, you said stand up and come forward, but I couldn't come forward because of my baby. Pastor, please give me the Word." So I spoke with her. At that time, 10 or more other people sat down and surrounded us. I talked to her about how Jesus forgave us of our sins, how our sins passed over to Jesus, how our sins became as white as snow, and how eternal redemption was accomplished. When I was finished, some people nodded their heads, and some people were so rejoiceful that they didn't know what to do. When I saw that, I was so happy that I couldn't sleep, even after I went home. It was really like that. I couldn't sleep, I was so thankful. I was being used for the work of God in leading souls, which could only be destroyed, into life! That's why I yell and testify to you until my throat hurts.

Loving folks, if you come before Jesus with an open heart, saying, "I truly have no hope in me. There is no good in me. There is nothing I can do well. I cannot help but be destroyed," you can all go home having received forgiveness of sin. However, some people think, "Still, I did this well. Deacon Kim, he's a complete fake. I think he's a phony, although he goes to church. But at least I'm truthful." People with this kind of heart have always gone against Jesus, even during Jesus' time. They have never received Jesus. It means that they could not truly rely upon Jesus.

Because Jacob was totally helpless, when he went out to his father, he could rely only upon his mother. Esau, however, was self-sufficient, when he went out to his father. "Hey, I will hunt and bring back delicious food. Why do I need to rely upon my mother?" As a result, he was cursed.

Folks, these words teach us about our heart in spiritual life. Do you think that they put this kind of story in the Bible to make the Bible thick because it would look shabby if the Bible were thin? No, that's not why. Every verse, every word, contains the sincere heart of the Lord, who truly wants to speak to us. Many people, however, don't know this. They think that it will be enough, if they try hard and work hard. There are so many people who do not know the will of God. I came here to spread the will of God to the citizens of

Busan. There are many great pastors here in Busan. Many of them have doctorate degrees, and there are many great pastors who I admire.

I'm not a great person or a person who has a doctorate from abroad. Long ago, I was truly a bad person. One day, while I was struggling in sin, I discovered that I am a person who could only be destroyed. It was then that I realized the secret of the precious blood of the Lord. The Lord washed all my sins, from head to toe. Jesus came into my heart, the moment I received forgiveness of sin. I was changed and the Lord has upheld me from that moment on. I'm not living a good spiritual life because I have faith. I can live a spiritual life because Jesus is upholding me. It's not that my heart is so strong that I do not commit sins. Rather, it is because Jesus gives me the strength to overcome sin. I can admit that, it is only because Jesus upholds me, that I do not end up in the dirty sewers.

Loving folks, reveal yourselves. I'm not telling you to shout out your failings here, but I'm telling you to acknowledge that you are dirty inside your heart. Throw away the thought that you are clean. "I can't do it anymore. I can only be destroyed. Jesus must save me. I cannot do it. Even if I try, I cannot do it. Even if I labor, I cannot do it. Even if I toil, I cannot do it." Today, at this time, Jesus will come looking for a person who has this kind of heart.

There was nothing that Jacob did. What did the woman caught in adultery do when she received forgiveness of sin? What did the thief on the cross do when he went to heaven? All they did was realize that they were people who could only die. Jesus always went to those kinds of people and showed them the path to salvation. Folks, are you a choir member? Are you a Sunday School teacher? Are you a baptized church member? Are you a deacon? If you think, "But still, I'm not like that," you must realize that you are the ones who are the most distant from God.

"I'm a sinner who can only be destroyed. Lord, have compassion on me." If there is a person like that, today, at this hour, I believe you will meet the Lord. Through Jacob and Esau, God is showing us a precious secret. Loving folks, a lot of time has passed. No matter how much you lick the rind of a watermelon, you cannot know the watermelon's true taste. No matter how much you chew on the shell of a chestnut, you cannot know the taste of the chestnut. If we only know the shell of the Bible, it is not meaningful to us at all. When you realize the spiritual secrets hidden inside the Bible, I believe that from that moment on, you will know the will of God and will live a blessed life.

3

The Woman Caught in Adultery

The Law of Grace
That Makes Sinners Righteous

Jesus did not judge the woman caught in adultery according to the Law of Moses. According to the law, she had to be stoned to death. However, Jesus judged her with the law of love and grace apart from the Law of Moses. We too are all sinners before the law. That is why we must go under the law of grace that makes us righteous.

3

The Woman Caught
in Adultery

Tonight, let's begin by opening our Scriptures to John chapter 8 of the New Testament. I will read to you from verse 1 to 11.

Jesus went unto the mount of Olives. And early in the morning he came again into the temple, and all the people came unto him; and he sat down, and taught them. And the scribes and Pharisees brought unto him a woman taken in adultery; and when they had set her in the midst, They say unto him, Master, this woman was taken in adultery, in the very act. Now Moses in the law commanded us, that such should be stoned: but what sayest thou? This they said, tempting him, that they might have to accuse him. But Jesus stooped down, and with his finger wrote on the ground, as though he heard them not. So when they continued asking him, he lifted up himself, and said unto them, He that is without sin among you, let him first cast a stone at her. And again he stooped down, and wrote on the ground. And they which heard it, being convicted by their own conscience, went out one by one, beginning at the eldest, even unto the last: and Jesus was left alone, and the woman standing in the midst. When Jesus had lifted up himself, and saw none but the woman, he said unto her, Woman, where are those thine accusers? hath no man condemned thee? She said, No man, Lord. And Jesus said unto her, Neither do I condemn thee: go, and sin no more.

I have nine sessions to preach the Word to you this week. I spoke to you last night and this morning, and this is our third session. During the remaining sessions, I hope in my heart that all of you will receive forgiveness of sin. I feel quite nervous and anxious because of this. A few pastors told me yesterday evening that I was speaking too fast and that they could not understand me. So I said, "That's why you need to buy the sermon tapes and listen to them two or three times more," and we laughed it off. I want to talk to you about redemption during this week, which is quite different from what you have generally thought about it. Thus, I think you will need to open your hearts wide.

Since the Bible speaks so clearly and precisely about redemption, you will be able to receive forgiveness of sin, if the Holy Spirit works as you listen carefully to these Words.

Folks, if you receive forgiveness of sin and take the Lord into your heart, I believe that I will see you in that eternal land, even if you return home and never see Pastor Park again. Last spring, I was invited by the pastor of the Jeonju Church to lead a conference in Jeonju at a place called the Anti-communism Hall. Many people received forgiveness of sin through that conference. At the end of the conference, I said, "There are twelve gates into heaven. Three on the east side, three on the west side, three on the south side and three on the north side. Folks, when we all meet in heaven, don't go in first. Those of you, who get there early, wait a while, and let's all meet at the middle gate on the south side and go in together."

The people who had received forgiveness of sin rejoiced, saying, "Amen, Hallelujah!" However, there are still some people here who cannot go to heaven, so I don't think you are very happy about this. Anyway, during this week, let's resolve the problem of sin that is tormenting your heart. This problem destroys your courage, every time you try to come out to God. Then we can meet at the middle gate on the south side of heaven and enter together. I have already promised the people in Jeonju, so it's going to be hard for me to promise to meet you at some other gate. If you would like to see me, wait for me at the middle gate on the south side. I hope we will have that joy of meeting each other and living together there, with the Lord, eternally.

Reading the Bible, I've always had many questions. I'm sure you've felt this way as well. I wanted to live a true spiritual life, not a superficial one, but that was very difficult. My biggest problem was the problem of sin. What does it say back here? It says, "The Secret of Forgiveness of Sin and Being Born Again." That means that if we have sin, we can never stand before God. I had so many questions about having my sins forgiven.

Among the many sermons I've heard, I have often heard sermons that sounded as if we could all go to heaven, just by attending church. They say you can all go to heaven because attending church is believing in Jesus. But when I would listen to those sermons, sometimes I would think, "How could anyone go to heaven just like that?" The Bible says, "Not everyone that saith unto me, Lord, Lord, shall enter into the kingdom of heaven." I was most curious about whether I could just believe and go to heaven. I was curious about one other thing. I heard that Jesus was crucified and died on the cross for my sins, and I was not sure whether my sins were really washed as white as snow. When I looked into my heart, I had so much sin. I was very curious about how my sins could be completely washed clean. Then, Jesus quietly called me, as I struggled because of sin, and I had time to lay my heart out before Jesus and have a conversation with Him.

The truly thankful thing is that, when we look in the Bible, there are many stories in which Jesus often had one-on-one conversations with people, although He lived a busy life, often preaching to three or five thousand people at a time. In John chapter 3, Jesus had a one-on-one conversation with Nicodemus. In John chapter 4, Jesus had a one-on-one conversation with the Samaritan woman. In John chapter 5, Jesus had a one-on-one conversation with the man who had an infirmity for thirty-eight years. It was just the two of them. In John chapter 8, Jesus had a one-on-one conversation with the woman caught in adultery. I often saw in the Bible that Jesus always had private conversations with a few of His disciples, after He had finished preaching to large crowds. During this conference, we will also have time for individual fellowship and counseling, after the main service, just as they had individual fellowship with Jesus.

I have heard many sermons, and I've also given many sermons about this story in John chapter 8. There are still many things that I am curious about when I read these Words. A woman was caught in the act of adultery. I am curious as to where the man went. Maybe he quickly ran away. Why did they drag the woman, caught in adultery, over to Jesus? What did Jesus write on the ground with his finger? I have these questions, when I read the Bible. At one point, when I read the Bible, the whole Bible was full of nothing but questions. I think that this is good, however, because just believing blindly can never work. People say, "Just believe. Just believe." Other things may be done that way, but faith can never be done unconditionally. If someone says, "I'm going to kill you, if you don't believe," then you may say, "I believe, I believe," but you cannot truly believe in your heart. Strangely, people with a burden in their heart cannot be forced to believe, as long as they carry that burden, because the heart flows according to a certain order.

There was an article in the newspaper a little while ago. Very bright street lamps were installed along the road leading to Gimpo Airport and were turned on before the Asian Games. The farmers, who worked the land alongside the Gimpo Airport road, looked carefully at their rice. The rice was growing, the blossoms were blooming, but the rice did not ripen. When they investigated the problem, they discovered that the rice directly under the street lamps did not mature. The farmers requested compensation for their loss. When the farmers said, "Our rice did not ripen, and we incurred this amount of loss because of the street lamps," the government officials questioned it, saying "How could that be? The rice did not ripen because of the street lamps? That makes no sense." As a result, they consulted a farming expert about the problem.

The expert said that even rice must sleep at night, especially at the end of the season. When rice is growing, the plants need long days with a lot of sunshine, but when it's time for the rice to ripen, the plants need shorter days. And as the nights become longer, they need to have a lot of sleep in order for the rice to ripen well. But the rice could not ripen because the bright street lights burned throughout the night, and the rice could not sleep. Thus, the farmers were saying that they should receive compensation. From then on, the street lamps were turned off at midnight.

There is a certain order in all things created by God in this world. I heard that scientists in America can put a mirror up in space to shine sunlight on certain cities in America, even during the night, but they dare not do it because it would destroy the life cycle, and they don't know what kind of plagues that might bring about.

Folks, likewise, our spiritual lives cannot be forced. If you drag someone and tell them to believe and believe, it does not work. Yes, they should believe, but the problem is that they try to believe in the absence of faith. And when that doesn't work, they say, "I believe!" and they even try screaming. If they can believe, then they can. But why should they have to say, "Lord, we believe in you!" and force it out? They are forcing themselves to believe because they are unable to believe naturally.

Although I believe in my wife, I never once said, "Honey, I believe in you." If one day I were to say to my wife, "Honey, my loving wife, I believe in you." How funny would that be? People who say, "I believe," are forcing themselves to believe because faith has failed them. That is not faith. Faith must come according to principle. Then, do you know what the real problem is?

You know that Jesus was crucified and died for your sins. You may attend the Sunday service, you may fast, you may give offerings, you may become a choir member, and you may even become a Sunday School teacher. You can do all of this through your own strength. But, folks, the faith that my sins have been washed as white as snow is somehow not so easily acquired. There is something in your heart that says, "No, I think that sin still remains." You know that Jesus was crucified to cleanse you of your sins, and with your mouth you may say that you are clean, with no sin in your heart. However, we can see that it is not completely accomplished inside of your heart.

Jesus did not try to cleanse our heads. He tried to cleanse

our hearts. You are unable to believe that Jesus cleansed your sins because you do not have faith in your heart. The first thing that comes to mind when you pray is sin. You say that if you believe in Jesus, you're joyful, happy, and thankful, but when you come forth to God, you cannot lift your face. You can only live a life of saying, "I am so ashamed. I am not good enough. I am wanting," because you are ashamed to stand before God.

Tonight I do not want to tell you that Jesus Christ was crucified for your sins. That is because there is no one who doesn't know that. Is there anyone here who doesn't know that Jesus was crucified for your sins? There is an old Korean proverb, "Nothing comes without some effort." It is a fact that Jesus Christ was crucified for our sins, but the sins in your heart must be washed away. If Jesus was crucified and sin remains in your heart, that is not faith. That is nothing.

Throughout my ministry, I have searched the Bible to read about how our sins were forgiven through the blood of the cross. Folks, if the faith, "Jesus died for my sins, to wash my sins as white as snow," comes into your heart, according to the Scriptures, your heart will not resist and you will enjoy peace and freedom. Only when that happens, the Holy Spirit will enter your heart, and He will lead you.

There are many stories in the Bible about forgiveness of sin. I cannot tell you about them all. I want to think about how we can cleanse the sin from our heart through the story of the woman caught in the act of adultery, who came before Jesus and received forgiveness of sin, as is told in John chapter 8.

Jesus went unto the mount of Olives. And early in the morning he came again into the temple, and all the people came unto him; and he sat down, and taught them. And the scribes and Pharisees brought unto him a woman taken in adultery; and when they had set her in the midst...

You all understand, up to this point, don't you? Now let's read the next verse, verse four, all together.

They say unto him, Master, this woman was taken in adultery, in the very act.

Yes, this woman was taken in the very act of adultery. She must have been very ashamed, right? And now I will read verse five to you,

Now Moses in the law commanded us, that such should be stoned: but what sayest thou?

Folks, there is an important story here. Here is a woman who has sinned. Moses said that this woman should be stoned to death. "But Master, what sayest thou?" The people were judging a sinner. Who first gave the judgment? The law gave the judgment. The law sentenced her to "death." How then, would Jesus judge this woman? A judgment completely different from that of the law came forth from Jesus. What did it say? It said, "Not guilty." This is the difference in the law. A person who sins can't help but to receive the death penalty.

The only way to save that person is to apply another law.

A sister sang a hymn just a little while ago. Suppose we are holding a singing contest. Just because you sing well does not mean you will win first place. How well or how poorly you do depends on the judging criteria. For example, if the judging criteria say the person who opens their mouth the widest will receive the most points, there is a good chance that a person like me would take first place. The reason is, there are not many people who have a mouth as big as mine. This means the result of how well or how poorly you sing will change, according to the judging criteria. In the same way, when people sin, the judgment of that sin will change according to the law. This woman committed a sin. Even though we want to save her, according to the law, there is no way we can save her.

Not too long ago, you would have been caught for violating the curfew if you had gone around after midnight. But is it still a sin to go around after midnight? No, it's not. That's because the law has changed.

A long time ago, even when the curfew law was in effect, there was no curfew in Gyeongju, on Jeju Island and in North Chungcheong Province. Say a person on the border between North Chungcheong Province and South Chungcheong Province was in South Chungcheong Province at around midnight, drinking and having a good time. Suddenly, the police come blowing their whistles, saying, "You're in violation of the curfew." If he runs away to North Chungcheong Province, is that a sin? That cannot be a sin in North Chungcheong Province because there is no curfew law there. However, if that person comes back to South Chungcheong Province, the police would come to get him. If he runs away to North Chungcheong Province, the police have no authority to arrest him. If you violate the curfew, while within the boundaries of South Chungcheong Province, you have to pay a fine, but you are free in North Chungcheong Province because there is no curfew law there.

The woman in John chapter 8, who committed adultery, did not just attempt to commit adultery, nor look at someone lustfully, or anything like that. It was so clear that she had sinned because she was caught while committing adultery. According to the law, that woman could not be delivered from destruction. I want to tell you this evening the true way this woman caught in adultery could be freed from sin through the Words in the Bible. What I say, may be very different from what you have all been thinking until now, but I hope that you will open your heart and listen to what I have to say.

Let's talk about this again. What happens if a person in North Chungcheong Province comes down to South Chungcheong Province past midnight? He will get arrested. Afterwards he goes up to North Chungcheong Province. Suppose right then the police follow him all the way to North Chungcheong Province and arrest him. Then what will the arrested man say?

"I will be judged at the court of North Chungcheong Province because this is North Chungcheong Province."

Suppose they go there, and he is tried. The judge sits there and asks, "What is your sin?"

"Curfew violation."

The judge then says, "What? Our province doesn't have night curfew violation."

Then the policeman says, "This man was out running around, even though it was past midnight. I'm sure of it. I saw it myself. We even have photos and eye witnesses."

"But he is not guilty."

"No, it was this person for sure. He was caught on the spot."

No matter how much he says that, the judge says, "Is that all you have to say?"

"Yes, I'm done."

"The defendant is not guilty, go back home, work hard and live a good life. . ."

There is no law to bind him.

What condemns us as sinners? The law condemns us as sinners. Sin cannot be sin without the law. Folks, suppose I were a person who does not believe in Jesus and suppose that I were a smoker. Would that be a sin? That cannot be a sin, according to the law of the Republic of Korea today. But if the Republic of Korea made a law that said, "If you smoke, you shall receive the death penalty," would it be okay for me to smoke? If I were to get caught smoking, I would immediately be taken away and be executed. Thus the law establishes sin. The Scriptures in Romans write that there was sin before there was the law. But when there was no law, sin was not considered sin.

Folks, what I'm talking about this evening may be a bit rigid and a bit hard to understand, but I'll continue. The woman caught in adultery came to Jesus, right? But did she walk over on her own two feet? Or did someone drag her there? The Bible records that the scribes and the Pharisees dragged her there. Actually, it was not the Pharisees and the scribes who dragged this woman to Jesus but the law. Could this woman be dragged to Him without the law? The law makes sin and the sin is what leads us to Jesus.

It is like the starter lamp for a fluorescent light. The starter lamp lights up and flickers before the fluorescent tube lights up. When the fluorescent tube lights up, the starter lamp turns off. Have you ever seen a broken starter lamp? The starter lamps need to blink and then turn off, but sometimes it doesn't turn off. If the starter lamp does not turn off, what does the fluorescent lamp do? You don't know what happens? If the starter lamp does not turn off, the fluorescent tube cannot shine brightly.

That's how it is with the law. Galatians tells us that the law is like a school-master who leads us to Jesus Christ. Without the law, you cannot know that it is bad, even when you sin. The law taught sin to us. "Ah, God does not like this kind of thing." "Oh, I shouldn't commit adultery." "Oh, I shouldn't commit murder." Folks, it is the law that made us realize this. Nobody would come forth in front of Jesus, if they did not realize sin. The law made you realize what sin is, which led you to want to receive forgiveness of sin. The law works as a starter lamp. After making us realize the sin inside of our hearts, the law must leave and Jesus Christ must come in. Folks, if the starter lamp is always on, the fluorescent tube cannot shine brightly. In the same way, when your hearts are continually caught under the law, the Holy Spirit can never be upon you. You must be freed from the law and only then will the Holy Spirit of God be upon you.

Let's continue. The people asked, "Moses in the law commanded us, that such a person be stoned, but what do you say?" Right then, what did Jesus say? He said nothing. Instead, He wrote on the ground with his finger. Many Biblical scholars have researched what Jesus may have written, and they have speculated a great deal on this. One day I was leading a Bible study and somebody asked me a question.

"Pastor, when Jesus was judging the woman caught in the act of adultery, what did He write with His finger on the ground?"

I answered to him.

"I don't know."

Among all the books that I've read in this world, there is no book as truthful, as clear and as definite as the Bible. This Bible misses nothing and has a match for everything. If we need to know something, it surely has been written about in the Bible. I read in the Bible that Jesus wrote on the ground with His finger, but it does not say what He wrote. How do I understand this? There is one thing that God wants to tell us. It is not the content of what Jesus wrote, but the fact that He wrote, on the ground, with His finger.

Then, what meaning does Jesus writing upon the ground have? I have searched in the Bible for the places where words were written with a finger. In the book of Daniel, it says that a certain man's hand appeared and wrote "MENE, MENE, TEKEL, UPHARSIN" on the wall. Afterward, when I looked where God wrote with His finger, I came to realize an amazing secret. God wrote with His finger twice in this world. The first time was when Moses received the tablets of stone on Mt. Sinai. It says that God Himself wrote the Ten Commandments with His finger. I want to tell you, here, what the difference is between the Ten Commandments God wrote with His finger on the tablets of stone, and what Jesus wrote with His finger on the ground.

Jesus did not write these things anywhere else, but He wrote them before the woman caught in the act of adultery. Why did He write this before the woman caught in adultery? Jesus wrote on the ground where He was asked to stand in judgment of this woman. The scribes and the Pharisees came and said, "This woman committed adultery. She was caught in the act. Moses' Law says that this kind of a woman should be stoned to death. But, Master what do You say? Please show us Your judgment."

Jesus was being forced to give His judgment. There is meaning in the fact that Jesus wrote on the ground with His finger before judging this woman. This woman should be judged by the law. The law first judged this woman. That law was written by God on tablets of stone on Mt. Sinai about 1,500 years before Jesus. If this woman had been judged according to the law that God had written with His own finger, on Mt. Sinai, then she could only die. If God had judged with the law He wrote with His finger on Mt. Sinai, not only would that woman have received destruction, but you and I as well. Ultimately, we can only be destroyed because no one on earth has ever kept the law perfectly.

Bible scholars have studied the Bible with the computer.

As a result, they discovered that the year Moses received the tablets of stone on Mt. Sinai was 1491 B.C. During the 1,500 years between Moses' reception of the law and the coming of Jesus, not one person kept the law perfectly. Because of that, whoever is judged by the law could only be destroyed.

Jesus Christ came to save this woman caught in adultery, this woman who could only die, this woman who could only be destroyed. Jesus came to save, not only that woman, but to save you and me this evening. But Jesus could not save her, nor could He save us with the law as it was. The Lord decided to change the law because through the law all people can receive only destruction. Change the law into what? He decided to change it into the law of love, the law of grace and into the law of faith, and that is why Jesus once again wrote with His finger on the ground.

These Words about the law are a bit dry, but they have many interesting aspects. The Bible says that Abraham was righteous. It tells us that he became righteous by faith. Abraham was a friend of God. Abraham was not without blemish. He took a maid servant named Hagar as his concubine, and he deceived people, saying that his wife was his sister. Abraham was a human being, just like us. He had many faults and committed many sins.

But how was he able to be so close to God? There were no laws between God and Abraham. At that time, people lived through God, without the law. Abraham's wrongdoing would not be acknowledged, even though Abraham may have done wrong things because there were no laws between God and Abraham. When the people of Israel left Egypt, they did not want simply to receive grace. They said, "We will live keeping the Word of God, so save us." Because the people of Israel were speaking so arrogantly, God said, "Okay, fine then, I will give you the law. Try keeping it. If you keep it, you will be blessed. If not, you will be cursed." "Okay, we will keep it all," they said. But no one could.

A law that cannot be kept is of no value. Suppose I made you a promise tonight, saying, "If you come here at two o'clock tomorrow morning, I will tell you about forgiveness of sin." Then I come here at two in the morning, as promised. You, too, had made the promise to be here. But if none of you come, that is a useless promise. Now, God needs to establish a new law for us because there is no one who can keep the law.

The Bible tells us about this in many places. It says "the law was added because of transgressions, till the seed should come to whom the promise was made." Should we rip up the Old Testament because we no longer need the law? That is not it. We come forth to Jesus Christ by realizing that we are sinners through the law. The book of Galatians calls the law a school-master. We live however we want to because without the law, we do not know that we are sinners. It tells us that we realize through the law we are sinners who could only die and that makes us come forth before Jesus. The law was not given to sanctify us, nor to make us righteous. The law was given to make us realize sin. Please repeat after me.

"The law was given for us to realize sin."

If you had been able to become clean by keeping the law, then He would have given us a law that we could keep. But God gave us the law that we could not keep. It's not because we lack in efforts, nor do we have weaker determination. By nature, we are the ones who cannot keep the law. Why? It is because the whole law should be kept, not just a part of it. Even though you may keep all of the rest but break one law, it is the same as breaking the entire law. When we try to keep the law, and we break it, we realize, "Oh, I am a sinner." Folks, there are so many people today, not knowing this, who are trying hard to keep the law, to go forth to God, to go to heaven.

The woman caught in the act of adultery in John chapter 8 represents not only this woman caught in adultery. This evening, this is actually talking about us. If anyone among you stands before the law to be judged, you can only die. The Bible says, "The wages of sin is death." It is because there is no one who has not sinned. Thus, Jesus had to change the law to save the woman. Jesus wrote on the ground with His finger.

First, God wrote the Ten Commandments of the law. Second, Jesus Christ wrote the law of love. Let's open the Bible. The book of Jeremiah comes after the book of Isaiah, in the Old Testament. Did you find it? Let's read Jeremiah chapter 31 verse 31.

Behold, the days come, saith the LORD, that I will make a new covenant with the house of Israel, and with the house of Judah: Not according to the covenant that I made with their fathers in the day that I took them by the hand to bring them out of the land of Egypt; which my covenant they brake, although I was an husband unto them, saith the Lord:

The law they received on Mt. Sinai was established the day they were led out of Egypt. Now, another law has been established.

. . . although I was an husband unto them, saith the LORD: But this shall be the covenant that I will make with the house of Israel; After those days, saith the LORD, I will put my law in their inward parts, and write it in their hearts; and will be their God, and they shall be my people. And they shall teach no more every man his neighbour, and every man his brother, saying, Know the LORD: for they shall all know me, from the least of them unto the greatest of them, saith the LORD: for I will forgive their iniquity, and I will remember their sin no more. (Jeremiah 31:32-34)

One day, perhaps about two years ago, my wife said, "Honey, I think you need a new suit." I didn't realize it, but my suit had gotten old and was worn out. So I went to the tailor with my wife and got a new suit. Why did I need a new suit? I needed a new suit because my old, worn-out suit would no longer do. Of course, these days there are a lot of people who get new suits, even though they have many good suits hanging in the closet. Folks, why do you need new shoes? If the shoes you are wearing now are worn out, you need to get new shoes.

There was the law between God and the people of Israel.

There was a covenant. God promised, "And all these blessings shall come on thee, and overtake thee, if thou shalt hearken unto the voice of the Lord thy God. Blessed shalt thou be in the city, and blessed shalt thou be in the field. Blessed shall be the fruit of thy body, and the fruit of thy ground, and the fruit of thy cattle, the increase of thy kine, and the flocks of thy sheep. Blessed shall be thy basket and thy store. Blessed shalt thou be when thou comest in, and blessed shalt thou be when thou goest out. But it shall come to pass, if thou wilt not hearken unto the voice of the LORD thy God, cursed shall thou be in the city and cursed shalt thou be in the field. Cursed shall be thy basket and thy store. Cursed shall be the fruit of thy body, and the fruit of thy land, the increase of thy kine, and the flocks of thy sheep. Cursed shalt thou be when thou comest in, and cursed shalt thou be when thou goest out." But, folks, no one among the Israelites could keep the law. No one kept the law perfectly, not only among the people of Israel, but among the many peoples of the world. Thus, it was pointless to God whether He had the law or not. Indeed, from God's perspective, this law was useless. God said that a new covenant, a new law should be established because there was no way we could go out to God through this law. This was prophesied in Jeremiah chapter 31.

Who established that law? God established it. Can Pastor Park change it? He cannot. And that is why Jesus Christ began to write on the ground with His finger. We don't know what He wrote. This woman is a sinner who could only die according to the Law of Moses. The law had to be changed into a new law because Jesus came to save sinners who could only die. Thus, He wrote the law of the grace of the Holy Spirit and this woman no longer needed to be judged according to the old law. Whose judgment does she receive now? She is now judged through Jesus' law of grace and law of love.

> . . . *He that is without sin among you, let him first cast a stone at her. (John 8:7)*

No one was able to stone her. They all went away. Jesus gave His judgment.

> . . . *Neither do I condemn thee: go, and sin no more. (John 8:11)*

Jesus judged the woman through the law of love because He himself bore all of her sins.

There are many of you who are indecisively going back and forth between the two laws. Sometimes you are under one law, the Law of Moses, and sometimes you are under the other law, the law of love. Sometimes you say you have received forgiveness of sin through the grace of Jesus. And sometimes you say, "I'm a sinner who could only die." Your spiritual life cannot grow because you are going back and forth. If you are going to stay under the law, you have to keep the law perfectly. If you are going to come out to Jesus, you need to forget the law and receive grace. You must choose one or the other. Of course, the law is not sin. The law is a good thing.

Some people these days cannot believe that Jesus walked on water. "How can a person walk on water? The specific gravity of a man is greater than the specific gravity of water." Is it not? But if Jesus does only what man can do, I'm not going to believe in Jesus. I believe because Jesus walked on water, because He does things I cannot do. If He does only what I can do, He's exactly like me. Why then would I believe in Him?

Jesus walked on water, right? I too know how to walk on the sea. You people in Busan live near the ocean. Would you like me to teach you how to walk on water? Do you want me to teach you? Of course, I didn't learn it through the Bible, but because we're on the subject, I'll teach you. It's not so difficult, this business of walking on water, so please listen carefully. Run fast toward the ocean at Haeundae Beach. When you get to the water, first, step with your left foot into the sea. Before your left foot sinks, step with your right foot. Then, before your right foot sinks, step with your left foot. If you step with your right foot before your left foot sinks, you can walk to Japan. You can even go to America. If you drown, doing exactly as I have taught you, I'll take the responsibility. But if you delay in stepping with your left foot because your right foot was sinking, I'm not going to take the responsibility. Go try it at Haeundae Beach. You won't drown.

This is funny, right? This is what the law is like. It'd be good, if you could keep the law, but the problem is that we do not have the power to step with our left foot before our right foot sinks. Keeping the law is also impossible for us. There is an old Korean proverb that says, "Don't even look up at a tree you can't climb." Even though you try hard, saying, "Lord," it still doesn't work. I don't know who taught you to do it like that. God gave you the law, knowing that you would be completely unable to keep it. How arrogant would you become, if you could keep the law? Because you cannot keep it, you say, "Lord, I'm a sinner," and you are humbled.

God knows us well. He knows what we can and what we cannot do. Thus, He made the law so we would be unable to keep it. But still we fall into the deception of Satan that says, "Try hard to keep the law," and we try to keep it with all our efforts and become completely blinded, unable to see the pathway of grace.

When I was receiving driver training, the instructor spoke about this. If a person is at a standstill, sitting in the driver's seat and looks straight ahead, he can see a total of 180 degrees to his left and his right. But when he is driving at 100 kilometers per hour he can only see 15 degrees. When I first went to Seoul from the country, the roads were so complicated, but I still had to drive my car. I would open the map with my wife and mark the places I had to visit. We would study how to get to a house before we had to go there. As I drove, I looked only straight ahead. I could not look to the left or to the right because I was unfamiliar with the roads.

I would come back home and talk with my wife. She would say, "Wow, we passed such and such a building today." Then I would say, "Did we pass that building?" I was too busy watching the signals and looking straight ahead, seeing only the traffic because I was so unfamiliar with the roads. Folks, when a person is relaxed and has time, he can see 180 degrees, or even 360 degrees, but when he is going at 100 kilometers per hour, he has a field of vision of only 15 degrees, and the surroundings pass by so quickly.

We are so busy trying to keep the law that we have no chance to look to the side because Satan has fastened our eyes on the law. We are unable to see where the road to forgiveness of sin lies, or what the law of grace is. We cannot see how our sins become forgiven. We try to keep the law. That is the spiritual life of most people.

"Ah! I sinned once again because of my weakness. Lord, please forgive this wretched sinner!"

Folks, even a good song is good only when you hear it once or twice. Would God enjoy you crying so miserably? God would say, "I'm sick of it." Wouldn't He say that? God wants to meet us inside joy. God is the One who gives us peace. God is the Lord of peace. When you are imprisoned under the law, you cannot taste joy, and happiness, or peace in your whole life. You can only cry and pray, "Lord, I am so wicked. Please forgive this sinner."

In addition, you can only say, "You have to get to heaven to know whether you can go to heaven or not." Because you have no faith because you are unable to believe the clear words of promise in the Bible, you can only say, "You have to get there to know it." I said to a certain person, "I live in Gangnam, Daechi Area # 316 in the Unma Apartments." If he answers, "I have to go there to know where it is," then that person does not believe in me. If a person believes in me, even though he has not been there, he will believe my words.

We ran out of cassette tapes when we were recording sermons, and the brother who was in charge called the cassette company in Seoul.

"Please send us 1,000 blank tapes."

Folks, because they trust us, they said, "Please deposit the money in our bank account," and sent us the 1,000 tapes before receiving payment. That person trusted us, and I'm thankful for that. This person was living in Seoul, and sent 1,000 tapes to someone in Busan he did not know. That is faith. "Oh, but what if he does not send me the money?" If he had that doubt, he would be unable to send the tapes.

God clearly promised, "If you do this and that, your sins are forgiven. If you do this, you can be saved, and if you do this, you can go to heaven." If you believe that, you know it, even though you have not been there. You say you have to get there to know it because you do not believe. But if you must stand before God to find out, it's already too late. When you get there, and it is not heaven, but hell, then what good is that? You are already in hell. He gave us the Bible and sent Jesus Christ so we can receive forgiveness of sin and go to heaven, before meeting the Lord on that day.

"Lord, I do not believe in You."

There is no one who says that. No one ever says, "I don't believe in You, God please have compassion on me." Most people think they believe, but if they do not believe in the promise of God, they do not believe in God. I have not been to heaven, but I believe that I will go there. It is because I know that Jesus is not a liar and that the Bible does not lie. This world is not my home. He clearly gave me the eternal land. The Lord promised that one day He would come and take me. He made me that promise. People who have not received the promise have to go there to find out.

Folks, Apostle Paul did not do something well to be saved. The thief on the cross did not do something well to be saved. He did not get saved by trying hard or by trying to keep the law. And that is also true of the woman caught in adultery, receiving forgiveness of sin. If we could keep the law and have our sins cleansed, and if we were able not to sin, we would not need forgiveness of sin. We need the law of grace of forgiveness of sin because we cannot do according to the law since we are sinners who cannot keep all of the law. How amazing that law of grace is! Making a sinner into a sinner is what the Law of Moses does and making a sinner a righteous person is what the law of grace does. Folks, I do not say that I can go to heaven because I don't have sin. It is not that I can go to heaven because I've never lied, nor stolen and have never once sinned.

A long time ago, there was a liar's contest. People who were known to be good liars got together and competed to see who could lie the best. The last contestant stood at the podium and said, "Loving folks, I am in the lying contest, but I have no confidence because ever since I was born I've never once lied. And so, I really cannot lie. I am here only because the people around me continually told me to be here. Unable to lie, I will just step down." At the awards ceremony, he won first place.

The person who says, "I do not lie," is the best liar. We are all people who have broken the law. We are all people who have sinned. But the Lord changed the law. He cleansed us and made us fit, we who had already fallen into sin. What did Jesus say, after writing on the ground with His finger?

"I do not condemn you. You have no sin."

Folks, before I realized this precious secret, every time I read the Bible I envied this woman caught in adultery. Although she was caught in adultery and was in a position to be beaten to death, I envied her that she had once heard Jesus, "You don't have sin." Another person I envied was the thief on the cross. Even though you're being executed, if you could go to paradise with the Lord, how blessed would that be? Later on, I learned that the woman caught in adultery was me. I came to know that the thief on the cross was me. Thus, I realized that the words Jesus had spoken to the woman caught in adultery were words spoken to me. I came to realize that the words He said to the thief on the cross were words He was speaking to me. I later opened my eyes and saw that the stories of David, the stories of Paul, and so many stories of others in the Bible, were all stories of me. The Lord said to the woman caught in adultery, ". . . Neither do I condemn thee. . ." Those words, I believed them as words the Lord was speaking to me. Jesus said that He does not condemn me. Jesus was saying that I was cleansed. Jesus said that I was righteous. Hallelujah! That is why I am righteous. Do you think Pastor Park is righteous because he does not sin? If a person becomes righteous by not sinning, it is through his own effort. If a person who has sinned much, like me, becomes righteous by Jesus cleansing them, this is through grace. Thus, I received forgiveness of sin by grace, at no cost, there was nothing that I did. There was no effort on my part.

"Sins of years are washed away.
Blackest stains become as snow.
Darkest night is changed to day,
when I to the fountain go.
I'm believing and receiving
while I to the fountain go.
In my heart, the waves are cleansing,
whiter than the driven snow."

It is not because I have not sinned. It is not because I have not lied. I am cleansed through believing that the Lord was crucified and died.

A lot of time has passed. I will say just one more thing and wrap it up for tonight. And we also need to have personal fellowship. Please open your Bible to Romans chapter 4, verse 4. I will read,

Now to him that worketh is the reward not reckoned of grace, but of debt. But to him that worketh not, but believeth on him that justifieth the ungodly, his faith is counted for righteousness.

Can God call a sinner righteous? He cannot. A sinner is a sinner, and a righteous person is a righteous person. Thus, God cannot call us righteous, if we are sinners. God did not judge us. He waited until He justified us so He could call us righteous. He waited until Jesus was crucified and died, to wash away all our sins. God saw that all our sins were washed away through the crucifixion of Jesus. God saw us after Jesus was crucified and said that we are righteous. When God sees us, all of our sins are washed away on the cross of Jesus. But how does this look to you? Among you, there are those who have the eyes of God, saying, "All our sins are washed away." People who believe so are justified by faith. But those who say, "But still I'm a sinner," are people who say that the crucifixion of Jesus did not wash away our sins.

There are many people who pray, saying, "God, forgive my sins." You are doing well, but let's think carefully about this. Folks, when Jesus was crucified, did He or did He not wash away your sins? If your sins are washed away, do you have to ask to have them washed away again?

"But we sin again."

Then those sins that you commit, are they not washed away? Here, we can see how the thoughts of those who have faith and those who don't differ. Those who have faith say, "Ah ha, my sins have been cleansed as white as snow." Those who do not have faith say, "But still I am a sinner."

Thus, those who have no faith do not rely on the grace of the cross of Jesus Christ, but on some effort of their own. They rely on their own works. And those who do not have faith can only fall under the law. They can only end up trying to keep the law. Galatians tells us that after faith comes we are no longer servants under the law.

I am sorry that I have spoken so dogmatically this evening. Anyway, in today's sermon, Jesus did not judge that woman according to the Law of Moses. If He had judged her according to the Law of Moses, that woman could only have been stoned to death. Jesus judged this woman through the law of love, the law of grace, a law completely different from the Law of Moses.

This evening, you cannot help but to be destroyed, if you stand before the Law of Moses. Please come forth to the law of grace of Jesus. Then this evening you will be able to receive the cleansing of your sins. Let's close our eyes and bow our heads.

Loving folks, we heard this evening the amazing words of how Jesus came and forgave all our sins, not through the law, but through love. I know that this one session is not enough for us to talk all about this. But you may think that you are just like the woman caught in adultery, thinking, "God, I am dirty and filthy. Just like the woman caught in adultery came forth to Jesus and received the promise of forgiveness of sin, I want to receive the cleansing of my sins before You, Lord, tonight. I want my heart to be freed from sin through the blood of the cross where Jesus was crucified. God, have compassion on me. Please save me." If you feel this way, please raise your hand. Is there any one of you who wants to have assurance of forgiveness of sin, who wants to become born again by faith and receive eternal redemption? Please raise your hand. Thank you.

4

The Man with
an Infirmity for 38 Years

Are You Trying to Become Righteous
by Keeping the Law?

Rather than tithes or morning prayer and fasting, Jesus commanded us to first have our sins cleansed. When our sins are cleansed, the Holy Spirit will be able to dwell inside of us and will guide us towards true change.

However, aren't you living with unclear expectations precisely like the man with an infirmity for 38 years, thinking to yourself, "my spiritual life will eventually get better"? We can never fully keep the law. Therefore, a person who attempts to become righteous by keeping the law becomes a hypocrite.

4

The Man with an
Infirmity for 38 Years

Let's read from John chapter 5, from verse 1 to 9 in the
New Testament of the Bible.

After this there was a feast of the Jews; and Jesus went up to
Jerusalem. Now there is at Jerusalem by the sheep market a
pool, which is called in the Hebrew tongue Bethesda, hav-
ing five porches. In these lay a great multitude of impotent
folk, of blind, halt, withered, waiting for the moving of the
water. For an angel went down at a certain season into the
pool, and troubled the water: whosoever then first after the
troubling of the water stepped in was made whole of what-
soever disease he had. And a certain man was there, which
had an infirmity thirty and eight years. When Jesus saw
him lie, and knew that he had been now a long time in that

case, he saith unto him, Wilt thou be made whole? The impotent man answered him, Sir, I have no man, when the water is troubled, to put me into the pool: but while I am coming, another steppeth down before me. Jesus saith unto him, Rise, take up thy bed, and walk. And immediately the man was made whole, and took up his bed, and walked: and on the same day was the sabbath.

Loving folks, how are you doing? I want to see how many of you received forgiveness of sin this week. Would those of you who have received forgiveness of sin this week please raise your hand? Raise your hand high, please. Thank you. Okay, put your hands down. Through attending this conference, which ends on Friday, I hope that every one of you will have the sins in your heart cleansed so that nothing may block you from God. Then Jesus can dwell in you and you in Him without any discomfort.

Long ago, there was a merchant in Kangwondo Province. He carried many different household items in his cart. Sometimes, he would go from town to town to sell his goods, and he would receive things such as crops, fruits, or honey as payment. One day, as he was going about, he came upon a certain village. As he was preparing to sell his goods, the old men of the village, who were playing chess in the shade under a tree, saw the merchant and said, "Hey! Mr. Merchant! Come over here!"

It didn't look as if they would buy anything from him, but he approached them anyway and said, "Yes, did you call me?"

"I once lived as a servant in the city. I eventually moved out here and founded this village. The land here is very fertile and vast. We are very well off here and live comfortably. I remember back in the city, however, that my master's son used to always study and read. We want to teach our children how to read. If you know of a good teacher, could you recommend one for us? Since you are a merchant, and travel all over the country, I'm sure you know of someone, don't you?"

The merchant listened, and thought, "These people in the mountains don't know anything. Okay, I won't go around selling goods anymore. I'll become a respected teacher, here in this town. How nice would that be?" He answered, "As a matter of fact, I taught reading in the city some time ago. Unfortunately, because of the unstable political situation, I had to leave. Now, I go around as a merchant, selling these goods."

Then the village elders thought, "That's great!" and were very excited. They told the merchant, "Starting today, we will build a school. Would you please be so kind as to teach the children of our village?" This merchant, however, thought it wouldn't be wise to accept right away, so he acted as if he was turning them down, but he eventually agreed to it.

That day the townspeople held a meeting. They built a school and a house for the teacher to stay in. They clothed him in beautiful silk pants, shirts, and jackets. They gave him an expensive hat and treated him like royalty. The merchant was now being fed well and living very comfortably. Finally, the school was complete, and they held an opening ceremony.

The day after the opening ceremony, 15 or so students came to the school to learn to read and write, but what could this uneducated merchant possibly teach them? Then he thought, "Well, I've come this far. I can't go back now." He decided to go forward with it. For a while, he stood there, blinking, and then he said, "Write this down."

"Yes, sir."

"House: H-A-U-S."

"Light: L-A-I-T."

"Class: K-L-A-S."

"Door: D-O-R."

"Okay, we will learn these four words today. Go home and memorize them."

The students were so happy that they were finally learning to read and write. It was so easy to memorize that all the students got everything right on a quiz.

"House: H-A-U-S. Light: L-A-I-T. Class: K-L-A-S. Door: D-O-R. Today, memorize these words." The students recited, "House: H-A-U-S. Light: L-A-I-T."

As a result, there was a reading boom in that little mountain village. Even the village women who were fetching water said, "Hey, why don't we learn to read and write? Let's learn from our children!" The school was becoming more and more beautiful each day. The elders of the village were so thankful to this teacher for his work, that they would bring him meat, cakes, furniture, and he received grand treatment in every way. The students would improve every day, and they would come to school the next day: "Bird: B-R-D. Knife: N-A-I-F. People: P-I-P-L. Ball: B-O-L."

They continued to learn in this way. Even the farmers began to learn. They would recite, "Hammer: H-E-M-R. Wheelbarrow: W-I-L-B-A-R-O." In the mornings, the only sound you could hear in the village was people memorizing and reciting. Of course, they had no books, but then they did not need books, the way they were learning. After about six months, this uneducated teacher began to run out of things to say.

"Teacher, last time you told us S-N-A-K is snake, but now you are saying S-N-A-K is snack? How could that be?" He began to become confused. "Sorry guys. That's just how it is."

"Oh, really?"

"Yeah, really. S-N-A-K is for both snake and snack. Isn't that easy?"

The students liked their teacher very much. From time to time, he would tell the students about his experience from travelling all over the country as a merchant. The students would listen with delight.

Then, one night, after much thought, the merchant realized, "The pitcher goes once too often to the well and at last it breaks. If I keep on being greedy like this, I'll get caught." Nevertheless, the students came to him once again the next morning. He said, "Students, I don't feel well today, so we will end early and you may go home," and he sent the students home early.

After sending them home, he packed up all the gifts he had received, took his money and packed his bags. Late that night, he ran off. The students did not know about it, however and the next morning came to school. They called out, "Teacher, Teacher!" But, he was not in his room, nor in the shed, nor was he in the bathroom. The children began to cry, searching for their teacher, but he was nowhere to be found. The entire village was so sad they did not know what to do.

"Our teacher, who had given us hope, who worked so hard to bring us joy, and who taught us how to read, where have you gone?" The students were all crying, as they went around looking for him. The elders could not bear to watch the students searching so sincerely for their teacher, so they picked two healthy, good, young men and sent them to the city to bring back a new teacher.

As the two young men were bringing home the great new teacher they had found in the city, they talked about many things along the way. They told him about how great the last teacher was and about how there had been a reading boom in their town. This new teacher, who was coming along with them, thought, "Will I be able to teach them as well as their former teacher, who was so popular?"

The next day, before he began to teach the students how to read, he told the students, "Recite everything you have learned until now." One student confidently said, "House: H-A-U-S. Light: L-A-I-T. Class: K-L-A-S. Door: D-O-R."

The students recited everything, exactly as they had been taught. The teacher was at a loss for words, but he couldn't just come out and tell the students that the teacher they had admired all this time was wrong. So he began to speak, saying, "Students, the man who has been teaching you until now is truly an amazing person. He taught you all how to read very well because he is such a special person, sent from the heavens above. However, I cannot teach you that well. Although, I cannot teach you as well, please learn from me also."

"Yes," they replied, and the students became tense and sat down to begin learning the lesson.

"Students, have you ever seen this word before?"

"No."

"This word is 'school.' Repeat after me, S-C-H-O-O-L."

"Teacher, I have a question. How could it be S-C-H-O-O-L? It's supposed to be S-K-U-L. That's wrong, Teacher."

"I know, that's what the great teacher taught you, but I am teaching you like this, so learn it this way from me."

But when he said, "school," one more time, there were some students who spelled it, "S-K-U-L," and others who spelled it, "S-C-H-O-O-L." It was a big mess.

"This is the second word that we are going to learn. This is the word, 'bee': B-E-E."

"Teacher, how could that be 'bee'? 'Bee' is spelled, 'B-I.'"

"Black: B-L-A-C-K," exclaimed the teacher.

"No, no it's, 'black': B-L-E-K."

"Purple: P-U-R-P-L-E."

"Purple: P-R-P-L."

"Home: H-O-M-E."

"Home: H-O-M."

Finally, the teacher gave up. He went to the elders of the village and said, "The village students learned under such an amazing and wonderful teacher that there is nothing more for me to teach them. Thus, I will have to leave." Upon saying this, he went on his way.

Deep in the mountain valley, there is no way to tell whether, "School: S-C-H-O-O-L," is correct or "School: S-K-U-L," is correct. However, if you learn how to spell words like that and go to a spelling bee, right away, your ability will be revealed. We cannot tell whether I am right, you are right, or who's right in the village, deep in the mountains. Since this is the easy way, it is taught, "Apple: A-P-L. House: H-A-U-S. . . ."

People, this is not something to laugh about. There are

many people today who carry on their spiritual lives in this way. Because they simply do not know, they live ambiguous, false spiritual lives. Although it may be difficult, you must learn everything correctly and precisely: "School: S-C-H-O-O-L. Black: B-L-A-C-K. Purple: P-U-R-P-L-E. Home: H-O-M-E." You must learn it like this, but because it's difficult, you let it slip by and say, "School: S-K-U-L is fine, and S-C-H-O-O-L is also fine." Folks, why do you believe in Jesus? Why do you go to church? Why did you come to the conference today? Why are you suffering from pain inside? Why doesn't your spiritual life work out? There is a reason for that. It is because we were cast out of Eden because of sin. You cannot go forth to God with sin because there is a wall of sin that is blocking us from God. A sheep that leaves the flock and goes deep into the mountains would be afraid, terrified, and in pain. That is how it is with humans who have left God. Although they have money, a pretty face, get good grades and hold a high position in life, there can be no true peace for anyone who has left God.

Why do you believe in Jesus? There is a wall of sin blocking the way between God and us. So we believe in Jesus, to wash away our sins, to restore our relationship with God and to allow us to go out to God, just as freely as Adam did before he and Eve committed sin. In that case, how do we wash away our sins? Saying, "Bird: B-R-D. Knife: N-A-I-F," is funny, but people trying to wash away their sins, according to their own thoughts, without knowing how and without looking for it in the Bible, is even funnier than that. Folks, I am not saying this to insult anyone. I asked some students, who had returned from a retreat, "What grace did you receive at the retreat?"

"We received forgiveness of sin."

"How did you do that?"

"The main lecturer told us to write all of our sins down on a piece of paper. Then we burned them in the campfire, and he said that would wash away our sins."

That's exactly the same as saying, "Bird: B-R-D," and "Knife: N-A-I-F." Where in the Bible does it say that writing your sins on a piece of paper and burning it is the way to wash away your sins? Is that what David did? Is that what Paul did? Is that what Peter did? If not, is that what Jesus told us to do? Because they don't know what's exactly right, "Bird: B-R-D," and "Knife: N-A-I-F," seem right.

An employee of Far East Broadcasting Station came to me and asked me to preach forgiveness of sin to our countrymen in China, North Korea, and the Soviet Union. I went to the broadcasting station and spoke about forgiveness of sin. I received many letters from pastors and ministers saying that the program was very good. Some people asked us to send some books written by Pastor Ock Soo Park, if there were any. I heard that one pastor used my broadcast sermons to lead the early morning services at his church every day. Some people, however, thought that something was strange because what I preached was different from how they had understood they could cleanse themselves of their sins.

I'm telling you as adamantly as I can. Let's stop living a, "Bird: B-R-D, Knife: N-A-I-F" type of spiritual life. We need to know exactly, according to the words of the Bible, how to receive the cleansing of our sins. Even though you may record all of your sins and burn them in the campfire, your sins are not burnt, destroyed, or washed away. This is an example of a, "Bird: B-R-D," and, "Knife: N-A-I-F," kind of spiritual life. Do you understand what I am saying?

We decided that the title of our conference here in Busan would be, "The Secret of Forgiveness of Sin and Being Born Again." What must I do to receive forgiveness of sin, and how can I be born again? How does the Bible say we can achieve forgiveness of sin? This is what you must clearly discover in the Word this week. How tormented you would be, if you had to go to hell because you thought that all your sins were washed away when you wrote them on a piece of paper and burned it in a camp fire? Heaven is a place you can enter only if your sin is gone. You can never enter into heaven if you have sin because the Holy Spirit cannot enter a sinner's heart. Speaking in tongues, prophesying, and casting out demons without taking care of the sin in your heart, is not Biblical. Speaking in tongues and prophesying are important, but more importantly, the sin inside of us must first be washed clean, as white as snow. When our sins are clean, only then will the Holy Spirit come into our hearts.

> *Behold, the LORD's hand is not shortened, that it cannot save; neither his ear heavy, that it cannot hear: But your iniquities have separated between you and your God, and your sins have hid his face from you, that he will not hear.*

That's what Isaiah chapter 59, verses 1 and 2 tell us. No matter how tall or handsome we are, no matter how rich or smart we may be and no matter how much knowledge we may have, the Holy Spirit cannot enter a person who has sin. That's why we need to receive forgiveness of sin.

A while ago, a young woman was demon possessed. This woman was not a believer, but she had married a believing household. Her parents-in-law were believers, but this lady had no faith. Her mother-in-law would always say, "Your faith is so small. You need to receive the Holy Spirit." She wanted to do whatever it took to receive the Holy Spirit, so she went up to the mountain to pray. For days, she fasted and called out, saying, "Father God, give me the Holy Spirit." You know that the Holy Spirit can never enter the heart of a sinner. Instead, the devil came into her, saying, "I am the Holy Spirit." This lady came back rejoicing and she had, indeed, changed.

She held onto her mother-in-law, crying and said, "Oh, Mother, I was so wrong for so long." The mother-in-law thought that her daughter-in-law's faith had become stronger, but after one or two days, her attitude changed. Some 10 days later, she went completely mad. You may pray with sins in your heart saying, "Holy Spirit, come into me." The Holy Spirit does not enter you, not because He does not want to, but because He cannot enter when there is sin. Thus, speaking in tongues, prophesying and receiving the fire before receiving forgiveness of sin are not through the Holy Spirit.

Folks, these things are clearly revealed in the Word. The devil acts as if he is the Holy Spirit to deceive us. He comes inside of us and works within us. The sin in your heart must be completely washed away for the Holy Spirit to work inside of you. When through the blood of the Lord, our sins are washed away as white as snow, only then will the Holy Spirit come into our hearts. We walk with the Lord from then on.

Our Lord Jesus Christ is holy. Jesus is the God of love. Also, our Lord Jesus is not a weathercock. He does not come and go as He wishes. He said that once He comes and washes away our sins, He will never leave us. He says, "I shall give you another Comforter, that I may abide with you forever." However, because most people today have not been cleansed of their sins, they rely on their feelings to be assured of their spiritual power. But such feelings quickly disappear. These things did not come from the Lord. Jesus tells you to be cleansed of your sins before you pay your tithe, go to early morning service, or fast. The Holy Spirit of Jesus will come inside of you, after your sins have been washed away. Then you will naturally change.

Folks, yesterday was October 7th. It was my birthday, the day I was reborn. I was born on July 20th, 1944, and I was born again on October 7th, 1962. So I have two birthdays. My first birth was of the flesh, through my parents. The other was the day I was born again, through the Holy Spirit of God, by receiving forgiveness of sin. Yesterday was the 25th anniversary of the day I was born again. I suffered much because of sin, and I confessed my sins every day. I was at the age when I needed a lot of sleep, but I prayed early in the morning, all by myself when nobody was at the church. Electricity was not well developed back then. The lights would go on and off in the middle of the service so I always had a spare oil lamp. I would turn on the oil lamp before anyone came and would ring the early morning service bell. I would kneel down and confess my sins. I would get sleepy, when I confessed silently, but I was afraid someone would hear me if I confessed out loud. So I confessed my sins before anybody could come. That was how I began my day.

"God, I lied yesterday. I hated someone. Please forgive me." Then, when I heard people coming to the early morning service, I would stop and attend the service. When people left after the service, I would confess some more. That day, I would try again not to sin. I was good at the sin you commit with your mouth, lying, maybe because I have such a big mouth. I lied even when I was just with my friends. They would ask me, "Hey, how much was that watch?" I would say, "I got it for 10 dollars," adding five dollars to the price. In Revelation chapter 21, verse 8, it says, ". . . and all liars, shall have their part in the lake which burneth with fire and brimstone: which is the second death."

I thought, "Oh, no. I'm going to hell." I would try not to lie, but when the next day came around, I had to confess again.

"God, I committed this and that sin, please forgive me. Please, help me not to sin today." I thought I should just not answer people because every time I opened my mouth, I would automatically lie. Whenever somebody would ask me a question, I would shut my mouth and say, "Hmmm, hmmm, hmmm," but that would last only until about 10 in the morning: after a while, my mouth would turn on, and I would be lying without even realizing it. It was so painful. Then one day I went to my pastor.

"Pastor! I may appear, on the outside, to be a good student, but actually, I'm a horrible person. I have these kinds of sins." I didn't care about being embarrassed. I made up my mind, and I confessed to the pastor. "How can I be forgiven of my sins?

"You must repent."

So, I did repent. When that didn't work, I went to ask the pastor again. He said that I must bear fruits of repentance. "How do I bear fruits of repentance?"

"If you stole from someone, give it back, and if you harmed anyone, repay them for it."

"Oh, I cannot do that. I guess I am not one of the chosen people." There was no way I could pay back all of the people I had harmed. When I used to go to school, I would take kids to the bakery and hit them, threatening them saying, "Buy me some bread." I lied, I hated others, I was full of jealousy and anger. How could I undo all of that? It was so disappointing to think that I was not one of the chosen people. I was in despair. It was very painful. "Heck, I'm going to go to hell anyway," I would say, "Let me sin even more and enjoy myself as much as I can before I die." or "I'll just go to hell." I tried drinking, smoking and fighting, but the more I sinned, the more pain came into my heart. I could not bear hearing the bell of the Sunday service from the chapel.

It was painful for me to come to church and painful to go out, I tried everything I could to resolve my sins. I tried confessing, repenting, crying, fasting, and praying all night long. The more I did, the heavier the sin in my heart became. After confessing, I felt lighter for a little while, but I would remember it all after a few days, and my heart would begin to fall into darkness again.

Folks, what are we supposed to do to receive forgiveness of sin? Loving saints, I've called you saints, but I don't know whether you are really saints or almost saints. "Saints" is exactly what it says, holy people, holy group. You must have no blemishes, no sins, and must be clean to be a saint. A person who has sin, is not a true saint. Isn't that so? We cannot just gloss over this. We must speak about it clearly.

"This pastor, what's his problem, digging into every little detail? It'd be good, if he'd just talk about faith and make us feel better and talk about how to receive the fire. That's why Pastor Park has problems." Is there anyone who thinks that way? Do you know why I'm being like this? I don't want to say to you, "School: S-K-U-L," but "S-C-H-O-O-L." So I hope that you will bear with me and listen.

This year I have gone to many churches and have led many conferences. Over the years, I have visited leper colonies, army bases, schools, prisons and have led many retreats. I've also done conferences on mountains. When I go to a church and ask people to raise their hands to receive forgiveness of sin, many people raise their hands, but although they may behave like gentlemen on the outside, they cannot deceive their own conscience. They know that they have sin in their heart that they have not resolved.

"Kids, c'mon, let's go to church." They put the Bible under their arm and appear gentle and holy. In the Bible there is a story that illustrates this very well. It is the story of Captain Naaman in 2 Kings chapter 5. On the outside, he wore a helmet, armor and everything was shiny, as a military captain. But on the inside, Captain Naaman was rotting away with leprosy. That may be the spiritual image of people today. They lead spiritual lives on the outside, as deacons, elders, choir members and Sunday School teachers. But on the inside, they are people who have not had their sins cleansed and are suffering in pain.

Let's go back to the story I talked about yesterday evening,

"The Woman Caught in Adultery." Many people had brought stones to kill her. Jesus said, "A person without sin among you, let you first cast a stone at her."

There was no one who could stone her. Why was that? They didn't have sin on the outside. It appeared that only this woman had sin, but on the inside, they were all sinners.

Folks, do not let the sin in your heart pass you by unnoticed. Unless it is taken care of, once and for all, you will surely regret the day you get to that land. Your certificate of church membership, your titles, and the plaques you have received will not help you. The only thing that will count is a pure heart cleansed of sin. The volunteer work you do for the Lord will not matter, unless every speck of sin has been washed away.

Then folks, how can we wash away our sins? What exactly does the Bible say we must do? People do not know. They believe for 10 years, 20 years, 30 years, yet they are still sinners. If they die like that, it's hell! Isn't that true? Folks, why do you believe in Jesus?

"We believe so we can receive forgiveness of sin."

"Have you received forgiveness of sin?"

"Yes, I have."

"Oh, then you should have no sin, right?"

"No, I still have sin."

There is something wrong with this. If all of their sin is washed away, they are not supposed to have any sin. But if sin is still there, even when they are cleansed, that means it is as good as not having had them washed away at all. Jesus was crucified to cleanse us of our sins, but if your sin still remains, it is as if the death of the Lord was for nothing. Isn't that true? We cannot talk about this problem, all at once, this morning, but I will address it, little by little. The condition of your heart is important in receiving forgiveness of sin because forgiveness is accomplished within your heart.

John Wesley, the founder of the Methodist Church, worked passionately for God. He visited homes to preach the gospel, helped the poor and went into slums to preach. People labeled him the Passionate Believer.

After working in England, he went to the United States to preach the gospel. There were no airplanes back then and no good ships like we have today. He had to cross the Atlantic Ocean on a small ship. Along the way, the ship ran into a storm. Wesley was so afraid, he was trembling at the bottom of the ship. Then, all of a sudden, he heard people singing praises. When he went in the direction of where the hymns were coming from, people dressed poorly were on the deck, pulling on ropes and tying down the ship. Although the sinking of the ship was imminent, they were singing hymns with peaceful faces. What kind of people were they, that they could be at such peace and have so much light shining on their faces, even before death? He could not understand. "I am a pastor, a missionary, and I'm not even like that. . . ." Thankfully, the ship safely arrived in the United States. When they arrived, a person, Spangenberg, who had been on board singing hymns and pulling on the ropes, spoke to Wesley.

"Mr. Wesley, may I ask you a question?"

"Sure, go ahead."

"Do you know who Jesus Christ is?" he asked the missionary.

"Yes, I know Him very well. Jesus Christ is the Savior that came to save all mankind from sin."

"Yes, that's right. So, did the Savior of mankind save you, Mr. John Wesley, from your sins? Are you now in sin or have you been saved from sin?"

To save means to rescue, right? But if you are struggling on the surface at Haeundae Beach, and you are saying, "I am saved, you are saved, we are saved," that is absolute nonsense. When a person who is struggling on the surface is rescued, then he can say, "I am saved." When a person is struggling in the grip of sin, and he says, "I'm saved," that is contradictory.

John Wesley could not answer. Of course, he could do more than answer, according to his knowledge, but he could not say anything in his heart. He just sat there with his head down. He eventually failed in his mission in the United States and returned home. There, he entered a small chapel and sat in the back. He listened to Martin Luther's lectures on Romans. There, John Wesley gained a clear testimony of having all of his sins forgiven. At that point, he changed. Apostle Paul was like that, D. L. Moody was like that, and C. H. Spurgeon was like that. The famous servants of God did not live spiritual life through their own names and their own efforts. They overcame sin through the power of Jesus, and they preached the Word through the power of Jesus.

Jesus once went to the pool of Bethesda. Once in a while an angel came upon the pool and troubled the water. The first person to enter into the pool, when the water was troubled, would be healed of whatsoever disease he had. People of various diseases were always gathered around the pool. The blind, the lame, the withered. If it were today, cancer patients would surely be there. Among those people were many invalids. One was a pitiful man, diseased for 38 years, who could not move. Jesus knew him, went up to him and asked him, "Wilt thou be made whole?" He could not be healed, however, because when the water was troubled, other people would go in before him. He was a pathetic fellow, always waiting for something to happen. Just as they say, "No one is loyal to a long disease," I don't know if his wife died or ran away, but he had no family as he had suffered from his disease for 38 years. He could not move, he could only stretch out his hands and eat the food people gave him. It was there he went to the bathroom. He lived with a vague hope that he would one day go into the water first, when the water was troubled and while everyone else was sleeping.

This morning, isn't your spiritual life like this? Like the man with an infirmity for 38 years, you try to do it, but it doesn't work. You are waiting for something to happen, vaguely thinking, "Won't my faith somehow get better?" Aren't you relying upon something untrustworthy, on some kind of unclear, unsure thing to come? Jesus came to this man, but no one knew who Jesus was. Our Lord comes upon your heart, from time to time. The Bible says,

Behold, I stand at the door, and knock: if any man hear my voice, and open the door, I will come in to him, and will sup with him, and he with me.

Jesus knocks upon the door of our heart. "Do you want to be made whole?" He asks. "Do you want your faith to become stronger?" "Do you want to have a life of victory?" "Do you want to receive forgiveness of sin?" Folks, can our Lord heal this man's disease right away? Yes He can! But what does the man think? He's speaking with Jesus, thinking, "I am not sure who you are, but I hope you will push me into the water when it is troubled." Folks, Jesus does not make you work harder or make you do better. He changes us from deep within. Right now, it is impossible for this man to try, on his own, to go into the water first, when the water is troubled.

Folks, there is something interesting here. Who does it say would trouble the water? It says an angel. What does that angel represent? In the Bible, it says that the law was given through angels. All verses in the Bible have mates. It is teaching us that trying to keep the law, to become righteous and to become holy, is as impossible as the man with an infirmity for 38 years, who cannot move, trying to go to the water when the angel troubles it. If that person could go in to the water when it is troubled and be healed, then there would be no need for him to look for Jesus. Isn't that right? Jesus came to deliver this person because he could not go into the water.

Let's look at another verse.

Now we know that what things soever the law saith, it saith to them who are under the law: that every mouth may be stopped, and all the world may become guilty before God. (Romans 3:29)

Please listen. Is the law a good thing or a bad thing? It is a good thing. The problem is that we cannot keep the law. If we could keep every part of the law, then there would be nothing better than the law. Because we cannot keep the law, it is useless, no matter how good it is. Do you understand this? Why are you a sinner? It is because you cannot keep the law. Indeed, the law speaks to those who cannot keep it.

"Do not lie. Do not commit adultery. Do not steal. Do not deceive." Who is it saying that to? It says that to those who lie and commit adultery. The law does not say that to the person who is doing nothing. God is telling us not to do such things because we are lying, committing adultery and stealing.

It is too late for us to go forth to God through the law. If a person says he can keep the law perfectly, he is a hypocrite because there is no one who can keep the law. He is a hypocrite who acts as if he keeps the law, although he is unable to.

But now the righteousness of God without the law is manifested, being witnessed by the law and the prophets. (Romans 3:21)

This is what God said to us in the Old Testament. He said that if we keep all of this law, then we are righteous. We tried hard to keep the law, in order for us to become righteous. But we broke every part of the law. A way to become righteous that has nothing to do with the law has now come to us.

Folks, here is a cup. Let's say that this one is righteousness and this one is the righteousness of Pastor Ock Soo Park. When I sin, does this righteousness break, or not? Yes, it breaks. Then wouldn't I put it back together and repair it? Because I can't go to heaven if I am not righteous, whenever I sin, I would say, "Oh Lord, please forgive me." I would try to put my righteousness back together, seal it and patch it up.

But in Isaiah, it says that our righteousness is like filthy rags. This broken and ruined cup is our righteousness. We struggle to patch it up and put it together, to decorate it and to go to heaven. But when we patch one side, the other side breaks. When we seal up the other side, this side starts to leak. It is all pitiful in the eyes of God. That is why God says, "Hey, don't wrestle with that. I will give you the righteousness of Jesus, so come to heaven with that." That's what He says.

You need righteousness to go to heaven. Folks, which righteousness breaks when I sin? It is my righteousness that breaks, not the righteousness of Jesus. If Jesus sins, then that is a big problem. There is no way for us to go to heaven, if that cup breaks. Folks, isn't that right? My righteousness is already rubbish, is already broken, and is already completely ruined.

The reason Pastor Park can say loudly that he can go to heaven is because he has received the righteousness of Jesus. No matter what mistake I might make, the righteousness of Jesus does not break. Thus, I take the righteousness of Jesus with me and Jesus takes my broken, dirty righteousness. God sees it and says, "Ah, He has sin and it's not going to work. Execute Him." That is why Jesus took our place and was crucified. All the bad things that we have done have gone over onto Jesus. On the other hand, all the righteousness of Jesus, of doing good things and truthful works, and obeying exactly the Word of God, has come upon us.

That's why, when you go to heaven, you cannot take your own righteousness of what you have done. Foolish people look at their own righteousness. They compare themselves to others and comfort themselves, thinking that they are a little bit better.

They cover and decorate themselves. They think they can go before God with their own righteousness. According to the standard of God, that is not good enough. That person is destined to go to hell. I cannot go forth with my things because all of my righteousness is already broken. So, trembling, I say, "It's not going to work." Then Jesus says, "Hey, Pastor Park! I will give you My righteousness. Go with My righteousness."

Then I go boldly forward with the righteousness of Christ. I am righteous, aren't I? A righteous person is not special, but merely someone who has righteousness. Tell me, who are the rich? If you have a lot of money, then you are rich. Who is a beggar? If you have no money and you are begging, then you are a beggar. That's right. Thus, a righteous person isn't someone special, but a person who has righteousness. That is a righteous person.

In the Bible, it says, "there is none righteous, no, not one." When you look at your own righteousness, there are no righteous people. But there are many righteous people who have the righteousness of Jesus, which came from God. It is said that Noah was a righteous person.

It is written in James that the effectual fervent prayer of a righteous man availeth much. In Psalms it says, the ways of the righteous are different from the ways of sinners. It says that God hears the prayers of the righteous. No one is righteous with his own righteousness, but if we have the righteousness of Jesus, are we righteous people or not? We are.

Folks, what do you need to get on the express bus? All you need is a ticket. Regardless of how you got it, if you have a ticket, then you can get on the bus. How can you go to heaven?

All you need is righteousness. You go forward with the righteousness of Jesus, the righteousness that came through the Lord, justifying us. That is why, there's a hymn that goes:

"When he shall come with trumpet sounds,
O may I then in Him be found;
Dressed in His righteousness alone,
Faultless to stand before the throne."

We can boldly go into heaven. Folks, suppose you have no money to buy a ticket, and I bought a ticket for you. Just because someone else bought it for you, would you feel insecure and be afraid to get on the bus? No, you would not. As long as you have a ticket, you will sit there peacefully and enjoy everything on the bus. When you go to heaven, you need to take righteousness, but to get on the express bus, you need to take your ticket. Because we go with the righteousness of Jesus, it does not matter what kind of human we may be. We go with the faith to believe in the righteousness of Jesus.

Before long, we will all go to that land. So what, if we suffer a little on this earth? So what, if we starve a little? And so what, if we get trampled on by others a little? So what, if we get cursed at? I carry my ID, my driver's license, and my credit cards in my wallet when I travel. No matter where I go, I always keep my license with me because it is always in my wallet. If I lose my wallet, I lose my license with it. And if it's found, they are both found. If my wallet is nailed, then my license is nailed also. If my wallet is burnt, my license will be burnt along with it. In the same way, all my sins are washed away and I am inside of Jesus through my faith in Him. The Lord is always with me, and I am in the Lord. If my wallet goes to Seoul, my license also goes to Seoul. If my wallet goes to Busan, my license also goes to Busan. If Jesus is in Seoul, so am I. When Jesus is in Busan, so am I. When Jesus goes to heaven, I go to heaven as well. Do you think that I have the skills to set up a ladder and climb it all the way to heaven? No, it is all accomplished through Jesus. Thus, we must be righteous, like Jesus, to come to Him because He is righteous.

That's what Romans chapter 3 verse 21 explains clearly. There is another righteousness of God that came to us, which had nothing to do with righteousness gained by keeping the law. That was the righteousness Jesus Christ gave us. Jesus was crucified for your sins.

Even the righteousness of God which is by faith of Jesus Christ unto all and upon all them that believe: for there is no difference. (Romans 3:22)

Folks, if I am standing here with another person, we cannot both be righteous in exactly the same way. One person must be better or worse than the other person. They cannot be exactly the same, if it is through their own actions. Folks, but we do not go with our own actions. We go through the grace Jesus gave us. Because the righteousness of Jesus is all the same, there is no difference. It truly has nothing to do with our works. In verse 23, "For all have sinned, and come short of the glory of God."

God sees you and says that you are righteous. If Pastor Park sees you and says that you are righteous, that's worthless because I don't have the power to guarantee my words. What about when God says, "You are righteous?" Can God call a person righteous who is not righteous? God cannot call a sinner righteous. I have sinned, so I cannot understand why

God is calling me righteous. I searched carefully to see how that could be. God loved me and to make me righteous, He sent Jesus to be crucified and He washed away all of my sins. He saw that they were all washed away and then, when He saw me, He saw that I was righteous.

"I received all the punishment for all of your sins on the cross 2,000 years ago. That is why you are righteous." This is what the Bible says. That's what we believe. We do not believe in Jesus who was crucified, but failed to wash away our sins. We believe in the Jesus who was crucified and who washed away our sins as white as snow. Some people say, "Jesus washed away our original sin, but did not wash away our daily sins." That is what many theologians of today say. The Bible does not say that. The Bible says that all of our sins were washed away with the crucifixion of Jesus. If Jesus washed away our original sin and did not wash away our daily sins, then how do we wash away our daily sins? We cannot wash sins away by our own effort. Jesus has to wash them away for us. Jesus did not say, when He washed away our sins, "I will wash away half, and you wash away the rest." Nor did He say, "Hey, I'll wash away 99.99 percent, and you wash away the remaining 0.01 percent." If you have 100 sins, and if Jesus washed away 99, you must go to hell because of that remaining one sin.

The blood of the cross is perfect blood. Because it is perfect, it is not blood that washes away some sins and leaves some behind. It washed away all sin perfectly. There are many words like this in the Bible. Yes, there are many words about receiving forgiveness of sin in the Bible. Over the last 25 years, I studied every single way to receive forgiveness of sin. How sins were washed away in the Old Testament, how David received forgiveness of sin, they are all there. What I am telling you is based on the Word of God.

We should not be confessing, "I stole," "I murdered," "I lied." We need to confess that we are humans by nature who could only sin. When a spy confesses that he is a spy, he does not confess, "I leaked top secret information." He confesses that he is a spy. There is no hope for us. Just as pears come from pear trees, and just as apples come from apple trees, we are evil humans who do nothing but sin. We are trees of sin. The harder we try, the more sins we commit. Go ahead, try not to sin. You'll end up sinning more. If you have tried, you would know. That's why Jesus must make us perfect.

When Jesus was crucified for our sins, He did not leave some sins remaining. He took care of all sins perfectly and was crucified. Folks, the word "Jesus" means the salvation of the Lord. Believing in the fact that He saved you from sin is believing in Jesus. Believing that all of your sins have been forgiven is believing in Jesus. Believing that your sins have been washed as white as snow is believing in Jesus. If your sins still remain, even though Jesus Christ was crucified, then it is as if He never died on the cross. If you buy an express bus ticket, but do not get on the bus, it is the same as not having bought the ticket at all.

How are our sins washed clean? They are washed clean through the blood of Jesus. Tomorrow morning, I will tell you in detail the process of how that sin that remains in your hearts, that sin that constantly makes you stumble, is washed clean through the blood of Jesus. Tomorrow I will tell you the process of how our sins are forgiven. The day after tomorrow, I will tell you the process of how to walk with the Lord and I will conclude by talking about how to live a spiritual life, after you receive forgiveness of sin.

Loving folks! Twenty-five years ago, I was in so much pain because of sin. It was not because I didn't go to church; at that time, I was a youth group member, a choir member, and a Sunday School teacher. I was in pain because of sin, but I received forgiveness of sin through the grace of God. When I read the Bible, after I received forgiveness of sin, my eyes were opened. The Bible talks a lot about forgiveness of sin, and I take it as my duty to testify about it. At one point, I was preparing to go abroad as a missionary. Everything was prepared, but God spoke to my heart, "Do not go abroad. Stay in Korea and preach the gospel to those who do not know forgiveness of sin."

It was difficult for me to turn from going out as a missionary, but by the hand of God, today I travel around Korea speaking about forgiveness of sin. I am not trying to please your ears. If these words enter you to remove all doubt in your heart and cleanse you of your sins, I would joyfully continue with this work, no matter what hardship it may bring.

Dear citizens of Busan, I have had many conferences in other cities. A few years ago I had a conference at Kimhae Air Force base, which is near here, but this is the first time I have had a conference of this magnitude in Busan. During this conference, I want to see the image of those people who can say, "I am free from sin," "I am born again," "The problem between the Lord and me is resolved," "I now have eternal life," and "Even if I die today, I am happy." I believe the Lord will be pleased with this. I sincerely hope that all of you can become such people.

5

The Chief Butler
and the Chief Baker

The Way to Salvation
and the Way to Destruction

Both chiefs committed sin, but the chief butler was freed and the chief baker could not avoid death. In order to live spiritual life one must precisely know the reason for the two people's life and death. If your heart is adding even one percent of your works, just like the chief baker, and not the blood of Jesus, you must quickly turn back from the way of destruction and turn towards the way of salvation.

5

The Chief Butler and the Chief Baker

We will read Genesis chapter 40, from verses 1 to 23.

And it came to pass after these things, that the butler of the king of Egypt and his baker had offended their lord the king of Egypt. And Pharaoh was wroth against two of his officers, against the chief of the butlers, and against the chief of the bakers. And he put them in ward in the house of the captain of the guard, into the prison, the place where Joseph was bound. And the captain of the guard charged Joseph with them, and he served them: and they continued a season in ward. And they dreamed a dream both of them, each man his dream in one night, each man according to the interpretation of

his dream, the butler and the baker of the king of Egypt,
which were bound in the prison. And Joseph came in
unto them in the morning, and looked upon them, and,
behold, they were sad. And he asked Pharaoh's officers
that were with him in the ward of his lord's house, say-
ing, Wherefore look ye so sadly to day? And they said
unto him, We have dreamed a dream, and there is no
interpreter of it. And Joseph said unto them, Do not
interpretations belong to God? tell me them, I pray you.
And the chief butler told his dream to Joseph, and said to
him, In my dream, behold, a vine was before me; And in
the vine were three branches: and it was as though it
budded, and her blossoms shot forth; and the clusters
thereof brought forth ripe grapes: And Pharaoh's cup
was in my hand: and I took the grapes, and pressed them
into Pharaoh's cup, and I gave the cup into Pharaoh's
hand. And Joseph said unto him, This is the interpreta-
tion of it: The three branches are three days: Yet within
three days shall Pharaoh lift up thine head, and restore
thee unto thy place: and thou shalt deliver Pharaoh's
cup into his hand, after the former manner when thou
wast his butler. But think on me when it shall be well
with thee, and shew kindness, I pray thee, unto me, and
make mention of me unto Pharaoh, and bring me out of
this house: For indeed I was stolen away out of the land
of the Hebrews: and here also have I done nothing that
they should put me into the dungeon. When the chief
baker saw that the interpretation was good, he said unto
Joseph, I also was in my dream, and, behold, I had three

white baskets on my head: And in the uppermost basket there was of all manner of bakemeats for Pharaoh; and the birds did eat them out of the basket upon my head. And Joseph answered and said, This is the interpretation thereof: The three baskets are three days: Yet within three days shall Pharaoh lift up thy head from off thee, and shall hang thee on a tree; and the birds shall eat thy flesh from off thee. And it came to pass the third day, which was Pharaoh's birthday, that he made a feast unto all his servants: and he lifted up the head of the chief butler and of the chief baker among his servants. And he restored the chief butler unto his butlership again; and he gave the cup into Pharaoh's hand: But he hanged the chief baker: as Joseph had interpreted to them. Yet did not the chief butler remember Joseph, but forgat him.

Loving folks, spiritual life appears easy, and it seems that you understand it, or that it goes well. But that is not the case. Of course, I do not have the power to solve these problems for you. There is only one condition that has allowed me to stand up here. It is the fact that for a long time I was tormented and in pain because of sin. But one day, I had the amazing experience of having all of my sins washed as white as snow.

Before stepping up here tonight, I received a letter. It was from my daughter, in Seoul. I have one son and one daughter. The older child is my daughter, who is in the 9th grade. My younger child is a boy, in the 6th grade. Because I have been away from them for a few days, I was extremely curious, and I quickly opened the letter. I'd like to read it to you.

"Dad, it's now a little bit past 12. I am writing you a letter because I am so happy in my heart. Dad, the devil was working, while you are doing the conference in Busan. Yeong Kook became sick with a high fever and was crying. Auntie and I prayed sincerely to God. When we finished praying, Yeong Kook's head did not hurt anymore. When I saw that he was fast asleep, I was so happy that I just had to write you this letter. Father, don't worry about Yeong Kook's sickness. God completely cured him."

I remember the day my daughter received forgiveness of sin. One day she had gone to the chemistry lab at her school. The students who had done an experiment earlier had left hydrochloric acid on top of a lamp and it had exploded. Unexpectedly, the acid spilled on my child's head, and she was covered in acid. The school nurse quickly rushed her to the hospital. The hospital cleaned her head with alcohol, bandaged her with gauze and sent her home. Upon my arrival at home, I heard what had happened to my child. I thought that she was fine because I knew that she had been treated at the hospital.

After 15 days, she was not healed. My wife took a look at her head. The skin on her head was rotting away. My wife immediately took her to the hospital where my sister-in-law worked. At the hospital, they were very surprised, saying that when hydrochloric acid spills, it must be completely removed, but it had been left there. They had to perform an emergency operation on my child's head. That day I didn't have any idea about what was going on and was on my way home, after preaching the gospel at Uhjungboo prison.

As we were passing the hospital, the pastor who had gone with me said, "A member of my church is hospitalized here. Let's stop by for a little while."

I pulled into the parking lot and parked my car. Just then, Yeong Kook ran out to me, saying, "Father, Father, Sister is in surgery right now." When I got there, the doctors had anesthetized my daughter and were beginning to remove the skin from her head. To me as her father, it was not a pretty sight. Afterwards, they wrapped her head with bandages.

She was admitted to the hospital and could not go to school for 10 days. I went to her school and told them that my daughter would not be able to attend for a while because she was sick. The principal said he wanted to see me. He said, "I am truly sorry for what happened. No matter how much her treatment costs, the school will bear the entire financial burden."

"I am a servant of God. These things do not happen by coincidence. I know surely the will of God is behind this," I told the principal. "Mr. Principal, I will not accept any money for her treatment. It cannot end just by me receiving money and treating her. I want to know why God has allowed this to happen." I refused to accept the treatment costs.

Because my child's aunt worked at the hospital, the expenses were taken care of. Ten days passed and Eun Sook had to go to school with bandages wrapped around her head. I could not let her ride the bus she usually took because it was so crowded. I am busy in the mornings, but for a month, I drove my daughter to school every day.

As a pastor, I don't have much time to spend with my family. I barely ever had an opportunity to talk with my daughter about her spiritual life. As I drove her to school each morning, I talked to her. I came to know that my daughter's heart was in agony because of sin. Sometimes I'd park on the side of the road so we could talk. At times, I'd park next to the school and talk to her about forgiveness of sin. When I told her, "Eun Sook, this is how your sins have been cleansed," amazingly, in the car that day, my daughter received forgiveness. She and I were able to taste the amazing joy of having the sin within her heart washed clean. On that day, my daughter began to change. The way she prayed changed, the way she read the Bible changed, the way she lived changed and the way she thought changed. I travel all over the country to hold conferences, so my children are often home alone. I have a thankful heart when I see them growing up well, by the grace of the Lord. I have heard that only fools talk with pride about their daughters and their wives, but I think it's okay to be a fool. For me, it's not a problem.

Not only my daughter, but whoever receives forgiveness of sin and has the sins in his heart washed clean, cannot help but change. When I go to conferences, sometimes my wife accompanies me. She came with me this time, as well. Since it is not good to leave our children home alone, we needed a sister who could help us. There was a sister who wanted to stay at our house, so she now lives with us. She is a sister who loves the Lord. We were able to see that because after she came to our house, the atmosphere of our house changed. My children became very free. Even more so, if Jesus comes into our hearts, we always change.

Jesus Christ does not sleep the days away. If He comes into your heart, He will take care of all your sins. When He becomes Lord of your heart, you will change. Your life will no longer be accomplished through you. There will no longer be a need for you to try to overcome sin, temptation, read the Bible, or pray. From that point on, it will be painful for you when you don't pray.

"How can I have Jesus enter my heart by faith, with no discomfort, and how can I have the sins in my heart washed completely clean?"

That is the problem. Folks, isn't that true? Of course, God is everywhere. On the other hand, God is not One who rests just anywhere. God can find rest only when He comes into a clean heart that has no sin. Folks, even if God wants to come into your heart, and if your heart is full of sin, God cannot enter. Even if He did come in, if He were to enter, He would be very uncomfortable.

Then how can we have our sins washed clean? This evening we read the words of Genesis chapter 40. What we read happened when Joseph was locked in prison for resisting the temptation of Potiphar's wife. One day, the chief butler and the chief baker of Pharaoh, the king of Egypt, sinned and were sent to the prison, where Joseph was also being held. As I read these words, I wanted to know exactly what it was God wanted us to realize from this story. It was impossible for me to know. Then, one day, while reading carefully, I learned an amazing thing.

Let's read the Scriptures together. Genesis chapter 40, verse 1, "And it came to pass after these things, that the butler of the king of Egypt and his baker had offended their lord the king of Egypt."

Please open your Bible and look at me. There are two people in Genesis chapter 40, verse 1. Who are they? They are the chief butler and the chief baker. Because Pharaoh was a great king, he had men in charge of his chariots; men in charge of his horses; men in charge of his clothes; and men in charge of the wine and bread. He had many ministers who were in charge of all sorts of duties. Genesis chapter 40, verse 1 tells us that the chief butler and the chief baker had committed sins. Which one had committed more sins? It does not say anything about that. It only states that they had both committed sins. We don't know who committed what sin, but they both committed sins and the two of them were imprisoned.

The Bible doesn't end it there. They both committed sins, but Genesis chapter 40 ends with one of them receiving salvation and the other receiving destruction. Heaven is not a place where people with sin can go. Although people may have all sinned the same, there are those to be saved and there are those to be destroyed. People do not go to hell because they have too many sins, and people don't go to heaven because they have only a few. When Jesus was crucified, with Him were two thieves, who had both sinned. One was saved and the other destroyed.

Can you tell why God recorded Genesis chapter 40 for us? The chief butler and the chief baker, these two people signify that all the people on this earth are divided into two classes. Everyone on earth has committed sins, but there are some who are saved and some who are destroyed. I believe that Genesis chapter 40 was written to teach us about this.

You too have all sinned. If you have committed sins, how can you tell if you are to be saved or destroyed? Do we have to go before God to know? No, we do not. These words were written by God for you to discover that if your faith is like that of the chief butler, you will be saved and that if your faith is like that of the chief baker, you will be destroyed. What kind of a person are you? Are you like the chief butler? Or are you like the chief baker?

"Pastor, before you talk about this story, teach us how the chief butler received salvation, and how the chief baker was destroyed."

Is this what you are thinking? Let's talk about it. The most important fact about receiving salvation is that when God saves us, it is not with our own strength. He saves us by Himself. When God made the heavens and the earth, did He make man first, or did He make a man last? He made a man last. Why did God make a man last? If God had made humans first and then had created the heavens and the earth, humans would have wanted to interfere so much that God would not have been able to stand it.

"Oh, God, the ocean is too big, and why are you making the sky so big, anyway? God, make the river shallow. We are going to drown. God, this rock is too heavy. Why don't you make it light?"

A long time ago, a man became tired after working and lay down under a chestnut tree to take a nap. Before he fell asleep, he thought, "God created the heavens and the earth? That makes no sense at all. God made the heavens and the earth, and this is how it turned out? Why does God make tiny chestnuts come from the huge chestnut tree? And why does He have big pumpkins come forth from those pumpkin vines that are skinnier than my pinky finger? What kind of God is He creating everything like this? If I were God, I would have made pumpkins that come from the pinky-thin vines as small as chestnuts. And on the big chestnut trees, I'd have made chestnuts the size of pumpkins. It would be so nice to pluck one of those huge chestnuts, steam it, eat it and share it with my neighbors."

As that person complained, he fell asleep and began to snore. All of a sudden, there was a "snap" and a cluster of chestnuts fell from the tree and struck him on the forehead. He was so surprised he woke up. Even before he picked the cluster of chestnuts from his forehead, he knelt down and said, "God, thank you. If these chestnuts were as big as pumpkins, my head would have been crushed. God, I thank you for making the chestnuts small."

Folks, we know nothing about the great wisdom of God. Right? We are like the man who fell asleep under the chestnut tree, aren't we? Most people cannot understand the things that God has prepared for us and often go against God with their petty thoughts and deeds. Although God wants to save people from sin, there are many people who are unable to be saved because they constantly complain and block the will of God, doing things their own way.

God didn't need help from a man when He created the heavens and the earth. God created the heavens and the earth in six days, and last of all, He created man. After the man was created and opened his eyes, what did God do? Did He run around, here and there, busily trying to improve the heavens and the earth? God had finished His work and was resting. From that moment on, there was rest between God and man.

Folks, do you know when that happy rest was broken? It was when man was no longer satisfied and tried to become better. Rest was broken when man was trying to open his eyes and when he tried to be like God by eating the fruit of good and evil. Unhappiness and pain came about from that point: Was it beneficial to us that humans were so careless? No, but we cannot do anything about it because we are descendants of Adam and Eve. Even now, it is because we are busily going around, trying to do something, that we cannot be saved.

When Jesus was in this world, he bestowed much grace and many blessings. Of course, not just anyone could come before Jesus and receive grace and blessings. Everyone who thought they could do well opposed, went against and complained about Jesus. They even tried to kill him. People who were helpless, like the woman caught in adultery, who I talked about yesterday, the Samaritan woman, the man who had an infirmity for 38 years, and people like the lepers, all received grace and blessings in front of Jesus. Folks, it is not that you are unable to receive forgiveness of sin because you are unable to do something. The reason you cannot receive forgiveness of sin is that you do things too well. It is because you think that you can do well, so you do not give God the opportunity to work. Rather, you try to do it yourself.

There was a certain woman in France. She lived alone, with her little white pig. It is more accurate to say that this woman was living with the pig, rather than raising it. She ate with the pig at the kitchen table, bathed with it and slept on the bed with it. One day, when it was the pig's birthday, as a present she bought a very expensive perfume, called Soir de Paris, which most people can't even think about buying. It was a perfume worn mostly by movie stars. I don't know French, so I don't know how my pronunciation is, but anyway, she bought the perfume. From time to time, she would bathe her pig in milk and put Soir de Paris on it. One day, she had to leave the pig and go on a long trip.

"I'm so sad. I'm very sorry, pig. Take care. I'll hurry back."

She set a table with food for the pig to eat, she prepared hot water for it to bathe in, and she made the bed with fresh sheets. She prepared many other things and went on her trip. Before she left, she put even more Soir de Paris on the pig than usual. While on the trip, she often thought, "How's my pig doing?" She couldn't concentrate on her work because she loved her pig so much.

After finishing her work, she hurried home and looked for the pig. The pig was nowhere to be found. It was not in the bathtub, in the kitchen, on the bed, or in the living room. The woman was about to cry, thinking, "Oh, I was wrong to leave my pig here all alone. It's all my fault." She looked everywhere for the pig. She looked for her pig in the garden. It was not under the tree. It was nowhere to be found. Later, she found it. It was in the dirty sewer, going, "Oink, oink." It broke this woman's heart to see her lovely pig, with its expensive Soir de Paris perfume, lying in the dirty sewer.

"Hey pig, get out of there," but the pig was the most peaceful and happy pig in the world. It wouldn't even consider coming out.

In the Bible, it talks about a golden ring in the nose of a pig, but this was Soir de Paris on the skin of a pig. Folks, pigs by nature like dirty things. The characteristic of a pig will not change, no matter what you put on the surface, Soir de Paris or whatever. The pig will always end up going back to the mud.

That's how it is with humans, as well. We have become dirty on the inside through sin. Without changing inwardly, we only decorate the outside with jewelry and diamond rings. You may do these things, but because your inside is dirty, you could only fall into sin and become dirty. It is very tiresome for a pig to be bathed in oil and milk and have Soir de Paris put on it, wear diapers and sleep on a bed. It is much more comfortable for a pig to roll around inside the sewers or in a pool of mud.

Folks, if you have sin within your heart, it is much more comfortable for you to go out and drink, and play and commit sins. It may also be very tiresome for you to sit here and listen to me. Because of that, there are many people who are bored and can't stand the one-hour of service they attend once a week. If they are happy to have the service, then why would that one hour be so boring? Sermons have become shorter and shorter because people have become bored with them. These days, it has come to a point where they have 15 or 20-minute sermons.

In Seoul, 1st session services are very popular. They say, "If a church member does not go to service on Sunday, but goes out to play, he'll have an accident." People become afraid, so they go to church. They attend the 1st session service, which starts at 7:00 and ends at exactly 7:50. In the trunk of their cars, they have a barbeque grill and beef ready to go.

"Hey kids, let's go to Yongin Theme Park today."

"Great, Dad!" The children stay in the car, while the parents attend the 1st session service. Then the children in the car become upset, as they wait because the service does not end sooner.

Folks, service is a burden to that kind of a person. They sit in the chapel, thinking, "Gee, the pastor is giving such a long sermon." When the service ends, like a bird freed from its cage flaps its wings and flies away, they start up their cars and off they go. Are these people interested in having service? Or are they more interested in going out and playing? They'd rather go enjoy themselves than have service. Deeds, such as these, reflect our heart.

Folks, when a person who is dirty inside because of sin, comes with the Bible under his arm, wearing a suit, with gel in his hair and walks around the chapel, then what is that? He must change inside of his heart. Jesus used to speak to the religious people of His time.

"You people are like open sepulchers! Didn't the One who made the outside make the inside also? Your insides are filled with dirty things." This is what Jesus said. Folks, these words not only apply to the scribes and the Pharisees of that time. Even today, if you do not have your sins washed clean, then you are the same as they. Will baptizing resolve everything when your heart is full of the characteristics of sin? Is it okay to become a deacon or an elder, when you are full of sin? No, it is not. That is Soir de Paris on the skin of a pig. You are a church member when you go to church and a worldly person when you go outside. Is that right? The light of Christianity is growing dim. The world is turning into a place where we can no longer see the bright light of Christ shining.

Folks, this evening I want to ask this of you. Don't try to show off that you are a good believer of Jesus on the outside, without having the problem of sin within your heart resolved. For many years, I have been ministering in Daegu, where I am known as the Redemption Pastor. Many people have come to me because of the problem of sin. Among them were many people who were Christians from birth or Christians who were baptized as babies, and sometimes deacons and elders and sometimes even pastors come. I tell them, "Elder, I am sorry. Elder, you cannot receive forgiveness of sin."

"What? An elder cannot receive forgiveness of sin? Does it say that in the Bible?"

"Yes, it does. Do you know who receives forgiveness of sin? Sinners receive forgiveness of sin."

No matter where you look in the Bible, sinners always receive forgiveness of sin. No matter how good God is at forgiving sins, God cannot wash clean the sins of a person who doesn't have sin. No matter how good a person is at saving drowning people, how can he save a person who is not drowning? Even though God wants to forgive sin, a person who thinks he has not sinned cannot have his sins forgiven.

"Are you an elder or a sinner? Please choose one of the two."

"It does not say in the Bible that Jesus washed clean the sins of an elder. Even if you are a deacon, you must become a sinner to have your sins forgiven. Even you, an elder, must become a sinner if you want to receive forgiveness of sin. Even a pastor must become a sinner, to receive forgiveness of sin."

When I say, "Raise your hand if you want to receive forgiveness of sin," many people would raise their hands. However, if I say, "Please, stand up," they stay seated. Why do they do that? It is because they don't want to show that they are sinners. When Captain Naaman was told to bathe seven times in the River Jordan, he was upset, saying, "What? How can I take off my clothes and shamefully show that I have leprosy?" If he's only at that stage, he needs to hear, "You are not qualified to have your leprosy healed. Go back and do whatever you were doing."

For some people, it is easy to receive forgiveness of sin, for others it is difficult. It is easy for people who are in despair, for people who have nothing to show for themselves, and for people who know that they could only be destroyed. However, people who think they have a good spiritual life, who think they are smart, who have a strong sense of pride, or people who uphold their reputations must know that they are light years away from receiving forgiveness of sin.

We take the easy way out. We are good at decorating our outsides, like putting Soir de Paris on a pig. We are good at doing volunteer work for the church. We clean, we wash the windows, we organize the children's shoe rack and lead the student meeting in the church. When there is a youth meeting, it is hard, but you provide financial support. When you go out to the streets, you witness to the children, telling them to come to church. We are good at those things, but when we hear, "Open your heart, become a sinner and receive forgiveness of sin," we do not like that.

Folks, today, when you look out in the evening in each city of Korea, you see many crosses. There are so many churches. People with a lot of money, poor people with a heart to love God, diligently make offerings, to buy expensive land and build beautiful chapels and expensive buildings. Those fancy chapels are built with passionate tears and the sincerity of church members. Folks, when they are asked to do those things, they do them very well. But when they are told, "Wash your sins clean," they quietly avoid it. How can this be?

There must be many of you here who have made offerings to God with all of your heart and soul. There are also many people here who have made offerings without having their sins washed clean. There are many people who fast and pray all night long for the church, but there are not many people who have had their sins washed clean. This is what hurts and disappoints the heart of our Lord. Do you know what the prophet Isaiah said?

Hear the word of the LORD, ye rulers of Sodom; give ear unto the law of our God, ye people of Gomorrah. To what purpose is the multitude of your sacrifices unto me? saith the LORD: I am full of the burnt offerings of rams, and the fat of fed beasts; and I delight not in the blood of bullocks, or of lambs, or of he goats. When ye come to appear before me, who hath required this at your hand, to tread my courts? Bring no more vain

oblations; incense is an abomination unto me; the new
moons and sabbaths, the calling of assemblies, I cannot
away with; it is iniquity, even the solemn meeting. Your
new moons and your appointed feasts my soul hateth:
they are a trouble unto me; I am weary to bear them.
And when ye spread forth your hands, I will hide mine
eyes from you: yea, when ye make many prayers, I will
not hear: your hands are full of blood. (Isaiah 1:10-15)

The book of Isaiah speaks more strongly and clearly about forgiveness of sin than any other book in the Old Testament. In places such as Isaiah chapter 44, verse 22, and chapter 53, it often talks about the cleansing of sins. It says that God will not receive tithe offerings or prayers, or no matter what they are, unless the donor's sins are washed clean.

Behold, the LORD's hand is not shortened, that it can-
not save; neither his ear heavy, that it cannot hear: But
your iniquities have separated between you and your
God, and your sins have hid his face from you, that he
will not hear. (Isaiah 59:1-2)

God will not receive things given by sinners. Folks, as we all know, when a priest made offerings before the Lord in the Old Testament, did God accept offerings that had blemishes, were lame, or from things that were wounded? No, He did not accept them. What does that mean? It means that God will not accept offerings or services from those who have sinned. He's telling us to first have our sins washed clean. But folks, there are many people among us who make their outside spotless, even though God does not care about the outside, while their insides are a mass of sin. Can that person really go to heaven? Does that person really stand on the side of Jesus? Can God really dwell within that person? He cannot. Folks, I am telling you again, that is Soir de Paris on the skin of a pig.

How can we be saved? I'd like to speak to you about how we can have our sins washed clean and stand before God.

If you look in Genesis chapter 40, the chief butler and the chief baker both sinned, but the chief butler received salvation and the chief baker was destroyed. We need to know the reason in order for us to live a spiritual life. If your spiritual life is like that of the butler, you can rest, but if your spiritual life is like that of the baker, you must turn it around to become like that of the butler.

Genesis chapter 40, verse 1, records that both of them sinned. But if you read down to the end, one person receives salvation and the other person receives destruction. Is the answer to why the butler was saved and the baker was destroyed found between Genesis chapter 40, verse 1 and the last verse? Would it not be there? Yes, it's there, because no other book is as organized and as systematic as the Bible. In elementary school, math books have blanks. There is a 30, and then a blank, and then a 50. Which number belongs in the blank? Forty goes there. That's the way the Bible is organized. God wants to teach us the answer through the Bible. I believe God recorded the Bible hoping that you'd have the same faith as the butler.

Let's look into the Bible together. When we look in chapter 40, verse 2,

And Pharaoh was wroth against two of his officers, against the chief of the butlers, and against the chief of the bakers. And he put them in ward in the house of the captain of the guard, into the prison, the place where Joseph was bound. And the captain of the guard charged Joseph with them, and he served them: and they continued a season in ward.

Here we must discover why the chief butler was saved. Then, we must find the reason for which the chief baker was destroyed. Folks, do you have your Bible? Then let's look into this together. Why did the chief butler get saved? Please look at your Bible and answer me quietly. Does it say that the chief butler went to prison and was remorseful and repented? Does it say he suffered for his sins and was crying for it? It does not say that. That's strange. God must have recorded the most important method for our salvation through the salvation of the chief butler, right? What do you think about this? To receive salvation, we must pray zealously, witness and repent with tears. This is what most people think.

Folks, if that was what God wanted, then surely the chief butler would have gotten up early in the morning and tearfully repented. That is what should have been recorded here. That is the logical way, isn't it? Is Pastor Park trying to forcefully make sense out of this? The amazing thing here is that it does not say that the chief butler repented at all.

Today most people think that we must do something to

receive salvation. But folks, that is missing from the Word of God. What did the chief butler do? Did he cry tearfully and was he in agony? I'm sorry, but nowhere in the Bible does it say that. Does this mean we don't need to repent? Does it mean it's okay not to cry? Is it okay not to pray? No. Folks, that's not what I am saying. I'm not saying there is no need to repent and that we don't need to pray. I am not saying that it's okay not to read the Bible. I'm not saying that it's okay not to volunteer. But the matter of salvation is far from these things. Salvation does not come about by way of such things.

In Genesis chapter 40, we must find the difference between the chief baker, who was destroyed, and the chief butler, who was saved. What is the difference? Folks, when I read chapter 40, there was no difference except that they had different dreams. Is that what you read also? Joseph went there that morning, and the chief butler and the chief baker were both sad.

"Why do you look so sad? Are you worried about something?"

"We had dreams and there is no way to interpret them."

"Aren't interpretations up to the Lord? Please tell me." The chief butler told him his dream.

"I had a dream last night. Because I was in charge of the king's drinks, I had to take the wine to the king, and I saw that my cup was empty. And I couldn't go to the king with an empty cup, so I looked everywhere. Then three branches came out from a vine in front of me. And it budded and blossoms shot forth. The flowers blossomed and the grape clusters ripened right away." The chief butler was worried because he had no wine to go forth to the king with. How happy he must have been when he saw the vine!

"Quickly, I picked the grapes and pressed them and made them into wine and served it to the king."

When Joseph heard that dream, he realized that it was a good dream. The chief butler and the chief baker were puzzled and asked why it was so. "Three branches are three days. Within three days you will surely be restored to your old position. You will be saved, and you will go before the king."

Folks, we must find out how that dream is a dream of salvation. He pressed the wine, but we have no idea what this means. That's because Pastor Park is not so smart. Sometimes, I am sure that the will of God is there, but I don't know what it is. Through praying and reading and reading it, while associating it with other Scriptures, God allowed me to understand this in my heart.

The vine represents Jesus Christ. Jesus is the true vine of our lives. Going forth to the king is going forth to the King of kings, God. But the chief butler had nothing in his hands to bring forth to the king. Why would he have nothing to bring forth to the king? Folks, that means that we have nothing to bring forth to God. But when he looked carefully, there was a vine, and it had fruits and they were ripe. When he pressed the grapes, they burst and juice flowed out. That is Jesus, who is the vine of life, being crucified on the cross, tearing His body and shedding His blood. The chief butler's dream was, "God, I need to go out to You. But there is nothing I could bring forth to God. I go forth only believing in the blood of Jesus, who was crucified for me. Please see this blood and receive me," the confession of our faith.

Because of that, when you go forth before God, you should take nothing other than the blood of Jesus Christ. Do you understand? Salvation can never be accomplished through such things as tithes, the 40 days fasting prayer that you do, or helping others.

Folks, God only asks, "Does your heart rely only on the blood of Jesus Christ?" That's the only thing God looks at when He saves us. Some people rely on the blood of Jesus, but they also mix other things with it. They mix in 20 or 40 percent of the good they have done with the blood of Jesus. Some people are so good that they mix in 60 percent. Some people mix in only one percent of what they have done to the blood Jesus shed for us when he was crucified, but even that will not do. It cannot be salvation, if even a little bit of my works, the good that I have done, is added. You must go forth relying only on the blood on the cross of the One who died for your sins, Jesus Christ. That was the dream of the chief butler. He had to go forth to the king, but his cup was empty. What was he supposed to do? How worried he must have been! While he was caught up in that, when he saw the grape vine, how happy he must have been! The blossoms came out, the flowers bloomed, the fruits shot forth, and the grape clusters ripened. "Wow, so glad to see you!" He picked them immediately and made wine. We try to go to heaven on our own, but we cannot and we don't know what to do. The chief butler's faith was the heart of seeing that our sins have been washed through the blood of Jesus, which was shed on the cross and going forth joyfully. This was the spiritual life of the chief butler.

Loving folks, we cannot live without sin. We cannot live by the Word of God, without breaking any laws. That's why God sent His Son, Jesus Christ. The blood of the cross that He shed on His forehead, on both of His hands, on His side, and on both of His feet, is more than enough to wash away our sins. Folks, we must go forth relying on that blood.

> "Those people then crucified Jesus.
> With three rusted nails.
> Sounds of hammering echoed in my heart.
> My sins were washed with that blood."

If the blood of Jesus didn't wash your sins clean, you must try yourself to wash your sins. If the blood of Jesus only cleansed half of your sins, you must labor and suffer to cleanse the remaining half. But if the blood of Jesus Christ cleansed all of your sins, then you cannot be a sinner. And that's why God calls us righteous. Folks, God calling us righteous is not because our actions are good, or because we have sinned little, or because we repented tearfully. He calls us righteous because the blood of His Son Jesus Christ completely and surely washed our sins clean.

Jesus Christ washed all our sins clean on the cross. He washed our sins clean forever. Many people do not rely on God, and they try to come forth with their own actions. When they do something well, they go forth to God happily; and when they do something bad, they feel terrible and their hearts cringe. Our hearts change up to twelve times a day. We are people who continually do wrong things. If we reach out to God with these actions, we can never completely come out to Him. Do you understand? You smile in the morning and are down in the evening. And then, in the evening, you smile and are down in the morning. Folks, isn't that how we are? Your heart when you are just leaving the service is not the same as your heart when you are on your way home. Isn't that true? Your heart, when you come to church, after a whole week, is down and out. If we try to go to heaven with our ever-changing heart, we come and go and come and go, and then, "Snap!" we fall off. That is why, folks, we must not rely on ourselves because our actions are destined to be destroyed. So we must go forth to God, relying on His grace.

Folks, suppose Pastor Ock Soo Park died today. Many people would cry, saying, "Oh no, oh no." Others might not be so unhappy.

Eventually, you would bury me, whether on a mountain here or on a mountain there or throw me into the river. I would go before the Lord. I would leave this world singing, "The bright shining path to heaven. . ." I would stand before the judgment of God. Then, let's say, the hoodlum called the devil shows up and says, "Now it's time. I am glad you are here. Have a seat."

The devil begins his prosecution: "God, Ock Soo Park was born in North Kyungsang Province on this month, this day, this year, and since birth he was very advanced in his ability to sin. We cannot say in words all the sins he committed. Now we will begin. This month, this day, this year, he attacked the peanut field; he stole and ate persimmons. . ."

The list would go on and on: "On this month, this day, and

this year, he fought, lied, and cursed."

"Gee, was I that bad?"

Maybe all of you will feel that way. Anyway, it may take years, just for the devil to present his case. "God, do you think that's all? The guy's a total rascal, so it is fitting that he goes to hell."

That's what the devil would say. Then, afterward, Jesus would step up with the defense. Listening to what the devil had to say, I would lose all my strength, but when Jesus comes forth, I would regain it. Jesus would say, "Don't worry, Ock Soo Park. I'm right here. Don't worry. Father God, as the devil has said, I acknowledge the sins that Ock Soo Park committed until now. But God, look at my side for a second. Why do I have this spear mark here? And the marks from the crown of thorns on my head? And why do I have nail marks on both of my hands? Isn't this evidence that punishment has already been given out for all the sins of Ock Soo Park that the devil has so exhaustively read off? When I was crucified, didn't I receive punishment for all that? Get thee behind me, Satan! Angels, you will now accept Ock Soo Park."

"Bam Bara Baam!"

"Do you have a crown prepared for Ock Soo Park?"

"Of course, we do."

This is just a rehearsal, you understand. Actually, I don't know if they have a crown for me or not. But when I get a crown in heaven, I want to wear it for just five minutes.

"Hey, camera, hurry up and get this." After the video camera films it, I will take off the crown. "Jesus, you know what? I think I'm going to have to take this off and give it to you. Jesus, what did I do? Jesus, You washed my sins. You gave me the Word, and you gave me the gift. This was none of my doing. I give this crown to You, Lord. Please receive it." I will put the crown at the Lord's feet, go home and watch the video.

Folks, the blood of the cross of our Lord Jesus Christ truly washed our sins cleanly. It washed us so perfectly that there is no flaw for the devil to pick on. Hallelujah! If the blood of the cross of Jesus could not wash our sins clean, the death of Jesus is the same as the death of a dog. The blood that he shed being crucified to wash our sins clean would be the same as unclean blood. Truly, however, the death of our Lord was not the death of a dog. He washed our sins clean and that is why we believe in Jesus. Because the blood of Jesus is enough, there is no need to add the good deeds that you have done. Because the blood Jesus shed is enough, there is no need for us to be punished again. God is satisfied with Jesus having received all of our punishment. Because of that, even a dirty and filthy human like me will be empowered by the blood on that day and will stand boldly before God. I may appear like this before you now, but on that day angels will be my guards.

"Angels!"

"Yes?"

"Go get me the fruit from the second branch from the top of the tree of life. Let me have a taste."

We can receive that kind of grace only through the blood of Jesus Christ. Today, the reason many people do not receive that grace is because they are constantly trying to add something to the blood of Jesus, even though they are not good at math. Now, let's subtract all the things you've added. Now, we must go forth, relying only on the blood of Jesus.

Joseph interpreted the dream of the chief butler.

"This is a very good dream. The three branches mean three days. You will be freed in three days. And when you are saved, please remember me and don't forget me."

The chief baker, when he heard about that dream, smiled and said, "I had a dream too."

"What kind of dream was it?"

"A dream similar to his. I saw in the dream that I had three white baskets on my head. . ." How excited do you think the chief baker was?

"On the very top, various different meats were laid out, and the birds began to eat them."

"That is not a good dream."

"How is that?"

"The three baskets here also represent three days. After three days, Pharaoh will cut off your head and hang you on a tree and the birds of the air will pick and eat your flesh."

Although that sounds dreadful, it was true. The white baskets represent Jesus Christ. When we take communion, we do it with bread and wine. Jesus is the bread of life. When the chief baker went forth, he should only have gone forth with his bread, but the problem was he kept adding something on top of the bread. The birds represent Satan. In the Bible, there are many parts that have two meanings. The word "capital" can mean several things. Such as capital city, capital letter and money. In the Bible, when they talk about Jesus Christ, they refer to him as the Lamb. They also refer to saints as lambs. The same applies to birds. In some places, they represent the saints of God, but the birds they are talking about here are just like the birds that ate the seeds that were sown on the wayside. They represent the devil.

Folks, when we go forth to the Lord, we must rely only on the Lord, who is the bread. God is telling us that because we constantly add things that we like, things that God cannot accept, we are destroyed.

This is what this story is telling us. Loving folks, in tonight's story about the chief butler and the chief baker, we looked into why they were saved and why they were destroyed. "I have nothing to bring forth to God. God, only sees the blood Jesus shed on the cross and that all of my sins have been washed clean, and with that, I hope that you will accept me." The chief butler represents people with this kind of a heart. The chief baker represents those who try to do things more zealously, adding something, although Jesus was crucified for their sins. The Bible is letting us understand that a spiritual life like that of the chief baker leads to destruction.

Because of that, those people who thought they had good faith, such as the scribes, Pharisees, and Sadducees persecuted Jesus when He was in this world. Those who accepted Jesus were all sinners such as the woman caught in adultery, the Samaritan woman, and lepers. The problem is not that we are not good at spiritual life, but often the problem is that we think we are doing well. If we really don't know how to do anything, the Lord will do it for us. If we cannot take care of our sins, the Lord will do it for us, but as long as I'm trying to manage on my own, the Lord can do nothing for me.

Loving folks, dung is dirty, but dung in the barn is not a problem because that's where dung belongs. But it is a problem if dung is on the dining table. Isn't that true? A sinner in this world, which is full of sin, is not a problem. But when we go to heaven, we cannot go there with sin. That is why you must have your sins washed clean here, in this world, before you go to heaven. Before you volunteer for church, make an offering, and sacrifice for the Lord, you must first have your sins washed clean.

One day, Leonardo Da Vinci went up a mountain in front of his house. There he saw a huge rock. He stared at the rock all day long. When it became dark, he went home and slept. The next day, he went back and looked at the rock again. For several days, all he did was eat, go to the mountain and look at the rock. Then one day he brought a hammer and a chisel and began to chip away at the rock. He would chip away after breakfast, and chip away a little more after lunch. Then, one day, a friend asked him, "Hey, Lenny."

"Oh, how are you doing?"

"Fine. What in the world are you doing now?"

"You have to come see. Look here, here."

"All I see is a big rock."

"Does that look like a rock to you?"

"It's a rock, of course. What is it then?"

"No, there is an angel inside of this rock, but the rock is covering it. I am breaking the rock that is covering the angel, and I am freeing the angel."

Da Vinci continued to chip away at the rock. One day, two days, one month, and finally two months had passed. Sure enough the image of an angel began to emerge from the rock. It was just an ordinary rock, in the eyes of normal people. But Leonardo Da Vinci saw the image of an angel inside of the rock. That is how the image of the angel emerged when he chipped and broke everything else away. You may be poor, ignorant and may be low in the eyes of others, but you are people who have the image of God when seen through the eyes of Jesus. You all have that precious image of God, but you are covered in sin. Just as Leonardo broke the rock with his hammer and revealed the image of the angel, Jesus, through the cross, uncovered the evil and dirty sins that had been covering you. Because of that, now the holy image of God can show through us. Just as Leonardo cut away at the rock, the Lord continually wants to wash the sin out of your lives. He wants to break down the insecurity in your lives. He wants to remove sadness and pain, and He wants to give you true peace and satisfaction, which belongs only to God. Believe in the Lord Jesus Christ. I hope that you will come to rely upon the Lord Jesus Christ.

What I would like to say to you citizens of Busan, is that Jesus Christ saved me from dirty sin. In 1962, on October 7, I was saved. Just as I received forgiveness of sin, I hope that every one of you will receive forgiveness of sin through the blood of Jesus. That is the only heart that I have. I experi-enced true happiness for the first time, the day Jesus came into my heart.

"Without him, I could do nothing,
Without him, I'd surely fail,
Without him I would be drifting
like a ship without a sail.
Jesus, Oh Jesus, do you know him today,
you can't turn him away.
Oh, Jesus, oh Jesus,
without him how lost I would be."

This is my testimony. I recall 1962, how I was before I knew Jesus. Wallowing in sin, deep in despair. Day by day, I began to change amazingly after Jesus came into my heart. If there is one reason I can stand here before you tonight, it is Jesus Christ. He was crucified and washed all my sins. There is no reason, other than this. I was a person who truly had no hope. I wanted to die, I was so tormented. I wanted to go to the army, but I failed the physical because my front tooth was broken. I was an utterly useless person, but Jesus accepted me.

The Lord wants to receive you this evening. He wants to embrace you to his bosom. Folks, receive forgiveness of sin. Come forth to Him and have all of your sins washed clean. I believe that you will be changed. Let's end the sermon here for now. Tomorrow morning, I will talk in detail about how our sins are washed clean.

6

Eternal Redemption

The Process of the Forgiveness of Sin
That the Bible Speaks Of

In the times of the Old Testament goats and calves were taken and offered at a holy place, and by their blood sins were washed. God sent his only son Jesus Christ on our behalf, and when Jesus was nailed and died at the cross he cleansed our sins for all eternity. The Bible teaches us in detail how our sins were washed by the blood of Jesus.

6

Eternal Redemption

Until now, we have spoken mostly about the mindset of a person who can receive forgiveness of sin. This morning and this evening, I would like to tell you specifically about how our sins can truly and completely be redeemed. Much is written about this in the Bible, beginning with the book of Genesis all the way through to the book of Revelation. I would like to address this by putting together some of the passages from the Bible that deal with redemption.

Also, when I ask you questions, please answer them in your heart, as you listen. I hope that this morning will be beneficial and worthwhile for all of you. I hope that these words will find a place in your heart, not as knowledge, but as faith, not as theory, but as reality.

We will begin by reading from Hebrews chapter 10, from verse 1 to 4.

For the law having a shadow of good things to come, and not the very image of the things, can never with those sacrifices which they offered year by year continually make the comers thereunto perfect. For then would they not have ceased to be offered? because that the worshippers once purged should have had no more conscience of sins. But in those sacrifices there is a remembrance again made of sins every year. For it is not possible that the blood of bulls and of goats should take away sins.

Now let's go down a little further and read from verse 10 to 18.

By the which will we are sanctified through the offering of the body of Jesus Christ once for all. And every priest standeth daily ministering and offering oftentimes the same sacrifices, which can never take away sins: But this man, after he had offered one sacrifice for sins for ever, sat down on the right hand of God; From henceforth expecting till his enemies be made his footstool. For by one offering he hath perfected for ever them that are sanctified. Whereof the Holy Ghost also is a witness to us: for after that he had said before, THIS IS THE COVENANT THAT I WILL MAKE WITH THEM AFTER THOSE DAYS, SAITH THE LORD, I WILL PUT MY LAWS INTO THEIR HEARTS, AND IN THEIR MINDS WILL I WRITE THEM; AND THEIR SINS AND INIQUITIES WILL I REMEMBER NO MORE. Now where remission of these is, there is no more offering for sin.

Folks, I live in Daechi-dong, Gangnamgu, Seoul. My house is within walking distance of the Olympic Stadium. During the last Asian Games, when they held competitions, such as the marathon, the roads were all blocked off and it was quite inconvenient. The headlines in all the newspapers said the Asian Games were a huge success. Among the successes, timing and computer calculating procedures have advanced to the point where they can measure time to one one-hundredth of a second and can transmit the recorded times immediately. I don't know the details, but from what I read in the newspaper, record keeping has become very convenient.

Sometime back, humans invented the semi-conductor and are now using them in everything. Semi-conductors were thought to be useless because they were not conductors nor non-conductors. Our lives, however, have become very convenient, since the advent of the semi-conductor revolution. Computers, electronic calculators, and similar kinds of products have become a part of our work and play, such that today semi-conductors have become an inseparable part of our lives.

Many useful machines have been invented or improved through the invention of the semi-conductor. Right now, we are filming this on video. I feel like the world has become a great place to live, whenever I watch the videos of our retreats and conferences at home. It is so nice to see that things I had forgotten from the conference are recorded for posterity. Even now, I see people walking around holding video cameras. I'm sure they have filmed all of your faces, allowing us to put you in this video and letting me see you whenever I think of you.

With advanced technology, we are even able to film parts of the body that we cannot see with our eyes, such as the heart, liver, and stomach. Unfortunately, however, we humans have not been able to make machines that can look into the hearts and minds of people. I don't know when such a machine will be invented, but when it is, I plan to buy one, no matter how expensive it is. I'm going to buy it and put it at the entrance of our chapel. When brothers and sisters come in, one by one, I will sit on the other side of the screen and watch, just like they do when you get on the airplane. They put the bag on the conveyer belt and they watch as it passes by. They check it with an X-ray. When you come to our church, I will set up a chair and sit behind the machine.

"Oh, who are you? So and so Kim, so and so Lee, Deacon so and so."

"Elder Kim, you still have sins in your heart. Elder, please come over here. Look, this is the picture we took of your heart, Elder Kim. See? You still have dirty sins. Repent!"

Folks, wouldn't that be nice?

"Brother Kim, come over here. Let's have a look to see if your faith is good or bad." We would take the picture, "Click."

"Wow, Brother Kim, all of your sins have been washed clean."

If that were possible, I think many people would come wanting to see if they have been cleansed of their sins. Would $5,000 per picture be too expensive? Maybe I'd give you a discount. How does $1,000 sound, then? Anyway, it would be wonderful to have a machine like that. People think and make plans the way they want to, but they know nothing about their own heart. They don't know how few or how many sins they have. People need to search their heart, but there is nothing from this world that will help them do it. In the Bible it is written,

The heart is deceitful above all things, and desperately wicked: who can know it? (Jeremiah 17:9)

These words say that nobody knows the heart. The truly interesting thing is that the words of the Bible mirror our heart.

There was a lady who went from Korea to Germany as a nurse. This lady had always gone to church, but when she went to Germany, she received forgiveness of sin and became born again. By the way, just because she was born again in Germany, does that mean she received German salvation? No. Whether you get saved in Korea, or in Germany, it's all the same. There is no such thing as domestic or international salvation. Salvation is made in heaven. Even though you receive salvation in Germany, that salvation is made in heaven.

This sister was so happy after being saved that she asked a German missionary "Is there a pastor in Korea who correctly teaches forgiveness of sin like this?" The missionary told her to look up Pastor Ock Soo Park in Daegu. He also told her that if she went to Pastor Park, she would be able to hear about forgiveness of sin. From Germany, she then wrote me a letter.

"Dear Pastor Park, I was saved through this and that. I heard about you through a certain missionary in Germany. Please tell me about all the conferences that you will be having."

We hold three or four conferences in large cities every year, and we have any number of smaller conferences in local churches. I received the letter when we were about to have a grand conference in Daegu. I wrote her a reply, saying, "We are having a conference in Daegu from this date to that date."

The sister wanted to invite her father to the conference and phoned him from Germany, at great expense. "Father, Father, please attend Pastor Park's conference in Daegu."

Her father was living in Namhae, which is in South Kyungsang Province. He was the president of Namhae Express Corporation. He attended a Confucian temple and would always say, "This is what Confucius said. . . . This is what Mencius said. . . ." He was a very old man. Since his daughter had spent a lot of money to make the phone call to invite him to the conference, there was no way he could not go. He had no idea what to do because never in his life had he wanted to go to where those "Jesus freaks" gathered. He was hesitant, and his daughter must have been worried about him, so she gave her friend, who was about to go on vacation, travel expenses and asked her a favor.

"I'll pay for half of your travel expenses if you go to Korea. While you're there, take my father to Pastor Park's conference."

As a result, her father was dragged unwillingly to the conference, like an animal being dragged to the slaughter. To let his daughter know that he was attending the conference, he came up to me and greeted me.

"My daughter is so and so, and I am so and so."

The conference continued, but he did not find it interesting in the least.

"All they ever talk about is how great Jesus is. They don't say much more than that," was his assessment.

He wanted to go home, even before the conference was over. He thought about how disappointed his daughter, who was living abroad, would be, if he returned home without staying to the end. So he spent each day at the conference, killing time. He was full of complaints and his face was always scrunched up, but whenever he would come to me, he would say, "Oh, Pastor. You are doing a great job." But he would become bored because there was no one to keep him company. He would sit here and there. He would go here and listen, and then he would go there and listen. The conference would end on Friday, and it was already Thursday evening. After the sermons ended, I would ask the people who wanted to receive forgiveness of sin to come forward, but this old man never came forward.

The conference was on a mountain and people had gathered around to talk about forgiveness of sin. It was too dark for this old man to be outside, and since he didn't know anyone, he just walked back and forth inside. After a while, he became curious and came to where we were. People continued talking. He went to the back of the room and took a seat. It is truly amazing how the Holy Spirit of God works. We say many things, but if just one Word comes into a person, that person can be changed completely. That Thursday evening, he sat down and listened, and because the Word of God has power, he received forgiveness of sin. He realized the secret of forgiveness of sin. Hallelujah! Then he wanted us to make the conference longer. He was so thankful and could not stop smiling. Afterwards, he returned to Namhae.

Some time passed, and I received a phone call.

"Pastor Park! I cannot ask you to come to Namhae just for me, but if you ever happen to pass through here, please stop by."

Since he asked me so sincerely, I decided to go there. He was so happy to see me. But there is one problem I always have when I go Namhae or Choongmu, and it is the same problem I have when I come to Busan. People who live by the sea always like raw seafood, but I don't really care for it. Since that is what the people who live by the sea enjoy, that is what they usually serve me when I visit. They sometimes ask me to eat small octopi that are still moving on the plate. Anyway, they say that the water of Namhae is the cleanest in Korea, and that Namhae seafood is the most delicious. He prepared a delicious meal for me, with all of his heart.

When we sat down, he told me, "Pastor, my only pleasure in life used to be getting up early in the morning and shooting arrows with the elderly people of the village. After the conference, within one month, I finished reading all of the Old and New Testaments." Before, he would go to shoot arrows. But now he would read the Bible, which he had never done before. It was amazing how the Holy Spirit of God was working. Then he made the observation,

"Pastor, there are some strange stories in the Bible."

"Which stories?"

"You know, I've been waiting to ask you about this, Pastor. I used to go to a Confucian shrine, and I always read the works of Confucius. Confucius would say things like, 'Be patient, benevolence breeds no enemies.' He said such precious words. The words of God are good, too, but in the Bible, there are some scandalous stories."

"Which stories do you mean?" I asked.

"When I read the Bible, I saw that a man had relations with his daughter-in-law, and daughters would have relations with their fathers. Why did they write such scandalous stories in this holy book?" There is the story of Judah having relations with his daughter-in-law, Tamar, and having a baby. Lot had relations with his daughters. There were even brothers who had relations with their sisters.

"I thought that the Bible was a good book. It should have only good stories. However, the Bible has all kinds of strange stories. These stories would make my face red and I couldn't continue reading. Pastor, why is that? Why did they write such stories?"

Pastors receive all kinds of questions, and there is no way to know how to answer them all.

One day, a school teacher told his students, "Children, if you have any questions, please ask them today."

"Teacher, how many hairs do you have on your head?"

"Don't be a wise guy, and don't ask impertinent questions. Ask about something in the book."

"Fine, then how many words are there in the book?"

Anyway, I am talking about those sorts of questions. This brother was truly following the Lord. He had thrown away all that was precious to him, and he had turned his faith to Jesus. If he had been a person I often spoke with, I could get by with saying, "Gee, I don't know about that," but with him I couldn't just make up some nonsense or say, "I don't know." Pastors often stumble into these awkward situations. Very briefly, I closed my eyes and bowed my head. "Lord your servant is so foolish that he cannot even answer this man's question. This is a question he is asking me for the first time in his life. Please give me the wisdom to answer it."

While I had my eyes closed for a second, God sent me a

realization. "Mr. Choi, that is the difference between the Bible and all other books."

"Does it have to have those scandalous stories in it to make it different from other books?"

"No."

Let's suppose I became old and died. As I lived in this world, there are the good things that I've done, and there are bad things that I've done. My disciples or my underclassmen, who are all pastors, would write about me in books, saying, "During his lifetime, Pastor Ock Soo Park accomplished this and that." They would write good things. They would not write about bad things, would they? If possible, they would do their best to hide the bad things. On the contrary because the Bible is a mirror of our hearts, it reveals our hearts exactly as they are in writing. People act as if they are calm and gentle, even if they have adulterous thoughts in their hearts. Even though they have the heart to hate others, they may have a hypocritical smile on their face, saying, "Hi, how are you?"

In the Bible, you can find many different kinds of stories. And yes, there are many adulterous and filthy stories. That is because we have those things in our hearts.

A father-in-law sleeping with his daughter-in-law, and a father sleeping with his daughters. You would not do those things. But folks, we all have adulterous hearts. The Bible has recorded this to reveal that aspect about us and make us realize it. If we did not have dirty things in our hearts, then dirty stories would not have been written. However, because our hearts are filled with dirty things, the Bible reveals everything and shows our hearts. When he heard my explanation, he said, "That's great. The Bible is indeed the truth. The words of Confucius are hypocritical, but the Bible is the truth." From then on, he read the Bible even more.

Folks, this morning, I don't want to tell you about how we've built chapels or a plan we have for our church. I want to talk to you about the problems in your hearts that you yourselves know nothing about. If I could say, "Look, this is your heart" and show you your heart, that would be great, but I cannot do that.

After the sermon on the first evening, I stepped down from the podium. One student said, "Pastor, what is sin? Can you please talk to me about sin?" I then explained sin to him.

"Pastor," he said. "How could that be sin?"

"Well, because you cannot see sin with your eyes, I cannot show it to you saying, 'This is what sin is,' but a thing called sin does exist." If I could draw out from you the sin in your heart, you would easily recognize it, saying, "Ah, so that's what sin looks like." For example, when you draw the blood of a person who has typhoid and look at it under a microscope, you can see the typhoid germs moving back and forth. Wouldn't it be nice if you could draw out your sin and look at it? Even if you take an X-ray, or draw blood and examine it, sin will not appear. Even if your sins have been cleansed, you cannot physically prove whether they are cleansed or not. Isn't that what sin is? So, there is only one thing that can prove this, and that is the Word of God.

In checking whether their sins have been cleansed, many people today do not want to rely on the Word of God. When they go to the mountain to pray, speak in tongues, and prophesize, they think that their sins have been washed clean. Many people hold the superstitious belief that their sins are washed clean when their tears start to flow, and their hearts become full of emotion. Those are just superstitions. Today, superstitions are becoming very popular in the church. A lot of people think their sins are washed clean when they feel good and not washed clean when they don't feel good. Regardless of how you feel, you must know how to wash your sins clean. Do you understand?

Folks, God, too, wanted to wash our sins. God not only cleanses our sins. God also specifically teaches us the process of having our sins washed clean. He wants you to realize, "Ah ha! So that's what's done to wash away my sins," and that is why God gave us the 66 books of the Old and the New Testaments. According to the Bible, we still need someone to explain clearly how to have our sins washed clean, because people do not know about these things. That is the duty of a pastor.

When you receive forgiveness of sin, the Word tastes sweeter than honey because the Holy Spirit is inside of you. You will miss service, if you do not go. Your heart will overflow with love, you'll be at peace, and you'll be able to live a good life. However, telling a person who has not had his sins redeemed, "Do not sin!" "Do not steal!" "Tithe," "Read the Bible," only adds burdens. Would they be able to do these things? People who have had their sins washed clean through this conference will feel that the Holy Spirit is in their hearts and that they have changed after just one night. There are people here who are like that, are there not? That is why the most important thing for us is to realize the secret of forgiveness of sin and how to be born again.

After coming here to Mugunghwa Hall, I looked around the facilities. The building is well built. I was touched when I read the introduction of how the Mugunghwa Hall was built. It said that this hall was built for the purpose of spreading the gospel and educating people in the Busan region. I am so thankful that I could come to this wonderful hall and give my sermons. Folks, this microphone picks up my voice as it should, doesn't it? This hall has a good speaker system. I have led many conferences in many large halls, but I've never seen a speaker system as good as the one here at Mugunghwa. It does not look so good on the outside, but it has great capabilities.

There is a microphone here. If this microphone line were cut somewhere, could it make sound like it does now? It could not. What would we need to do, if that happens? A technician would come and find where the line was cut, and then reconnect it. Then it would work again. Folks, if the Holy Spirit goes inside of you, you cannot help but to change. If you still love the world, after you've received forgiveness of sin, if you still live a fleshly life, there is some kind of a problem. When the wall between God and us disappears, and when all the problems between God and us are resolved, from that moment on, we are able to walk with Jesus.

We ask you to raise your hands and come forward every night. There is a reason that we have people here in every corner preaching the Word. Why are we doing that? This place is like a hospital. When you go to the hospital, there are doctors. If a doctor is too busy and there are too many patients, does the doctor gather the patients together and throw a bunch of aspirin at them, telling them to pick them up and swallow them? He cannot do that. Just because a doctor is busy, he or she cannot merely pass out painkillers to everyone, or send them home after swabbing them with iodine.

He gets the stethoscope and diagnoses the patients one by one. When he asks, "What symptoms do you have?" the patients must answer precisely. When they get a prescription, they can get the medicine they need. It is the same with the disease of the spirit. If I end by finishing the sermon, it is like throwing aspirin for everyone to come and pick up. That would not do, would it? And so, we ask those of you who want to receive forgiveness of sin to please come forward after the sermon is over. Then we have counseling time with the servants of God who are here with us. They find out what the problem is and they prescribe medicine accordingly. They find the medicine in two places, in the Old Testament and in the New Testament. Then, when you take the medicine, the sin in your heart vanishes, as if it were washed away. Just like indigestion melts away, you feel light when your sins are washed clean. You change, saying, "Hallelujah." You are a changed person. Our pastors and ministers are walking around with the two bags of medicines, the Old Testament and the New Testament, and they listen to what each person has to say.

"Ah, this person's condition is like the Samaritan woman, so this Scripture will be good for her."

"He needs this Scripture because his condition is like that of Nicodemus. . ."

That is why whenever I have a conference, I invite 40 or 50 pastors to join me, and we come together. When you go to a hospital, they have external and internal medicine, with many departments. Even within internal medicine, they have the general internal medicine department, as well as other departments. These pastors' expertise is how to deal with sin. They have a professional license, and they specialize in and deal with the problem of sin. Yesterday evening, after I preached the Word, I saw some people going home, after having received forgiveness of sin. I saw them rejoicing. They couldn't get a hold of themselves. I smiled as I stood behind them. "I had tasted that kind of joy myself, a long time ago." It made me happy, remembering the time when I received forgiveness of sin. Folks, let's all receive forgiveness of sin. Let's not have anyone here go home without receiving forgiveness of sin. On that day, if someone says, "Oh, Pastor, I came to the conference, but I went home early because I was so busy and couldn't receive forgiveness of sin, and now I'm here in hell." How sad would that be?

There are so many things I want to say, and I'm sorry that I have not yet spoken about the words we read earlier. There are many passages about forgiveness of sin all over the Bible such as Genesis, Exodus, Leviticus, Numbers, Deuteronomy, Joshua, and Judges . . . But in the Bible, it does not label them, "This is how you can have your sins forgiven." What did I say yesterday evening? I talked about the chief butler and the chief baker. They had both sinned, but one was saved and the other was destroyed.

I explained through that story how our souls can be saved and how they can be destroyed. That's how the Bible is. Your eyes will open if you receive forgiveness of sin, and you will realize it. There was a time, long ago, when I did not know this, but when I read the Bible after receiving forgiveness of sin, my eyes were opened.

"Oh, this is how to receive forgiveness of sin."

"This is another way to receive forgiveness of sin."

One time I painted the whole Bible red.

"Oh, this is the way to receive the forgiveness of sin. Ah, I suffered so badly because I didn't know this."

I would color the Scriptures with a red pen. I colored it with colored pencils, and after a while, it looked as though the whole Bible was painted red. I had to get a new Bible. Folks, there are so many passages in the Bible about receiving forgiveness of sin. I cannot speak about them all, so let me just tell you one thing. I hope you will listen well to this one thing and receive forgiveness of sin.

When the Israelites under Moses were coming out of Egypt, they made the tabernacle. The man who made it was Moses. Let's read Hebrews chapter 8, from verse 1 to 5.

Now of the things which we have spoken this is the sum: We have such an high priest, who is set on the right hand of the throne of the Majesty in the heavens; A minister of the sanctuary, and of the true tabernacle, which the Lord pitched, and not man. For every high priest is ordained to offer gifts and sacrifices: wherefore it is of necessity that this man have somewhat also to offer. For if he were on earth, he should not be a priest, seeing that there are priests that offer gifts according to the law: Who serve unto the example and shadow of heavenly things, as Moses was admonished of God when he was about to make the tabernacle: for,

See, saith he, SEE, SAITH HE, THAT THOU MAKE ALL THINGS ACCORDING TO THE PATTERN SHEWED TO THEE IN THE MOUNT.

You have no idea what these words mean, although you just read them, right? Here, there are two tabernacles. In the earlier part of the reading it says, ". . .We have such an high priest, who is set on the right hand of the throne of the Majesty in the heavens; A minister of the sanctuary, and of the true tabernacle, which the Lord pitched, and not man." (Hebrews 8:1-2)

In verse 2, we can find the words sanctuary and tabernacle, right? What kind of a tabernacle does it say it is? It's okay even if you are wrong. If you were knowledgeable about this, you would be up here talking about it. Why would you be sitting down there? When I first began broadcasting, I was very clumsy. I didn't know what to do. I said, "I can't do broadcasting. I keep making mistakes," but the announcer told me, "Pastor, anyone can make mistakes when they talk. It's okay to make mistakes with words. But the truth, you cannot make mistakes with the truth. We announcers, however, cannot make mistakes when we talk. But, Pastor, for you, making mistakes could be your charm." Maybe she was just saying that to make me feel good, but, anyway, it is okay, even if you are wrong.

Here it says the "true tabernacle." Is it made by man or by God? It was made by God. Let us look at verse five.

Who serve unto the example and shadow of heavenly things. . . (Hebrews 8:5)

There are two altars, two sanctuaries, two tabernacles and two temples.

Folks, have you ever heard that there are two tabernacles and two temples? There really are two. There were sanctuaries where they gave offerings to God. One of them was made in heaven and the other was made by Moses on earth.

Folks, when the Israelites were leaving Egypt, God called Moses, "Moses."

"Yes!"

"Come up to the summit of Mount Sinai."

So Moses went up to the summit of Mount Sinai. Folks, you have seen the movie, "Ten Commandments," right? God gave Moses two tablets of stone, with the Ten Commandments, when he was there starving for 40 days and 40 nights. Afterward, God showed Moses a vision with everything from the tabernacle in heaven. The altar was there, the bread table was there, the ark was there, and the water pot was there. He showed Moses all of it. Then He said, "Moses, make one of these in this world, according to what I have shown you here on the mountain." Now I will read Hebrews chapter 8 verse 5.

Who serve unto the example and shadow of heavenly things. . .

Now do you understand it?

. . . as Moses was admonished of God when he was
about to make the tabernacle: for, See, saith he, that
thou make all things according to the pattern shewed to
thee in the mount. (Hebrews 8:5)

So when we read this verse, God revealed the temple, the ark, and the altar in heaven, and told Moses to build them on earth exactly as he saw them. He brought down from heaven the image of the altar, exactly as it was and told Moses to build it on earth. So, the image of the altar in heaven was brought down, and humans made the altar on earth. Where is the original of that, then? It is in heaven. The one on earth is just a replica. Because of that, every time the Israelites sinned, they made offerings before the altar. The priests wore ephods, killed lambs, sheep, or cows and sprinkled the blood about. Now I will speak about how these offerings were given to wash away their sins.

Please open your Bible to Leviticus chapter 4 of the Old Testament. I'll read from verse 27.

And if any one of the common people sin through igno-
rance, while he doeth somewhat against any of the com-
mandments of the LORD concerning things which ought
not to be done, and be guilty; Or if his sin, which he
hath sinned, come to his knowledge: then he shall bring
his offering, a kid of the goats, a female without blemish,
for his sin which he hath sinned. And he shall lay his
hand upon the head of the sin offering, and slay the sin
offering in the place of the burnt offering. And the priest
shall take of the blood thereof with his finger, and put it

upon the horns of the altar of burnt offering, and shall
pour out all the blood thereof at the bottom of the altar.
And he shall take away all the fat thereof, as the fat is
taken away from off the sacrifice of peace offerings; and
the priest shall burn it upon the altar for a sweet savour
unto the LORD; and the priest shall make an atonement
for him, and it shall be forgiven him. (Leviticus 4:27-31)

Here it says, "place of the burnt offering," "altar of burnt offering," and also "altar." These things are all inside the tabernacle. People of the Old Testament wanted to make offerings by killing a lamb because they had sinned. Can they make an offering just anywhere? At home, on the street, or on a mountain? No, they cannot. They must come forth before the altar when they make an offering. Let me explain this for you to understand better.

Folks, this story is very important. Please listen carefully. I have just read how to make an offering to have your sins forgiven, as it is written in the Old Testament. Now, suppose a person committed a sin. Let's read Leviticus 4:27 together.

And if any one of the common people sin through igno-
rance, while he doeth somewhat against any of the com-
mandments of the LORD concerning things which ought
not to be done, and be guilty; Or if his sin, which he hath
sinned, come to his knowledge . . . (Leviticus 4:27-28)

So, not just anyone can receive forgiveness of sin. There are qualifications to be met. The qualifications to receive forgiveness of sin are, first, you must have committed a sin. No matter how great you are, if you have not committed a sin, you cannot be forgiven. Secondly, you must realize your sin; you have to realize that you are a sinner. Then a person is qualified to receive forgiveness of sin. Because the wages of sin is death, the sinner must bring a kid of the goats, a female without blemish, a life that will die in his place.

Let's go back 3,500 years. We have entered a time machine and have now gone back. It is now the Old Testament era. What year are we in now? It's 1,500 B.C. This man must now bring a kid of the goats, a female without blemish. Now this man has brought a kid of the goats, a female without blemish. Does this goat have sin? No, it has no sin. But what about this man? He has sin. Then, upon which one will the wrath of the judgment of God fall? Of course, it will be upon the man. That's why he says, "Goat (lamb), I'm sorry. Please die for my sins, for my sake." Having said that, he brings the goat over. One is a sinner and the other is a clean goat, free from sin.

If this goat (lamb) is to die for this man, the man's sin must shift over to the goat. Unless the sin is shifted, it cannot be punished. Then how does the sin shift over? If sin were a pen, he could just take it out, and if sin were a suit, then he could just take it off. But we cannot touch sin, nor can we pick it up and move it. Folks, we cannot see sin with our eyes, but God sees sin with His. Verses 28 and 29 say,

Or if his sin, which he hath sinned, come to his knowledge: then he shall bring his offering, a kid of the goats, a female without blemish, for his sin which he hath sinned. And shall lay his hand upon the head of the sin offering. . .

The sin offering is either a lamb or a goat. Thus, the sinner lays his hands on the head of the goat. Why does he do the laying on of hands? Look here. Electricity that we use now is made at the power plant. Cables are connected to bring the electricity here from the plant. Folks, what must we do to transfer sin? It is recorded in Leviticus 16:21 that sin moves over through the laying on of hands. Please read it carefully when you go home tonight. Look at nothing else, but please listen carefully. Because sin moves over through the laying on of hands, this person must do the laying on of hands to move his sin over to this side so the goat (lamb) will die instead. Now we will do the ceremony of moving sin over. Let's go back to 3,500 years ago. I am the priest.

"For you to move your sin over to the goat (lamb), you shall do the laying on of the hands upon its head."

Now this sinner has done the laying on of hands upon this clean goat (lamb). Then did this sinner's sin transfer to the goat (lamb)? What moved over? I didn't see anything. Folks, when he did the laying on of hands, we could not see whether his sin moved over or not. So, you can never know that your sin has moved over by seeing it clearly with your own eyes. Even if you look at it through a magnifying glass, you cannot see it. When you look through the eyes of faith, however, sin, transferred with the laying on of hands because that's what God promised. If you see it with the eyes of faith, the sin moves over when you lay on your hands. Whether you believe it or not, it is your choice. In the Bible it is recorded that sin moves over by the laying on of hands, so the sin must have moved over, right? Folks, let me ask you. Would God lie? Even though we are not really happy to see each other, we act as if we are, saying, "Hey, it's great to see you!" We often put up a front like that. Many people say they caught a fish as big as their arm even though they caught a fish only as big as their hand. If we listen to a smooth talker, the fish he caught can become big or small. But God cannot do that. He says exactly what is in His heart. If something is in God's heart, He says such-and-such is in His heart. He is unable to say otherwise. He says the sin moves over because it does move over. He cannot say sin moved over when it did not. So do you believe in this God? If you don't want to believe this, then there is nothing I can do about it because somebody else can't have faith for you. If somebody could believe for you, then I would believe for all of you because I know how to believe. But because I cannot do that, isn't that why I am raising my voice now?

Now, he did the laying on of hands. First of all, after the laying on of hands, does sin remain in this man? No. What about in this goat (lamb)? In the Word of God, after the laying on of hands, there are no more sins in this man, and this goat (lamb) becomes the sinner. Not a sinner, but a sin goat (lamb), so to speak. What does the priest do with it then? He takes a sharp knife, at his side, and grabs the goat's (lamb's) neck, and stabs the artery to get its blood. The goat (lamb) sheds its blood, falls over, and dies. Then the priest takes the blood of the goat (lamb) and sprinkles it onto the altar. There are horns on the altar. He makes the horns red by painting the blood on it. Because the wages of sin is death.

"God, a life shed its blood, and died for this man's sin." They paint the blood as proof that something has died for his sin. The rest of the blood is poured under the altar. Then, all the leftovers, such as the dung or the intestines, are burned, and the offering is finished. The man has now had his sins washed clean. This is the sin offering in the Old Testament. Repeat after me, "Sin offering." It is an offering for the redemption of sin. So this man now has had his sin washed clean. Is he righteous? He is not righteous? Does he have sin? He does not. So he is happy, "Da da da da," he lives on.

Starting now, today, October 9th, 1,500 B.C., this person becomes holy. From October 9th, 12 o'clock, noon, he became clean. And the time "tick, tick, tick," passes by. His life of holiness is safely kept and he is fine, for one hour, two hours, and perhaps for 10 days. Then, after ten days, he meets his family's enemy.

"We meet again." He cursed his enemy, hated him and fought with him. Now is he righteous? Is he holy? No, he is not. After getting into a big fight, he quietly thought, "Oh, I paid a lot of money for that goat (lamb), to kill it and give it as an offering to wash away my sins. Now my righteousness is gone. Oh, it's all because I met that idiot, my enemy." The man suffered and cried. He had no choice but to go and get another goat (lamb) and bring it over. He goes to the market and looks for a goat (lamb). He touches the head, lifts up the left leg, looks at the chest, looks at the tail, and if there are no blemishes, he brings it back and makes another offering. This kind of offering continued in the Old Testament. It says that blood flowed like a river at the altar.

Folks, have you heard that Solomon once made a thousand offerings? Although people with money can give a thousand offerings, if one goat (lamb) costs 100 dollars, then that's a hundred thousand dollars. Even if we want to make such an offering, we cannot afford it. Let's think about this from God's point of view. God truly loves humans, but He cannot pour His love upon them because sin is standing in the way. God's heart is saddened about this, but this person killed a goat (lamb) and made an offering, so God was very pleased. "Wow, this is great."

But after a couple of hours, he sinned again. When God was about to show him His love, he goes and sins, again and again. It'd be very tiring for God to love us like that. No matter how many offerings we give, it will not work because it can only wash that one act of sin. So, offerings made by killing and giving goats (lambs) are not the actual, but an example. There is a reason God gave us that example. A goat dies at the altar in the temple of heaven and our sins are forgiven. Priests in the Old Testament killed many goats or lambs and gave them as offerings for us to realize that.

Eventually, however, in the actual temple of heaven, God wanted to make an offering that would forgive man's sins eternally. Because the eternal offering cannot be given through a lamb or a goat, God sent His only begotten Son, Jesus Christ, as a lamb for us.

Jesus came to this earth for our sins as the Lamb of God. If that is the case, should our sins not transfer onto Jesus? How could we have our sins move onto Jesus? Most people do not know about this. So they say that they do not know whether their sins go over to Jesus or not. The devil is so good at deceiving us. We can't see sin, even with our very eyes. When the devil says, "Hey, you have sin. You sinned. You lied."

"Oh, yeah, that's right. Oh, Lord. I am a sinner. Sob, sob, sob," and people begin to cry. Every morning, they cry and sob miserably. Because of that, real estate prices near churches fall, and people around the churches come to hate church-goers.

Now, our sins must move over to Jesus. What can we do to move them over? When they killed lambs in the Old Testament as offerings, they had to do the laying on of hands, to move sin over. Then, how can the millions and billions of people who have been born on this earth all come to Jesus and do the laying on of hands on Him? Clearly, they cannot. If we all do the laying on of hands on him, then Jesus' head will wear out and fall off.

If you go to the cathedral in Rome, Italy, there is a bronze statue of Peter. Pilgrims from all over the world come and pass by to kiss his feet. I heard that one of Peter's feet, which was made of bronze, became completely worn out and now he is missing a leg. Now they've put him in a glass case, to keep people from kissing his remaining foot. Even if just a few people were to come and kiss it, the whole leg would eventually wear out and fall off. If millions of people come and lay their hands on Jesus, His head can only become worn out, too.

In the Old Testament, when one person sins, he lays his hands on the lamb. But if a whole nation or congregation sins, they do not all do the laying on of hands. Rather, they have a representative do it. If you read in the Old Testament, in Leviticus chapter 4, verse 1, it tells about this. Read it when you go home. Thus, we need a representative to do the laying on of hands to move our sins onto Jesus. Let's look into that process. Open your Bible to Matthew chapter 3, verse 13.

Then cometh Jesus from Galilee to Jordan unto John, to be baptized of him. But John forbad him, saying, I have need to be baptized of thee, and comest thou to me? And Jesus answering said unto him, Suffer it to be so now: for thus it becometh us to fulfill all righteousness. Then he suffered him.

Look, ladies and gentlemen. Suppose this brother is Jesus, and this one is John the Baptist. John the Baptist was baptizing in the River Jordan, and Jesus came by.

"Baptize me," said Jesus. What did John say in response?

"I need to be baptized by you and you come to me?" What did Jesus Christ say to that?

"Suffer it to be so now, for thus it becometh us to fulfill all righteousness."

How can righteousness be fulfilled by Jesus being baptized by John the Baptist? Because righteousness is the opposite of sin, thus fulfilling all righteousness means that our sins are forgiven. Then John goes down to the River Jordan and baptizes Jesus. Folks, when baptisms are performed, do they lay their hands on the person? Yes, they do. This laying on of hands by John the Baptist, who is the representative of all of mankind, is the process of transferring the sin of mankind onto Jesus. Do you understand? When he was baptized and came up out of the water, the heavens opened and there was a sound from the heavens.

This is my beloved Son, in whom I am well pleased. (Matthew 3:17)

That's what God was pleased of. Why? It was because God had sent Jesus to this earth and told Jesus to bear all the sins of the world and die. Here He was carrying upon Himself all the sins of the world. That is why He is the beloved Son, the obedient Son. That is why God gave this answer.

John the Baptist did the laying on of hands upon the head of Jesus and performed the baptism. Then, since John the Baptist is the representative of all mankind, all sin transferred over to Jesus. Loving Folks, please answer me clearly. When did your sin transfer onto Jesus? Did it transfer when you believed? Suppose your sins transfer when you believe, and you believe now, but Jesus died two thousand years ago. Doesn't that mean that Jesus did not die for your sins being passed over to Him? Jesus had to die two thousand years ago, after having our sins transferred to Him. Only then could the death of Jesus have an effect on us. If Jesus had died when our sins had not transferred, no matter how He died, it would have had nothing to do with us. We could not say that He died for our sins. Isn't that so? Do you understand?

And that is why, it is not important when we believe that our sins transfer. Long before we were born into this world, all of our sins had already moved over onto Jesus. That's right. Jesus bore and carried the sins of, not only you people, but of your children, and of your grandchildren, and of all mankind, forever, before God. You did not see that with your own eyes, but it is a fact that your sins passed over. This is the Word of God. Let's open the Scriptures, and read John chapter 1, verse 29. We will read it together.

The next day John seeth Jesus coming unto him, and saith, Behold the Lamb of God, which taketh away the sin of the world.

The first day, when John was baptizing at the River Jordan, Jesus came to him and was baptized. The next day, Jesus came again to John at the river. So, this was the River Jordan where the blue waters flow, and where John was baptizing. He was crying out, "repent and be baptized," when Jesus came from the other side. Then, what did John say?

Behold, the Lamb of God, which taketh away the sin of the world. (John 1:29)

Was Jesus carrying a heavy load on His shoulders when He came? John said, *...Behold, the Lamb of God, which taketh away the sin of the world.* We could not see that He is carrying sin. He had been dipped in the water the day before, and He was baptized. Other than that, He was wearing wrinkled clothes because His wet clothes had dried. The same Jesus from yesterday had come along. We could not see with our eyes that our sins had moved over onto Jesus, but the eyes of God could see it. John the Baptist saw it, as well.

Behold, the Lamb of God, which taketh away the sin of the world.

Are your sins excluded from this? Although it may include all other people's sins...

"Yes, I think my sins are excluded from that, Pastor!" There are many strange people, and that is why God said, "I am your eternal enemy, from generation to generation, so I took away everyone's sin except yours"? No, it's not.

the Lamb of God, which taketh away the sin of the world.

Folks, a lamb carried away sin by the laying on of hands in the Old Testament era. Jesus, who is the Lamb of God, came to take away our sins, and He bore them all. Do you understand? So now, Jesus must be punished. Who has the most sin in the world? It is Jesus crucified on the cross because the sin of the whole world was upon Him. Because He had so much sin and was dirty, even God turned his face away from Him, right? And that is how He bore our sin. And Jesus, who was the Lamb of God, was crucified. That is why in Isaiah 53, verse 4, it says,

Surely he hath borne our griefs, and carried our sorrows: yet we did esteem him stricken, smitten of God, and afflicted. But he was wounded for our transgressions, he was bruised for our iniquities . . . (Isaiah 53:4-5)

It says that Jesus was crucified for our transgressions and our iniquities.

Folks, you cannot check with your own eyes, if your sins have been moved over to Jesus because sin is invisible. If a pregnant woman has a child, she knows that she has given birth because the child is tangible. You can tell with your eyes, if something was there and then it is no longer there. But sin, whether it is there or not, cannot be seen with the eye. All you have is the memory of sin in your heart. Because we remember sin, Satan uses our memory to deceive us, as if we still had sin. If our sin remains because we have it in our memory, would that mean our sin is gone, if we don't remember it? Were that the case, we'd all receive forgiveness of sin, if we got amnesia. No, that is not it. You may remember it, and at times you may feel guilt in your heart, but that sin surely passed over to Jesus Christ. That is what the Bible tells us. Believe it if you want to, and don't believe it if you don't want to, folks. Because your sin passed over to Jesus and received judgment, there is nothing left to be judged. That's why it says in the children's hymnal,

> "There is no more judgment for me.
> The Lord's blood covers my sins.
> Because Jesus died for me,
> the judgment is not upon me."

Do you know this hymn? When we go to receive the judgment from God, He says, "I finished your judgment."

"When?"

"At the cross."

Yesterday because my car was so dirty, I went to the car wash with one Minister. I was about to pay, after they finished washing the car, when the Minister said, "Pastor, I've already paid for it."

"When?"

"Just a little while ago."

So, is there a need for me to pay again? Jesus received all

of the punishment we needed to receive without consulting us and without so much as getting our permission. Folks, that is how much He loves us. Please do not receive that love in vain. After Jesus was crucified, if your sin still remains, the Lord would have such a heartache.

Let's search through the Bible and talk about this in more detail. Please open your Bible to Hebrews chapter 9. I will read verse 11.

But Christ being come an high priest of good things to come, by a greater and more perfect tabernacle, not made with hands, that is to say, not of this building.

Jesus did not enter the tabernacle built by the hands of man in the Old Testament. Rather, He went to the real tabernacle in heaven. Then, in verse 12,

Neither by the blood of goats and calves, but by his own blood he entered in once into the holy place, having obtained eternal redemption for us.

Here it says, "Neither by the blood of goats and calves. . ." When they made offerings in the Old Testament era, they needed the blood of goats and calves, remember? But they did not use that for the offering in the sanctuary of heaven. Jesus entered once and for all, the Holy place, through His own blood. The offerings given according to the example of lambs and goats wash away sins. But people had to continually kill goats and lambs, every time they would sin because the sacrifice cleansed only the sin of that time. Jesus Christ, when He was crucified and died, washed away not only the sins of that time, but all our sins, eternally. And that is why there is no need for Him to be crucified again. If He needs to die again, even now Jesus would not refuse to come down to be crucified, but He is sitting at the right hand of the throne of God because there is no need. Read verse 13,

For if the blood of bulls and of goats, and the ashes of an heifer sprinkling the unclean, sanctifieth to the purifying of the flesh:

Even when they gave offerings through killing goats and calves, were people's sins washed clean, and were they sanctified? Yes, they were sanctified. Even the blood of goats and calves can wash sins away. Then, more so, why wouldn't the blood of Jesus Christ, the Son of God, be able to wash away our sins? Do you believe that? Don't just believe with your mouths. Do you truly believe? Raise your hand if you believe. The Lord will rejoice. I did not do anything, so you may believe. Because Jesus shed His blood for you, the Lord rejoices in you, who believe. You say that you believe Jesus washed away your sins, but when you are asked, "Do you have sin?" You answer, "Yes, I have sin." That is not believing. You must believe that the Lord washed your sin perfectly clean. Then your heart can be freed from sin. Now, I will talk to you from another perspective, but you must be clear about forgiveness of sin. There should be no doubt or problem in your heart.

Let's read, Hebrews chapter 10, verse 10, together,

By the which will we are sanctified through the offering of the body of Jesus Christ once for all.

Folks, what makes us holy? We are holy because Jesus

was crucified. Because you don't know this, you try hard yourself to become holy, but that makes no sense. I told you last night, it's Soir de Paris on the skin of a pig. No matter how much Soir de Paris you put on a pig, on the inside it's just a pig who likes to wallow in the mud. What can you do about that? Folks, how can we, who enjoy sin, become holy? We cannot become holy, but we are holy because Jesus was crucified and shed His blood. Verse 11:

> *And every priest standeth daily ministering and offering oftentimes the same sacrifices, which can never take away sins:*

That washes only my sins, which are right then, right there. Verse 12:

> *But this man, after he had offered one sacrifice for sins for ever, sat down on the right hand of God;*

What offering? The eternal offering. The effect of the offering is eternal.

> *. . . sat down on the right hand of God; From henceforth expecting till his enemies be made his footstool. For by one offering he hath perfected for ever them that are sanctified. (Hebrews 10:12-14)*

God made us eternally holy and also has perfected us forever, through the blood of the cross. Believe that you have been made holy. I hope that you will come to believe in the cross that has perfected you, so there'll be nothing more for you to do for your sins. Verses 16 and 17:

THIS IS THE COVENANT THAT I WILL MAKE WITH THEM AFTER THOSE DAYS, SAITH THE LORD, I WILL PUT MY LAWS INTO THEIR HEARTS, AND IN THEIR MINDS WILL I WRITE THEM; AND THEIR SINS AND INIQUITIES WILL I REMEMBER NO MORE.

God said that He no longer remembers your sins and iniquities. If you did something bad to me, and if I knew about it, you would feel uncomfortable coming to me. But what would happen, if I forgot all about it? Then everything would be fine.

Between my wife and I, there are times when she does something wrong. Then, I chastise her, saying, "Why did you do that?" When she does it again, I say, "You did that last time, too! Why do you keep on doing that?"

"When I do something wrong, you just nag at me, on and on, about it."

"Fine then, I won't mention it again." But later on, without realizing it, I end up mentioning it and nagging her again.

"You said you were going to forget about that, but you never let it go. You keep it in your mind."

People are that way. They say that they will forget about something, but then, when something else happens, they remember it all over again. Even though we try not to remember, we cannot help but to remember. Sometimes we try to remember, but no matter how much we think, we still cannot remember. That's how humans are. But if God does not want to remember, He does not remember. He remembers when He wants to. He does whatever He wants to. If God says He does not remember, then He completely forgets about it, just like deleting a file on a computer. Because of that, God does not remember our sins whatsoever. Hallelujah! I praise the Lord.

Loving folks, you have done a great job, sitting in those small chairs for nearly three hours. This evening I would like to talk to you from a different perspective, how your hearts can become freed from sin. I'm thankful that I can come to Busan and stand before you, loving citizens of Busan. I have a thankful heart toward pastors who invited me and also to you, for attending.

I have nothing to show you for my gratitude, but the forgiveness of sin that I received, this amazing salvation. I hope that you, too, will be able to receive it. As you listen to the Word, I'm sure there is much that you do not understand. Many people bought the sermon tapes yesterday. We are providing them for you, so those of you who do not understand, if you listen to the tapes two or three times, I believe that your faith will become firmly rooted.

Anyhow, those of you who are attending this conference, I hope that every one of you continues attending, this evening, tomorrow morning, and tomorrow evening. When we go to heaven, I hope that not so much as one person here will be left behind. Let's meet each other joyfully in that land. There are twelve gates into heaven. Three on the east side, three on the west side, three on the south side, and three on the north side. Let's all meet at the center gate on the south side and go into heaven together. In that land, I hope that we will all be able to live eternally with the Lord.

7

The Man
Who Fell among Thieves

Who Meets with
the Good Samaritan?

What did the man who fell among thieves do to receive salvation? Nothing. He could only lay down half dead. To this man, a Samaritan, who is a picture of Jesus, came and bound up his wounds, pouring in oil and wine, set him on his own beast, brought him to an inn and took care of him. Jesus appears to those people who cannot do anything by themselves and leads them to eternal salvation.

7

The Man
Who Fell Among
Thieves

We will read the Scriptures, in the New Testament, Luke chapter 10, from verse 25 to 37.

And, behold, a certain lawyer stood up, and tempted him, saying, Master, what shall I do to inherit eternal life? He said unto him, What is written in the law? how readest thou? And he answering said, THOU SHALT LOVE THE LORD THY GOD WITH ALL THY HEART, AND WITH ALL THY SOUL, AND WITH ALL THY STRENGTH, AND WITH ALL THY MIND; AND THY NEIGHBOUR AS THYSELF. And he said unto him, Thou hast answered right: this do, and thou shalt live.

But he, willing to justify himself, said unto Jesus, And who is my neighbour? And Jesus answering said, A certain man went down from Jerusalem to Jericho, and fell among thieves, which stripped him of his raiment, and wounded him, and departed, leaving him half dead. And by chance there came down a certain priest that way: and when he saw him, he passed by on the other side. And likewise a Levite, when he was at the place, came and looked on him, and passed by on the other side. But a certain Samaritan, as he journeyed, came where he was: and when he saw him, he had compassion on him, And went to him, and bound up his wounds, pouring in oil and wine, and set him on his own beast, and brought him to an inn, and took care of him. And on the morrow when he departed, he took out two pence, and gave them to the host, and said unto him, Take care of him; and whatsoever thou spendest more, when I come again, I will repay thee. Which now of these three, thinkest thou, was neighbour unto him that fell among the thieves? And he said, He that shewed mercy on him. Then said Jesus unto him, Go, and do thou likewise. (Luke 10:25-37)

We talked in detail about how, through the Bible, our sins were transferred to Jesus Christ. Actually, our sins do not burden our shoulders, but they do make our hearts heavy. Sin wounds the core of our heart, rather than infecting our flesh. Because of that, when most people receive forgiveness of sin and become freed from the burden of sin, they give testimonies of many different kinds of disease being cured automatically. A certain foreign doctor said, "When we get rid of the burden of sin in the heart, 437 different kinds of diseases are automatically healed."

Most of our diseases originate in the heart. I often experience that myself. When I become worried and concerned, I cannot digest my food, and I lose my appetite. However, when my heart is light and happy, I have no problem, no matter what I eat.

Folks, we all know that it is good to be freed from sin, but most people don't know how to be freed from sin. If there is a tree of sin, then people live a spiritual life plucking the fruit of that tree, one by one. Apples, persimmons, grapes, and peaches grow only once a year. Once you reap the fruit, there is no more to pick. However, the tree of sin bears its fruit anytime, anywhere. Isn't it? That fruit comes while you are sleeping, when you wake up, after breakfast, and it comes even when you are walking down the street. So most people waste their lives every day, picking this fruit. Not once do they stand before God with a bold, confident, joyful, or peaceful heart because there is no end, no matter how much they pick. That is the condition of most people's hearts.

Our Lord did not try to discipline the fruit of sin. The sins we commit are the result of sin. He resolved the sin in our heart from its origin; uprooting the tree of sin.

On the first evening, I said that sin and crime are different. A cold and a runny nose are different. A cold is also different from a cough. Of course, you do get a sore throat, a runny nose, and you cough when you have a cold, but the cough and the runny nose are not the cold. We steal, we lie, and we hate others. All people who have sin do such things. However, we do not call stealing sin. Stealing is the result of sin. We call stealing a crime. If we have sin in our hearts, it makes us commit sins. This morning, I talked to you about how the sins we had, from top to bottom, were transferred to Jesus Christ. This evening, I want to talk to you from a different perspective.

How does our salvation come about? How can we enter into heaven? How can we be eternally freed from sin? How can we boldly come before God, like long ago, before Adam and Eve sinned? That's what I want to talk to you about.

Folks, we think that such things are impossible, but because God has many methods and great power, He can make such dirty and filthy humans like us clean.

I will talk specifically about these problems, based mostly on the words in Luke chapter 10.

Long ago, a young man worked at a port in London, England. He had no family or loved ones. He couldn't even get married, and he lived very poorly. With the few pence he made working all day long, he would buy some bread. He slept anywhere. His job was carrying luggage on and off ships that went back and forth between England and the United States. From time to time, he heard from the people who came from the United States that it was a land of opportunity and that it was a good place to live.

So this young man began to think, "I've been living here, and I've worked hard, only to ward off starvation. Why don't

I go to America and make some money?"

He began to save up for passage to go to America. Since he did not make a lot of money, he would hide the little bits of money he made in his suit pocket. He would pull out his money and count it, whenever he had time.

Back then, there were few ships that went to the United States; perhaps only one a month. One day, he went to the ticket booth and asked the price of passage. He counted all the money he had in his pocket. It was just enough to buy a ticket. He could buy the ticket, but he was worried about what he would eat onboard, and what he would do when he got to America. He thought, "If I'm going anyway, I might as well not delay, but leave now. Everything will work out, somehow." He made up his mind to buy the ticket. Back then, it took a ship one week to get to the United States from England.

He thought, "I won't die of starvation in just one week. As soon as I get to America, there will be food, and I'll be able to make money." He got on the ship.

"Farewell, Port of London."

He turned his back on England with no hesitation, and to the sound of the ship's horn, off he went to the United States. Now, the people on board got together and were excitedly talking about all the possibilities in the United States. He would sit and listen to them, and at times, he also talked. When it came time for lunch, "Ring, ring!" The bell rang calling the people to come to the dining room to eat. Everyone went to eat, but he could not go because he had no money. The person next to him said, "Young man! Let's go eat."

"Oh, I got indigestion from breakfast," he said, "So I think

I'll pass up on lunch."

"But still, you need to eat."

"No, I'm fine."

"Then fine, go ahead and skip lunch." Everyone had eaten and was returning, saying, "That was delicious."

Now, this young man was so hungry that he could not bear it. However, he still said, "I'll make it through, I can suffer this once."

When it was dinner time, the bell rang again, "Ring, ring!"

"Young man, you didn't have lunch, so you must be starved. Come, let's go eat."

"Oh, no. I'm fine. I go for days without eating."

"If you skip meals like this, it's going to be bad for your health."

"Oh, don't worry about me."

So everyone else went to dinner, and once again, he went hungry. He would talk with them and have a good time, but when it was mealtime, when they would ask him to join them, he would become very down and say, "No, you guys go ahead."

"Young man. Why are you starving yourself?"

"It's none of your business whether I starve or not!" he would say and become angry. The other people began to say that he became strange at mealtime and stopped inviting him. Two days passed, three days passed, and after he had starved for five days, he felt like he was about to die. In two days they would arrive in the United States, but it felt as though he would starve to death before even making it to America. On the morning of the sixth day, there was an announcement on the ship.

"Attention, passengers! We truly apologize, but we will arrive in America five days later than scheduled, due to the storm." He thought he could somehow make it through, if it were only one week, but now he felt doomed.

"Now I'm going to die." He had no confidence that he would make it through the next five days, so he made up his mind. "Look, if I'm going to die anyway, they say, if you eat, you at least look better when you die. Therefore, let me eat, and then die. I'll go to the dining room and eat something. When they tell me to pay, I'll wash the dishes, do the laundry, or whatever!"

So he went into the dining room at about the time the other people were finishing their meal and leaving. The waitress asked, "What would you like to have?" He thought, "Well, if I'm going to die anyway, I'll eat as much as I can."

He ordered five steaks and a lot of other food. The waitress then asked, "This is for how many people?"

"It doesn't matter how many people eat. Just bring the food."

The waitress brought over the food he had ordered. He was eating for the first time in several days, so he ate without knowing whether the food was good or not. He ate one plate, two plates. . . . He had eaten so much that his stomach was about to burst, but in his heart he began to worry about paying.

He thought to himself, "The waitress is going to ask me to pay for the food. What will happen when I say that I have no money?" He was nervous and began to stall. All other employees had left and one waitress stayed behind to clear his table. After finishing his meal, he sipped the water slowly and said, "Excuse me. May I have the check?"

The waitress said, "Pardon?"

"I said, please bring me the check. How much does this come out to?"

"Is this your first time eating here?"

"Please, just bring the check." Now, he had really made up his mind.

"Are you eating here for the first time?"

"First time or second time, it doesn't matter. Just bring it."

"We don't charge you for food."

"What?"

"When you bought your ticket, all of your meals were included."

"Oh, my God! If I had known that, I wouldn't have starved myself."

As he thought about how he had starved for five days, without knowing that he had already paid for his meals, you can imagine how resentful and angry he felt. Folks, this is not something to be angry about, compared to the person who is going to hell. Do you know why people go to hell? Do you think people go to hell because they have committed too many sins? They go to hell because they have not realized the Word of God. That young man suffered miserably for five days because he did not know that the meals were included in his ticket. If it had not been for the storm, he might have starved the entire week and not have made it to the United States, at all.

The reason we go to hell is because we do not know the will of God. When a mother gives birth, doesn't the mother prepare diapers and clothes because she knows that the baby will urinate and defecate? In the same way because God knew how evil and dirty man would be and that we would sin, God prepared everything for us.

People who do not know what God has prepared for us, who have so many sins, do not rely on what God has prepared, but try to do things for themselves.

One day, a certain mother had to go out of town for a while. She told her son, "Come home early from school today, okay?"

"Why, Mother?" he asked.

"Because I have to go out of town for a while."

"Okay, Mom, I'll come home early."

The boy forgot about it and went to play soccer instead, and came back home at around sunset. The mother had left, after waiting as long as she could. Before she left the house, however, she prepared dinner for her son, as well as his breakfast for the next morning. She also left rice in the pot. Now if the son did not know that his mother had prepared his food, wouldn't he have been running around, looking for something to eat? In the same way, people who do not know the secret of what God has prepared for them try to do things for themselves. The lawyer in Luke chapter 10, which we read earlier, is that kind of a person.

Let's read together from chapter 10, verse 25.

And, behold, a certain lawyer stood up, and tempted him, saying, Master, what shall I do to inherit eternal life?

Folks, please listen. The question the lawyer asked,

"Master, what shall I do to inherit eternal life?" implies a very deep meaning. This lawyer thought that he had to do something to receive salvation and eternal life, so he tried hard to keep the law. Did he receive eternal life? He thought that he could achieve eternal life by doing that, but eternal life was beyond his grasp. That is why he came forth to Jesus and asked the question, "What shall I do to inherit eternal life?" What was Jesus' answer? In chapter 10, verse 26, Jesus says,

What is written in the law? how readest thou?

These are very important words. Did He ask only, "What is written in the law?" No. He asked, "What is written in the law, and how readest thou?" He asked two questions.

Folks, we can discover spiritual secrets hidden inside the Word when we read the Scriptures carefully. The question Jesus asks, tells us that the words of the law can be read and understood in different ways, depending upon the person. What is written in the law? Yes, words such as, "Thou shalt not commit adultery," "Thou shalt not steal," "Thou shalt not murder," and "Thou shalt not give false witness," are written in the law. It is true that these are recorded, but "how do you read it?" In other words, "how do you accept the law?" That is the question. Jesus asked the lawyer, "How do you read that? How do you accept it?"

Most people who live spiritual lives in Korea today know what is written in the law, but there are problems in how they receive it. I would like to ask you this evening. In the law it says, "Thou shalt not steal," "Thou shalt not commit adultery,"

"Thou shalt not murder," and "Thou shalt not covet." Does it not? How do you receive these words? There are two kinds of people. Some people say, "Well, the Word of God said, do not steal, so I'd better not steal. And God said, 'Do not lie,' so I'd better not lie." They try hard to keep God's Word. There are people who accept the law in this way. There are other people, however, who try not to steal, not to commit adultery, not to lie, not to hate, not to murder, but are unable to do so. They say, "God, I just can't do this. There is no way I can do this. God, you do it for me. I cannot do it." They give up, waving a white flag in front of God. People understand the law in these two different ways.

During the Asian Games, this time around, Korea won many gold medals in boxing. In boxing, two people, standing in a small ring, hit each other. The person who is better, lands many hits, but the person who is not as good, cannot help but to get hit. Gloves fly all over the place; to the head, to the stomach, to the face. When one person can no longer withstand the punches, and when he goes down, it must be so peaceful. Don't you agree? If you just fall, all those punches that were pounding down upon you cease, and you hear only the sound of the count. How peaceful that must be. Of course, in a boxing match, you should fight to win, but in the match between God and us, we need to get knocked out quickly. We must surrender and pass out quickly. The more we struggle to do something for ourselves, without falling down, the more painful it is for us. People who went to church, not out of formality, who have tried to live a true spiritual life, sincerely and unanimously agree that the more they are determined to not commit sin, the more sin they actually commit. I'm sure that those of you who have experienced this know exactly what I'm saying.

I'm sure many of you here have smoked, right? Raise your hand if you have ever had the experience of smoking. I, too, have smoked. People who smoke must have thought at least once about quitting.

Today is October 9th. Suppose I decided to quit smoking on October 10th, at midnight. If I were a person who usually smoked a pack a day, I would smoke two packs on October 9. To see if what I'm saying is true, those of you who have had that experience, please answer me. Isn't that right? Suppose I want to leave my notebook here and go somewhere for a second. You would not even think of looking into my notebook, would you? You would think, "Pastor Park left his notebook there," and go on about your business. But if as I was leaving, I said, "Folks, it's okay for you to come up here and do whatever you want, but please do not look in my notebook. You must absolutely not look in this notebook. If you do, you'll be in big trouble. I am saying, you must absolutely not look in this notebook."

Then I leave. If I had said nothing, you would not have given a second thought to looking in it, but because I told you that you should never look in it, you would badly want to see the secrets inside. Isn't that right?

A long time ago, there was a certain teacher. In the middle of class, he would stop teaching, go to the cupboard, pull something out and eat it. The children would ask, "Teacher, what is that?"

"You little rascals, this is what you call dried persimmons."

"What are dried persimmons?"

"If kids eat it, they die."

One day, the teacher went somewhere and left the children alone in the classroom. "So, what, exactly, are dried persimmons, that when adults eat them, it's okay, but when children eat them, they die? Would we really die? Let's eat some and see what they're like."

Then, one child ate a little bit. Did he die? Not even close. Instead, it was so delicious. He ate one whole dried persimmon. He still didn't die.

"Hey, guys. Get over here! Let's all have some. We might as well all sin."

The children got together and ate all of the teacher's dried persimmons. They finished eating, but then became afraid when they thought about being spanked by the teacher. They thought, "What shall we do?" Among them, one witty child said, "Just do as I say."

"Okay, what are we going to do?" The student dropped the ink stone the teacher valued very much and "crack!" It broke. Then he said, "All of you! Quick, get on your stomachs on the floor!"

All the students laid down on their stomachs. The teacher was now returning. When he entered, the students were all on their stomachs on the floor. "Hey you little rascals! What are you up to?"

When he said that, the smart student said, "Teacher, we have sinned and deserve to die!"

"What happened?"

"Well, while we were playing around with one another, we broke the ink stone you value so much. That was a terrible sin! We felt so guilty that we decided we should die, so we ate the medicine you told us would kill us. Now we are waiting to die. We ate it, but nothing's happening. We're starting to worry. Maybe it's because we ate too little of it. We would like to eat more, but there is no more."

This is an amusing story, but the reality is that we are deceived by Satan. We think that if we make up our minds not to sin, that we will not sin. On the contrary, the more determined we are not to sin, the more sins we commit. Do you understand?

There was a certain daughter. Eventually she became an adolescent. She became infatuated with her boyfriend and could not study. Because of that, her father locked her door so she could not go out, and he made her study. The daughter tried to control her heart, thinking, "Okay, now I will study."

Then the father would come and say, "Are you thinking about that boy again?" She was not thinking about him, but her father stirred up her heart. Do you know what I am saying? It is not that we are determined to sin, but if our heart falls into sin, then we become dragged along by it.

Once, when I was leading a Bible study in a prison, one of the prisoners said that he wanted to meet with me privately. I spoke with the warden, and then I had a meeting with the prisoner. He said he had a very bad habit. Whenever he got drunk, he would always cause huge problems. Once, after having caused a big accident, he was determined not to drink again. He quit drinking entirely. One day, he was passing by a bar. His friends said, "Hey, Jin Suk! Come here and have a drink with us!"

He turned his head because he didn't want to go in. After a while, he was in front of the bar. He was determined not to go in, but his heart was already there. The legs follow the heart, not the mind.

"Okay then. Just one drink. Only one," he thought. And he really did have only one drink. The only problem was that he had that one drink too many times. When he later sobered up, he was at the police station. He had no idea what had happened.

Folks, God is not deceived. He knows that we are not people who can avoid sin, only because He tells us to. No matter how much He tells us not to sin, we are humans who can only sin. So instead of telling us not to sin, He gives us the strength to overcome sin, so we won't fall into sin. We need to receive the strength that comes from God for us to be freed from sin. We can never overcome sin by our own effort and determination.

"Do not murder," "Do not commit adultery," "Do not steal." When people try to keep the law, but are unable to, they say, "Ah, it doesn't work for me, even when I try. God, I can't do it." The law was given to us for us to surrender. God made the law so you cannot comply with it, even if you try zealously. That is why there is no one who has kept the law perfectly. People who cannot keep the law, even when they try, no longer try to do it themselves.

That is why Jesus asked, "How do you read the law?" One type of person thinks they have to try to keep the law, as it is recorded. The other says, "I cannot do it. Jesus, you must do it for me."

Jesus always enters and works upon the second type of person. Those people who only say with their lips, "I can't do anything. What is it that I can do?" continually come forth on their own, even though they say, "I cannot do anything." People who have realized, "There is only evil in me. I only have filthiness. I am so dirty," no longer try to do it themselves because they know it's pointless to do so. The Lord works upon this kind of person.

What did the lawyer say? He knew the law, but he did not know the true reason why God had given the law. That's why he thought that he could accomplish something if he worked hard.

. . . THOU SHALT LOVE THE LORD THY GOD WITH ALL THY HEART, AND WITH ALL THY SOUL, AND WITH ALL THY STRENGTH. . . (Luke 10:27)

This makes no sense either. Can you love the Lord, your God, with all your heart? I don't think I can do that. I drive my own car, and I average about an hour each day on the road. I calculated the total distance I travel each year, and I also calculated my usual average speed. I spend, on average, more than 365 hours in the car. When I added up all that time, I felt like so much time was being wasted when I drive. I can't afford to have another person drive for me, so I decided that I should use the time to memorize Bible verses, pray, or contemplate the Bible. One time, I stopped at a red light, and there, with the Bible open on the seat next to me while I waited, I thought about something from the Bible. I fell into the words and had been reading for a while, when I heard honking from behind. When I looked up, I saw that the cars in front of me had left, and I was there in the middle of the street by myself. The light had turned green.

When I drive, the car tells me, "Master, if you are going to use me, please pour all of your heart upon me." That's what it says to me, so I can't give my heart to God while I'm driving. My heart is too busy driving.

With all of your heart, with all thy soul, with all thy strength, and with all thy will.

Raise your hand if you can do all that. If you love the Lord with all your strength, then what strength are you going to eat with? People who don't know, want to do it and say, "Lord I believe in you. Please have me do this."

In other words, the wisest person in boxing is the one who gets knocked down by his opponent as soon as the first round starts. It's better than getting beaten up and then getting knocked out, after having had his nose broken, his forehead torn apart, his eyes blackened, and after becoming all bloody. Of course, you shouldn't actually do it like that in a real boxing match, but in the competition against God, that is the wisest way. God does not care for you until you pass out, give up and surrender completely.

This lawyer says,

THOU SHALT LOVE THE LORD THY GOD WITH ALL THY HEART, AND WITH ALL THY SOUL, AND WITH ALL THY STRENGTH, AND WITH ALL THY MIND; AND THY NEIGHBOUR AS THYSELF. (Luke 10:27)

This is what you get if you condense the Ten Commandments into a single sentence. The first four commandments tell us to love the Lord, but starting from the fifth commandment, it tells us to love our neighbor. What did Jesus say? He said, "Thou hast answered right: this do, and thou shalt live."

If you live only when you do them, it means you will die if you cannot do them. In the Old Testament, Deuteronomy chapter 28 says,

And all these blessings shall come on thee, and overtake thee, if thou shalt hearken unto the voice of the LORD thy God. Blessed shalt thou be in the city, and blessed shalt thou be in the field. Blessed shall be the fruit of thy body, and the fruit of thy ground, and the fruit of thy cattle, the increase of thy kine, and the flocks of thy sheep. Blessed shall be thy basket and thy store. Blessed shalt thou be when thou comest in, and blessed shalt thou be when thou goest out. (Deuteronomy 28:2-6)

But it also says, ". . . if thou wilt not hearken unto the voice of the LORD thy God, to observe to do all his commandments and his statutes which I command thee this day; that all these curses shall come upon thee, and overtake thee: Cursed shalt thou be in the city, and cursed shalt thou be in the field. Cursed shall be thy basket and thy store. Cursed shall be the fruit of thy body, and the fruit of thy land, the increase of thy kine, and the flocks of thy sheep."

Folks, is this a blessing or a curse? It's a blessing to the person who can keep all of the law, but it's a curse to the person who cannot. People do not realize this and simply say, "This is a blessing! Blessed you are when you come in, blessed you are when you go out." They are so blinded by the blessing that they try to keep the law without knowing whether they can or cannot keep it. We must understand the Bible correctly. Apostle Paul, before he came to believe in Jesus, had persecuted and killed people who believed in Jesus. It's not that Paul had not read the Bible. Even when you read the Bible, knowing the words and knowing its main point are completely different. If you know only the words of the Bible, you try hard to do something. But when you know its main point, you will rest and God will work. Do you understand?

When the lawyer said that, the Lord said unto him, "Thou hast answered right: this do, and thous shalt live." The Lord said, "Alright, if you can keep all the law, go ahead and do it."

Can you keep the whole law? You cannot. Raise your hand, if you're confident you can keep the entire law. Nobody has raised their hand. You are very wise people. I hope that you will not only not raise your hand, but that you will say in your heart, "I cannot do this." People who only say they cannot do it, constantly try to do it. The people who know in their heart they cannot do it, do not even try because they know they will fail even if they try.

When Jesus says, "Thou hast answered right, this do and thou shalt live," it means go ahead and do it and you will live. What does that mean? This is the same as the way to walk on water I talked about two nights ago. How can you walk on water? You run onto the water, and before your right foot sinks, you take a step with your left foot. Before your left foot sinks, you take a step with your right foot. Then you can walk all the way to Cheju Island. You can even walk all the way to Japan or Taiwan. But folks, if you wait until one foot sinks and you drown and die, then that's not going to work. Try it. If you do exactly as I told you and you drown, I will take full responsibility, but I won't take responsibility, if you do not do as I told you. Who would attempt to walk on water upon hearing this? If you already know that this is not going to work, as you listen to me, then you will not even try it. If you are a wise person, you will realize that you are unable to perform under the law. You know that you will fail. However, this lawyer wanted to justify himself and said, "Who is my neighbor?" That's what he asked. Then Jesus told him the story of the man who fell among thieves.

A certain man went down from Jerusalem to Jericho, and fell among thieves, which stripped him of his raiment, and wounded him, and departed, leaving him half dead. A priest passed by. Did he help him? No, he did not help him. Afterward, a Levite passed by. Did he help the man? No, he did not help him, either. Then a Samaritan passed by. Did he help him? Yes, he went over to him, poured oil and wine upon his wounds, put him on his own beast, and took him to an inn. There he gave two pence to the inn keeper.

Jesus is saying that this man who was hit by robbers represents the lawyer. Folks, what happened to this man who was attacked? He was stripped of his clothes, beaten and left there half dead. What did he do to be saved? All he did was lie there. He was unable to do anything. The Samaritan, who represents Jesus, approached him, poured oil and wine upon his wounds, bound him, set him on his own beast, took him to the inn, and took care of him. At that point, salvation was accomplished.

Everyone, what does an appendicitis patient do, when he comes to the hospital for surgery?

"Come here doctor. Perform the operation right here. Please use a scalpel made in America. Please disinfect the tweezers and be careful when you are administering the anesthesia." At this point, no doctor would want to perform the surgery.

"Please go to a different hospital."

"Do it yourself," the doctor would say.

Do you know what a doctor does to a person who has appendicitis? Before the operation, he tells the patient to sign a contract, a document that says it's okay for him to make a mistake. Then he administers the anesthesia and with leather cords, ties and binds the patient's arms and legs. When the doctor is able to do whatever he wants to do, he picks up the knife. He cuts when and where he wants to cut. When he wants to remove something, he removes it. When he wants to stitch, he stitches.

"Ah, cut a little deeper here. A little bit to the right. That thing at the bottom, hurry up, take that out. Now, hurry up and disinfect it!" If the patient talks like this, the doctor will walk away. Folks, all of our thoughts and our heart must be cast away for our soul to be saved. Then the Lord can cut and stitch.

"Lord, I leave it in your hands. Do whatever you want." At that point, Jesus makes it perfect. If the man who fell among thieves had been alive and well when the Samaritan approached him, he would have cursed the Samaritan and told him to go on his way. The reason is that the Jews looked upon the Samaritans like dogs. But he didn't care whether it was a Samaritan, a pig, or a dog that had come to save him. He was dying. There was no longer any pride or dignity he needed to protect. Whoever could save him, whether that person was black or white, it didn't matter. That's what this is all about.

Ten years ago, a certain pastor nearly drowned. We were getting ready for a retreat, and there was a flood. I know how to swim a little, so I was able to swim across the stream. The pastor must have thought, "Well, I'm more athletic and stronger than Pastor Park and, if he crossed it, why shouldn't I be able to?" With that in mind, he jumped in. He began to drift away, pulled by the water. He was only twenty meters from a water fall when some high school students rescued him. He would not be here today, if they hadn't reached him. Afterward, he said that it is a lie when they say that a person who is drowning screams, "Help me!" When he was actually drowning, he couldn't bring himself to utter a word.

Folks, when you throw a rope to a person who is drowning, does he ask, "What brand of rope is this?"

"Is it reliable?"

"Is it made in America, or is it made in Korea?"

"How many pounds can it hold?"

"Please give me a stronger rope."

If he says anything like this, then he is not in trouble. A person who is really drowning can't even say, "Help me!" He just goes, "Bloop, bloop," and tries to hold onto whatever he can. If there is anyone among you who has not received forgiveness of sin, you must first realize that, without it, you can only be destroyed. A person who realizes this, does not question it. Because you're full, because you are unable to realize you can only be destroyed, you have a lot of reasons and problems of your own.

Everyone, before I received forgiveness of sin, I realized that I was a sinner who could only go to hell. I felt that if someone could come to me and tell me how to receive forgiveness of sin, it would be worth becoming that person's servant for the rest of my life. When did the man who fell among thieves become saved? When he was looking death in the eye; when he was powerless to do anything himself. Do you know what kind of people Jesus sought out when He was in this world? The Lord was not close to those who were smart, prayed glibly, read the Word well, or who had a good spiritual life. Jesus was always near those whose only alternative was death, who could do nothing, and who had no hope in this world.

Folks, that's how Jesus is this evening. Do you have no hope? Do you have nothing to look forward to? Are you a person who could only be destroyed? If so, then Jesus is right there next to you. But if in your heart, you say "Although, I'm desperate, I'm not that bad off. I'm a good believer, but let me listen to how I can be saved," you are very far from Jesus. The man who fell among thieves was half dead. He was in a situation where he could only die, unless someone came to the rescue.

In Luke chapter 10, verse 33, it says,

But a certain Samaritan, as he journeyed, came where he was: and when he saw him, he had compassion on him,

What does this say? It says that the Samaritan had compassion on him. Not only did the Samaritan have compassion on him, but what did he say afterward? What did he do afterward? Who went close to whom? Did the man who fell among thieves come close to the Samaritan? Or did the Samaritan come close to the man? Did the one who would be saved come close to the savior, or did the savior come close to the one who needed to be saved? Who approaches whom? Does the person drowning in the water come close to the person who is rescuing him, or the other way around?

"Wait there. I'll be right there. Then you come and save me." Is that what they say? That makes no sense. Are you a person who needs to be saved, or are you the savior? If you are a person who needs to be saved, you do not approach. Rather, it is the Lord who must approach you.

Today, so many people struggle, trying to come close to God. Even though they struggle, it doesn't work. When a person is drowning, the wise person does not jump in right away.

He waits until that person loses all of his strength. If he jumps in while the other person is still full of strength, the drowning person will grab onto him and both of them will end up going under. He has to wait until the strength of the person drowning is completely sapped. After the person drowning loses his strength, the person who will save him takes his shoes off, warms up a little bit, and goes into the water. If that other person is still struggling, saying, "I'm dying!"

"Ah, you still have strength in you. Not yet."

"Ahhh! Please help me!"

"Hmmm. No, hold on. Should I warm up a little more? Should I play a game of checkers?" He would stall and wait. When the person drowning loses all his strength, then the rescuer jumps in and rescues him. This is the way of salvation. If the person who had fallen into the water is still full of energy and struggling to survive, he cannot be rescued.

A little while ago, a high school P.E. teacher, who was a very good swimmer, went to the beach in Pohang with his students. The teacher was sitting in a tent, when some students ran up to him and said, "Teacher, Teacher! Kids are drowning in the water!" He ran over and saw five students struggling in the water. The teacher quickly went in and swam to them. The students immediately grabbed him and held on. The teacher and the students all died. Another student, a little farther off, was not able to grab onto the teacher. She put her feet down and saw that the water was only chest deep. The students and the teacher had all died in shallow water. They didn't need to struggle; all they needed to do was put their feet down and stand. I don't know what the name of the school was, but this is something that actually happened.

What must we do to receive salvation? The Lord has shown us tonight in the Scriptures. The man who fell among thieves did nothing. The Lord did all the work. The Lord will work for your salvation. I hope that you will rest now. Let's rest. Did the man say, "Oh, look at me! Save me! I'm right here! Let me go a little closer to you!" Is that what he did? He was just lying there, doing nothing. Who came to him? The Samaritan, who Jesus represents, Jesus went to him. He went to him and poured oil and wine on his wounds.

When I read the Bible, I take every word apart. Let's do that. Usually, when there's a wound, they pour wine and oil on it. That's what we learned, when we were being trained to go out as missionaries. Liquor with high levels of alcohol is good for disinfecting. After disinfection, you apply Vaseline to the wound. If you put some oil, like Vaseline, on a wound, then other germs cannot get in.

You're not supposed to apply the oil first, but here we see that they did. No matter how much I thought about this, I couldn't understand why they did it that way. After some time, however, I finally realized why. The oil in the Scriptures represents the Holy Spirit, and the wine represents joy. Pouring oil and wine upon us means that when we first receive forgiveness of sin, the Holy Spirit enters us and brings us joy.

Folks, when joy enters people's hearts, they think that they have received the Holy Spirit. They wait for some kind of joy to come, but it doesn't come, no matter how long they wait. The Holy Spirit comes in first. Also, alcohol is very volatile, but oil does not evaporate very well because it is viscous. The Holy Spirit does not leave us, but joy often evaporates and disappears. Let's not become too attached to the joy that comes with forgiveness of sin because joy does not last. Joy can leave you quickly, but once you receive forgiveness of sin, the Holy Spirit does not leave you and is with you forever. Pouring oil and wine upon the wound, and then what does it say? The wounds were bound. It means that the Lord binds our wounds, our blemishes, and everything wrong about us.

. . . set him on his own beast. . . . (Luke 10:34)

Thankfully, He seated us where He should be sitting. It is the Lord who is walking in the humble position with holding the animal's reins, where we should be walking.

Folks, these things are not through us, but through the living Christ. Let's draw a conclusion. Many people know that Jesus was crucified for our sins. Some people have actually been freed in their hearts from sin. Some people say that Jesus died for their sins and that their sins have been washed clean, but they are still in pain because sin remains in their hearts. Some people have all of the sin in their hearts washed away and are resting in joy. The question is, why don't other people have that faith, although they know that Jesus died for their sins?

One time, Jesus was walking along a road, and a certain woman touched His garment from behind. This woman had a disease of an issue of blood for twelve years and had been suffering all that time. She tried many different ways to treat her disease, but nothing worked. One day, the thought arose in her, "If I just touch Jesus' garment, I will be made whole." That faith made this woman whole.

Folks, you must have faith that your sins have been taken care of, not just the knowledge of it. When the knowledge comes into you, you may know that your sins are taken care of, but there is still a sense of discomfort about it. When faith comes in because your sins are taken care of, you can come to realize that you do not have to do anything more for your sins. You are able to enjoy true freedom from sin.

Folks, it is not about trying to know in theory that Jesus died on the cross to forgive your sins. What I'm trying to tell you is that your heart must be completely freed from sin. Your sins must be washed as white as snow. You need to be completely freed from sin, just as Adam and Eve were in the Garden of Eden, before they fell into sin.

To what kind of people does that faith come? People who try to do something for themselves may know that Jesus died for their sins, but the faith to be freed from sin does not come into their heart. People must first have given up on themselves.

"I can't wash my sins clean by myself."

"Even if I confess, I cannot do it."

"Now, if the Lord will save me, then I will be saved. If not, I can only die." The Holy Spirit can alight upon this kind of heart. The Lord is searching the hearts of those who are sitting here today.

"God, I cannot do this. I am now truly waving the white flag. I am helpless, God. Jesus, you must do it." I don't know which of you have this heart, but Jesus can go inside that heart. Such people do not need pride. They need not defend themselves, saying, "I am a deacon." "I graduated from the seminary," or "I am an elder." They say only, "I am a sinner who can only die. Please save me. That is the only thing." These thoughts must arise from the heart. The Lord searches and comes upon people who think that way.

You ask, how do I know about this? For many years, I spoke to many people about receiving forgiveness of sin, after I had received forgiveness of sin myself. Although people may sit in the same row of seats and listen to the same thing, some only know it in their head but have not learned it in their heart. Thus, they suffer from it. But there are others who rejoice, having received forgiveness of sin. I have seen their lives begin to change.

With the passing of time, I have discovered that no matter how much you talk to people about the secret of forgiveness of sin, people who think that they can do something themselves are not able to be freed from the sin in their heart. Because of that, they can never be freed from saying, "I am a sinner." This evening, what kind of a person are you? The problem is not that you don't know that Jesus was crucified for your sins. Folks, that is not the problem. The problem is that your thoughts must be broken down. Only the heart that says, "I cannot do anything," is a heart on the verge of salvation.

In Daegu, there is a big church called Samduck Church. Although he has now passed away, there was a pastor named Dae Wee Hong who ministered there for a long time. I admired Pastor Hong very much, and those of you who are a little older may also remember him. He ministered in Mangju when he was young. He was the pastor of a Presbyterian church in a small village. There were two churches in the village. The other one was a Methodist church. The churches were very hospitable to each other. At Christmas, Pastor Hong would send gifts from his church to the other church, and the other church would send Pastor Hong gifts as well. When there were events, they would work together. They were very friendly to one another and treated each other with a lot of love. One year, there was a revival at the Methodist church, near Pastor Hong's church. A Norwegian missionary, named Mary Monsen, had come to lead the revival. She preached a sermon entitled, "You Must Be Born Again." Many people from Pastor Hong's church attended and received forgiveness of sin and were rejoicing.

Because they were receiving so much grace, they came to the pastor and said, "Pastor, Pastor. That church over there is having a revival. Let's all go."

The pastor did not think it was worthwhile, so he did not go. But on the last day, he thought he should go because his church members were asking him so sincerely to come. He put on some casual clothes, so as not to stand out as a pastor, and went late to the meeting.

Missionary Mary Monsen gave a sermon on forgiveness of sin. The pastor had graduated from the seminary, so, of course, he already knew about it. The people there, however, listened with a different attitude from when they were listening to him. His church members concentrated on every word.

Finally, the service ended, and people began to leave.

As they did, the missionary moved to the entrance of the chapel and shook everyone's hand, one by one, and asked, "Are you born again?"

Pastor Hong was a pastor, but he never had the actual experience of being born again.

"Am I born again? What should I say, if she asks me?" He was hesitating and most people had already left. Only a few people remained. He didn't want to be the last one there because he didn't want to be an inconvenience to them, so he was trying to leave quickly. The missionary held out her hand and asked, "Sir, how are you doing? Sir, are you born again?"

Of course, she didn't know that he was a pastor, and that his own church members had been there. How could he say that he was not born again? So he answered, "Yes, I am born again." That's what he said.

"Wow, God, thank you very much. Hallelujah! I am so happy to meet a person who is born again."

She held his hand even tighter and was so thankful and happy, she didn't know what to do. Then she asked him, "When were you born again?" He sloughed it off, telling her it had been some time ago. The missionary walked him all the way to the door, thanked him, and waved good bye to him. Beginning then, the Holy Spirit began to work on Pastor Hong's heart. "You are a liar. You lied at least twice."

Folks, you know who you really are when the Holy Spirit begins to work. Even though we are fake humans, who can only be destroyed, we don't know, in truth, how fake we really are.

When the Holy Spirit works, you discover how deceitful you are. When the Holy Spirit works, you discover that you are the sinner. Pastor Hong realized that he was a sinner. "Lord, have compassion on me. I am a sinner."

He felt deeply that he was a sinner who could only be destroyed. After that experience, he was easily born again. Pastor Hong wrote many books. They are so old, I don't know if they are still in print, but he wrote a book entitled, *The Road to Redemption*. Loving folks, if you ask someone if they are born again, they really hate that, don't they? Why is that? From time to time, when pastors would ask me sincerely about my spiritual life, I'd ask them, "Pastor, are you born again?"

Strangely, there are two responses to this question. There are people who become very angry, and there are those who become very joyful. Asking if you are born again is not a horrible curse, but the people who are not born again hate it very much. On the other hand, if a born again person is asked that question, he is very happy to hear it. That is the difference.

When the man who fell among thieves realized that he couldn't do anything for himself, he allowed just anyone to do whatever they wanted to him. At that moment, the Samaritan came to him and did what he wanted to do. Salvation was completed and accomplished for him, not by the methods of the man himself, but by the methods of the Savior. After a while, he was lying down at the inn. The Samaritan gave the inn keeper two pence. One pence at that time for the Jews was one full day's wage and the cost of one day's living. Two pence represented two days. The Lord said that one day is like a thousand years and a thousand years is like one day. This promises that the Lord will return to take us in approximately 2,000 years.

Loving folks, I don't know when, but I believe that the Lord will return. He will come on His cloud to take us. Do you have the confidence to stand before the Lord? Are all your sins washed clean? Have you truly received redemption? Are you really born again? Can you be lifted up with the Lord on that day?

We have prepared this conference for you. We have this evening and tomorrow evening remaining. Do not delay it until tomorrow. Humble your hearts this evening, and break everything down, saying, "Lord, save me this evening. I'm a sinner. Have compassion on me."

Come forth to the Lord with an open heart. I hope that this will be the day your name will be written in heaven, in the Book of Life. The day you can never forget:

"Happy day. Happy day.
When Jesus washed my sins away."

I hope that this will be that day. Let's bow our heads together. Quietly, close your eyes. Loving folks, how did the man who fell among thieves receive salvation? What did he do to be saved? It's not that something has to be done for salvation to be accomplished. He received salvation because he couldn't do anything. Are you a sinner? Are you evil? Are you filthy? Are you trying to resolve your sins, but are unable to? It doesn't work, does it? Those of you who say you can do nothing, I believe that the Lord will bestow salvation upon you.

8

The Power of Samson

A Life of Walking
with the Lord After Being Born Again

If you have surely been born again after receiving the forgiveness of sins, you will now live by the guidance of the Holy Spirit. We are no longer alone, for Jesus walks with us until we hold his hand to cross the river of death and into the eternal kingdom. However, many people think that they can live spiritual life on their own now that they have received salvation, but a person who has received forgiveness of sins certainly needs a leader.

8

The Power of Samson

After yesterday evening's service, I heard the testimonies of several people, of how they received forgiveness of sin. They had been suffering deeply from sin. When I saw how touched they were that during this conference they had received forgiveness of sin, I had a thankful and a glowing heart before the Lord. I haven't heard every one of your testimonies. However, I know that if I ask anyone of you to give a testimony, there are many of you who will testify that this has been an unforgettable conference, that it has allowed you to receive forgiveness of sin and freedom for your spirit. I know all of these things are through God, who loves the people of Busan. I glorify the loving Lord.

This morning, I'd like to talk to you about how we are supposed to live after we have received forgiveness of sin.

When people are first married, they are very nervous. That anxiety later leads to arguments. It is always that way when a man and woman do not know each other well. After a few years, however, they come to understand each other. At first, their love is only emotional. Eventually, it becomes a deep love, where the family can truly be at peace. This morning, I would like to talk about the problem of how we can live the rest of our lives peacefully with the Lord after we receive forgiveness of sin and take Jesus into our hearts.

Please open your Bible to Judges, chapter 15 in the Old Testament. I will read from verse 13 to 20.

And they spake unto him, saying, No; but we will bind thee fast, and deliver thee into their hand: but surely we will not kill thee. And they bound him with two new cords and brought him up from the rock. And when he came unto Lehi, the Philistines shouted against him: and the Spirit of the LORD came mightily upon him, and the cords that were upon his arms became as flax that was burnt with fire, and his bands loosed from off his hands. And he found a new jawbone of an ass, and put forth his hand, and took it, and slew a thousand men therewith. And Samson said, With the jawbone of an ass, heaps upon heaps, with the jaw of an ass have I slain a thousand men. And it came to pass when he had made an end of speaking, that he cast away the jawbone out of his hand, and called that place Ramathlehi. And he was sore athirst, and called on the LORD, and said, Thou hast given this great deliverance into the hand of thy servant:

and now shall I die for thirst, and fall into the hand of the uncircumcised? But God clave a hollow place that was in the jaw, and there came water thereout; and when he had drunk, his spirit came again, and he revived: wherefore he called the name thereof Enhakkore, which is in Lehi unto this day. And he judged Israel in the days of the Philistines twenty years.

A long time ago, there was a certain Prime Minister. He did not know how to care for his family. He worried only about the country and was a very faithful Prime Minister, loyal to the king and the people. This Prime Minister didn't even use the salary he received from the government for himself. He always used it for his country. Therefore, his way of life was very poor. As a result, even in the palace, many people admired him. The king worried about this Prime Minister, so, he would send his servants to see how the Prime Minister was doing, and at other times he would send him food.

This Prime Minister was loved by all, but he had no children. The king became very worried about that in his heart. Therefore, whenever the king had a chance, he would ask the Prime Minister's wife, "Are you pregnant yet?" From time to time, the king would make herbal medicine for her and give it to her. There were still no signs of pregnancy, however. As a result, with no children, the Prime Minister lived a very lonely life. When they reached the age of 50, the Prime Minister's wife finally became pregnant. Upon hearing the news, the king and the rest of the palace were so happy.

Because the Prime Minister was not well off, the king sent maids to the Prime Minister's wife, and good medicine to strengthen her body. Finally, it was time for the wife to go into labor. When she had a son, everyone was very happy. The Prime Minister was happy, too, and as soon as he was done with his work for the country, he would come home and spend time with his child. He was happy to see that his son was growing up as healthy as a tiger.

The Prime Minister's son was the center of attention at home, to the king, and all the people of the palace. But there was one problem. Whenever he returned from playing outside, he would always come home beaten up by other kids. Whenever he had anything good or delicious, the other kids would take it. As time passed, rumors began to spread that the Prime Minister's son was an idiot. The Prime Minister eventually became very old. The son turned fifteen, then sixteen, then seventeen. It was finally time for him to get married. Whenever the Prime Minister thought about his son, he thought, "How will that boy lead our family?" He was so worried that he couldn't sleep.

One day, he made up his mind. There was a famous gangster who was unmatched in his toughness and recklessness so he went in and out of prison as if it were his own house. Early one morning, the Prime Minister told his servants to bring the gangster to his house. Because this gangster had done so many bad things, when he heard that the Prime Minister was calling for him, he thought, "Oh, no," and began to tremble. When he arrived, he knelt down in the yard of the Prime Minister's home. He was lying on his stomach, with his head bowed. The door opened. The Prime Minister came out and said, "Hey, why are you lying down like that? I have invited you as a guest. Please come inside."

The gangster had no idea what was going on. Upon hearing this, he did not know how to behave, but immediately he entered the Prime Minister's house. At that moment, breakfast was served. As he was having breakfast with the Prime Minister, the gangster thought to himself, "Oh, because I did so many bad things, after he feeds me, he is going to have me killed." He was trembling so much that, when he thought about his imminent death, he could not swallow his food.

"The reason I called you is that I have a favor to ask of you. It may be difficult, but would you please do me one favor?"

"Only say what it is. My life is yours, to do with as you wish."

"My son has come of age. However, since I was too busy working for the country, I have not been able to take him around to see the country. I will give you as much money as you need. Could you please take my son and show him around the country for three months"

The gangster thought, "What is this, a free lunch?"

"Take just one pony." Upon saying that, he gave the gangster a pony, which one person could barely ride, and told him to go.

"Okay, we will be on our way now, Mr. Prime Minister," the gangster said. After saying that, he said to the son, "Sir, please get on." The gangster took hold of the reins, and they started on their way. They passed through Seoul, through Noryangjin, through Youngdunpo, and continued on. As they were going around a mountain, the gangster said, "Sir?"

"Yes, what's the matter?" asked the Prime Minister's son.

"Sir, your legs seem quite strong."

"That's right! Do you know how strong my legs are? I could easily walk fifteen miles."

"Oh, that's so true, sir. I, on the other hand, am weak, and my legs are not in good shape. That is why I am always limping."

"Oh, really? Yeah, that's right. Your legs do look awfully weak."

"Would it be okay if you were to take the reins, and I ride for a while?"

"That sounds like a good idea."

Then, the Prime Minister's son held the reins and the gangster rode. After a long while, the Prime Minister's son's legs started hurting, and his feet became swollen. The Prime Minister's son then said, "Let me ride the pony, now."

"Sir, you are the Prime Minister's son. You know, they say that a man's words are more precious than gold. You said that you have strong legs. I don't understand what you are saying," replied the gangster.

"Oh, yeah. That's right. My legs don't hurt. I'm fine. Keep riding."

With that, the gangster began to pick on and take advantage of the Prime Minister's son. Whenever there was a good food to eat, the Prime Minister's son didn't get any, and the gangster would eat it all. The Prime Minister's son would eat only leftovers. When the Prime Minister's son thought about this, although he received many compliments, his legs were hurting and he felt like he was dying. However, he did not know how to bring up the matter. Finally, after a while, he gave up thinking about his reputation, and said, "Now, I am going to ride the horse."

"Oh, sir," protested the gangster.

"No. I am going to ride."

"Sir," he said again.

The Prime Minister's son became angry. After they had been traveling for a long time, whenever they ran out of money, they would enter a little town. The money for their travel expenses would be sent from Seoul to the head of the town. When they were moving through Cheonan and were nearing Daejon, the Prime Minister's son said, "Let me eat this, and you eat only a little bit," and he would fight with the gangster; but the Prime Minister's son was way behind the gangster in wits, so all he could do was complain. He couldn't really do anything to the gangster, so everything always went the way the gangster wanted. As they continued on, from Daejon to Junju, and down to Namwon, the Prime Minister's son's complaints became worse and worse. No matter how hard he thought and challenged the gangster, he could do nothing because the gangster was always a level ahead of him.

"We'll see how it is when we get to Seoul. I think my father has a major problem. How could a person running the country be this stupid? Of all people, he chose this nasty, sinister gangster to travel with me?"

He now began to worry about the country. They had passed through Chungmoo, Samchunpo, through Busan, Ulsan, Kyungju, and were around Daegu. By that time, the fights had become more open and direct. Whenever there was food, they would tell each other, "Get out of my way," and start to eat. They continued to fight, as they went along the road. However, as they came closer to Seoul, the gangster thought, "I'd better not go on like this," and said, "Sir, please eat as much as you want."

"Okay, fine, you get nothing. You had a lot of fun torturing me, didn't you? Do you think I'll give you a break, just because you are being nice now?"

"Oh, sir, please ride the horse."

"Oh, I see. You're singing a different song, now that we're getting close to home."

"Why you little. . . Sir. Please don't be so harsh."

"Shut up!"

In this frame of mind, the two men came to Seoul. When they finally arrived home, the Prime Minister was so happy to see his son home safely, he had set up a nice dinner table. The son then came forth to his father, and said, "Father, I have made it back safely, through your grace."

"Wonderful. Did you enjoy going around the country?"

"Yes, but Father, there is something I need to say to you."

"What is it, my son?"

"Father, if I tell you this, you may think of me as a bad son, but Father, exactly how do you go about handling the matters of our country?"

"Why? What is that supposed to mean?"

"Of all the people you could have sent with me, why did you send this gangster, who made me suffer so much? Father, how could you do such a thing, and still take care of this country? I feel sorry for the king, who trusts you as the Prime Minister."

The Prime Minister was overjoyed, and his eyes began to well with tears. "You are right. You are indeed right, my son. My son is not an idiot. We were just too overprotective. He is, indeed, my son."

Folks, how happy do you think this Prime Minister was? If the son hadn't gone through such an experience, he would have lived his whole life with people thinking he was an idiot.

Folks, are there people here who have received forgiveness of sin through this conference? Ah, many people have their hands up. Hallelujah! Please listen. Do you know what happens inside of you when you receive forgiveness of sin? There are many things for me to say about that.

Over the past 25 years, I have done many conferences about forgiveness of sin. During that time, I have seen many people receive redemption. In addition, I have seen that some people were joyously living blessed lives in Jesus, after receiving forgiveness of sin. But often, I saw that people were not able to live close to the Lord, although their sins had been forgiven. This is what I would like to speak to you about tonight. If you have received forgiveness of sin clearly, the wall between God and you is now gone. As that happens, the Holy Spirit of Jesus enters your heart, without you even knowing it. If that happens, we live through the Holy Spirit. The Prime Minister's son had the power and wisdom within, but he became an idiot when he did not know how to use what he had. Likewise, if we don't live via the Holy Spirit even though our hearts are filled with the Holy Spirit, but through our own worldly ways, we end up living a life exactly like a person without the Holy Spirit.

Let me give you an example. Suppose my daily income is

three hundred thousand dollars. My problem is, I can't spend that much money in a day. Let's say that I came to Busan and come upon two people I know very well. They are both poor.

"Hey, why are you so poor?"

"Pastor, we are poor because of this and that."

"Oh, really? Well, let me help you. Mr. A, I will give you $10,000 a day. Mr. B, I will also give you $10,000 a day. I'll deposit the money every day in both of your accounts. Spend it however you like."

The two of them hold onto my hands and begin to cry, saying, "Oh, Pastor, thank you so much," and were very happy.

Mr. A takes his account book and runs home. "Wow, $10,000 a day! That's $20,000 in two days. After three days, four days! Great, I'm rich! Honey, come here! How much money do we have?"

"We have about one hundred dollars." He takes the hundred dollars and bought a safe. He wraps his checks and the money in plastic, and places them in the safe, and hides the safe in his room. Every night, he would lie down, and think, "Ah, all that money in the safe, and I get $10,000 richer every day. Life is great!"

Mr. B went home and said, "Honey, worry no more. I've only made you suffer, but now I will finally make you happy." Ten days later, Mr. B withdrew $100,000 and bought a nice house, a nice car, nice furniture, clothes, and shoes. "Kids, let's go to the mall. Get in the car. Tell me what you want."

"A piano! A violin!" Because they had more than enough money, he could buy his kids wonderful things like clothes, toys, and musical instruments. Everything had changed.

A month later, I return to Busan to see how the two of them are doing. When I go to Mr. B's house, he is living in a big, fancy house, with security guards walking back and forth in front of the gates.

"Excuse me, is this Mr. B's house?" The security guard says, "That's right."

"I am Ock Soo Park from Seoul. I've come to see Mr. B."

"He's too busy. You cannot see him."

"Would you please call him anyway?"

"Mr. B, there's a guy out here named Ock Soo Park from Seoul. Shall I kick him out?"

"What? Pastor Park? Please hurry. Show him in. He's the reason I can live this well." When I entered the house, I saw a beautiful garden with a tennis court and a swimming pool. Everything had changed. The owner comes out and said, "Pastor, all of this is because of you." The way he ate, what he wore, and everything he did, had all changed. I had a good time at his house.

The next day, I go to see Mr. A. When I arrive, his whole family was living in a small, rented room. As I knock on the door and stepped in, he greets me saying, "Pastor, please come in." However, what he eats, what he wears, where he sleeps, and the things he does are exactly the same as before. There was no change in his life.

"Hey, didn't I give you any money?" I asked.

"Sure you did."

"Then where is it?"

"Because it is so precious, I wrap it all up and put it in my safe."

Although they received the same grace, everything had

changed for one person, while nothing had changed for the other. We must know how to live a spiritual life after we receive forgiveness of sin. If you live with the grace of God, your life cannot help but change. But folks! When you don't know this, you return to your old ways, even though you are receiving grace. Just like a dog returning to its vomit, or a pig returning to dirty places after being washed. It is important how you enjoy the grace that God gives you, after receiving Jesus Christ and forgiveness of sin.

Before going to the military, I was trained to become a missionary to go abroad. I heard that when you go to uncivilized countries, you may have to catch and eat bugs. I received the training necessary to be a missionary, training such as how to sleep anywhere and to eat any kind of food. As I was preparing to go abroad, I was called to the military. When I was about to be discharged, I received guidance from the Holy Spirit, telling me, "Do not go abroad. Stay home and preach at home to people about forgiveness of sin." Since then, day by day, God has amazingly opened paths before me. I am standing here today, through the grace of God.

After being discharged from the army, I didn't know what to do. I wanted to witness in Kimcheon, which was one hour from Daegu by train. I had no money, no house, nothing. Faith arose in me saying, "God is with me and will lead me in all I do." I was discharged on June 8, 1968, and went to Seoul. In Sinlimdong in Seoul, a tent was set up and they were holding a conference. Many children came, and I was invited to talk to them about the Bible. I was happy to hear that and went. It was where Seoul National University stands today, but back then, it was just a field. For a week, between the services, I would sit the children down, talk to them about the Bible, and preach the gospel. After I finished, the sponsors thanked me for my work and gave me 3 dollars and 50 cents. Men who were drafted into the army back then received a salary of 35 cents a month, so I had been given nearly one year's salary, all at once.

For me, it was a lot of money. I thought, "I am going to take this money, go to Kimcheon, get a room for myself, and preach the gospel." I decided that I would live however God led me, eat when I eat and starve when I starve. I was not afraid because Jesus was with me. I went to Kimcheon and looked for a room. There were two little rooms available for rent. They wanted a deposit of $70, which was out of the question. I went high and low in Kimcheon, searching everywhere. There were pool halls, cafes, ping pong halls, and many other places and buildings.

"Father God. Even the gods of this world give their people a place to work, but why aren't you giving your child a building, which he needs to preach the gospel? Please give me a building." That's how I prayed. Nevertheless, I still had no building. I prayed for one day, two days, but there was no answer. After I had received forgiveness of sin, all of my prayers had been answered, but at that particular moment, there was no answer. "What am I supposed to do? Does this mean I am not supposed to witness here?" Many different thoughts crossed my mind. I had no money, but whenever I had the time, I went to Kimcheon to find a place. One day, I was on my way home from searching, when I met a foreigner on the bus. He was about 10 years older than me. We struck up a conversation.

"What do you do?" I asked. He said, "I'm a missionary."

"Where are you going?"

"I am traveling."

"What are you traveling for?"

"Oh, I'm just sightseeing."

"You are a missionary, who gets paid to be a missionary. You are not witnessing, but traveling around?"

I thought to myself, "I want to do the work of God, but I can't because I have no money," so I chided him. The strange thing was that he listened patiently. When I finished, he asked, "Mr. Park?"

"Yes?"

"May I spend a day at your house?"

"Okay, come with me."

There was a place, deep in a mountain valley, close to Habcheon where I was trained to become a missionary before going into the army. There are no ponds or people with toothbrushes there, and we had to drink water from the creek. While the missionary stayed with me, he had some creek water. After that, he was constantly going back and forth to the bathroom. It was quite bad for him. Later, he even said, "Mr. Park. If I die, I hope that you will send my body to my wife." One week later, as he left, he said, "Mr. Park, I would like to come live with you for a year. Will you allow me to do that?" I said, "Sure. Soon we will go to Kimcheon to do the work of God. Go and find a place for yourself, in Kimcheon and come back here." Then he left. A while later, the missionary came to us.

"Mr. Park, please listen to what I have to say. We need a

building. I brought $350 that God has given me. This is not from me, so please take it and use it." He was so worried that I would not take the money, he did not know what to do.

"That's fine, but I did not receive this money from you, missionary. You have given this money to God, and I receive it from Him."

"That's right. It was not I who gave it to you."

God had miraculously provided us $350. I have never had to reach my hand out to anybody when I do the work of God. Whenever I talk about the miraculous things that have happened to me, my eyes become teary and I have difficulty speaking. Because we are children of God who have received forgiveness of sin, God hears all our prayers. What did I know about this world, when I went out into it? For $350, I could buy the best house in Kimcheon. Without even knowing it, I leased a house for $200. We spent the remaining $150 on this and that, while going about witnessing.

Just because you believe in God, it doesn't mean that hardship will not come to you. Although we face hardship, God allows all things to work together for good. The landlord had pledged the house as collateral for a loan he received from the bank. He then went bankrupt and ran away, without paying off the loan. At that time, I was always busy, going around the country, leading conferences. One day, one of my church members came and told me, "We have a big problem! We've lost the house to the bank!" A month later, the branch manager came to see me. Since the bank now owned the house, they were evicting us immediately. I had no idea what to do because I had nowhere to go. I prayed to the Lord,

"Father God, I made this mistake because I know nothing about this world. What am I to do? I have nowhere to go. God, You do not want Your servant to sleep under the bridge? Please, give me a house."

There was no answer. One day, I had the heart, "Don't just pray, go out and get a house for yourself." So, I went out to the city to find one. There was a two-story house with a very big hall and a lot of rooms. I met the landlord, who said that the deposit was $200. I accepted, but I had no money. Whenever I would go away to conferences and would return home, people would tell me that the branch manager had stopped by several times, looking for me. One day, early in the morning, I was once again leaving. Because it was usually difficult to meet me, the branch manager had come early.

"Why is it so hard to catch up with you?" he asked.

"I'm busy. I'm leaving now to go to a conference."

"Don't you have time to talk?"

"I'm really busy right now."

"I guess I have no choice, I will come with you." Then he and I both got on a bus. I was hesitating whether I should tell him that I was a believer because if I had told him I believed in Jesus, he might have tried to take advantage of me. Then I thought, "If I go on without saying I believe in Jesus..." I prayed to God. "Is this a problem that God has to take care of, or a problem you have to take care of? Aren't you trying to take care of this? Then shouldn't I say it? That's right. If I cannot do anything, then God has to do it. I need to say it. That's right!" so I made up my mind.

"Mr. Branch Manager. It's not that I'm not moving out

because I didn't receive my $200. Even though I want to move out, there is no place for me to go. I have told my Master about it, but He has not yet replied. As soon as I hear back from Him, I will leave. So please take this and go back." Then he asked, "Who is your master?"

"My Master is a very good person. He is Jesus Christ."

He opened his eyes wide. "Mr. Park, are you that kind of a person?"

"Yes, I am," I told him about how Jesus had helped me until then. Then he took my hand and said, "Mr. Park, I have no religion, but after listening to you, I feel something. Anyhow, please pray harder and resolve this matter quickly."

I was praying, but I was worried. Whenever I led conferences, I was able to forget everything, but as soon as I got on the bus and went home, I would become worried. The building had an attic, and one day, I went up to the attic, closed the door, and prayed. Without knowing it, I was crying and praying loudly. I heard later that the other people in the house were surprised and frightened.

One day, as I was praying, I received the heart, "Why don't you go to that two-story house you saw the other day?" Because the house was cheap, I thought it would have been sold already, but when I went there, it still had the, "For Lease" sign out front. I thought, "Ah, God wants me to have this house." Even though I had no money, I had gone there. Only the children were home. I told them that I was the person who was interested in the second floor and would be back later. That evening, I returned and said, "I'd like to rent your second floor."

"You're the person who came this morning."

"Yes." Little by little, I explained everything to them. "I am a servant of God. I came to this city to testify the Word of God. Someone here caused me a lot of financial trouble, and I have to move from the place where I am now staying. I have no place to go. I have prayed to God for a month to resolve this problem for me. I still don't know how God is guiding me, but I think that this is the house God has prepared for me. Still, I have no money. If you would like to give me this house, then give it to me. If you do not want to give it to me, do not give it to me. Regardless, please do not pity me because God has surely prepared a place for me somewhere."

I spoke to the owner for 30 minutes. After I finished, he thought for a while and said, "I am an elder of a certain church in the city. God has given me such a nice building next to the freeway. If a servant of God wants to use it, how can I turn him away?"

I was so happy, I could not tell whether what I was experiencing was reality or a dream. Just then, the elder's daughter was playing hymns on the piano in her room. Listening to her play, I felt as if I was in heaven. The Lord was indeed living. My tears flowed, and I was so thankful. I was about to leave when the elder held my hand and said, "If you come empty-handed, we will both feel uncomfortable. How much money can you come up with? Please prepare as much as you can. I don't care how much it is."

Then, without knowing it, I said, "I'll give you $80." Having said that, I gasped and placed my hand over my mouth, but it was already too late. His reply was, "That's fine. Then, it's settled."

I would move in a week later. Eighty dollars was a lot of money. There were many brothers and sisters at the time, but if I had told them what happened, then I would only make them worry.

"God, I said eighty dollars without even realizing it. You must take responsibility for this." I knelt down and prayed. Whenever the gate would squeak, I would wonder if it was somebody bringing me money. One day, two days, three days had passed, but there was no sign of any money. On the afternoon of the fifth day, a woman was walking by and said, "I think this is the house," and came to the door. I looked carefully. It was someone I knew. When I had first come to Kimcheon and contracted for the house, I had left fifty dollars as a deposit. Since the house was lost to the bank, the mortgage was canceled. The lady was charged with returning my fifty dollars. I had gone several times to retrieve the money, but there was never anyone there. One day, I went to talk to them at 11 p.m. They said, "Sir, please take some of our furniture. We have no money to give you." I thought there was no way I would ever get my money back, so I had given up and forgot about it. A year had passed, and the woman had shown up at my door.

"I really must apologize. I am so much in debt, that my creditors bother me every day. Even if I can't pay the others back, I have to pay you. I don't know how, but today, I received forty dollars. If I take it home, the creditors will take it from me, so I brought it here. Please take this forty dollars now, and I'll pay the other ten dollars later."

You know, a person's heart is so strange. "Forget about the

ten dollars." I don't know why I couldn't say that.

"Thank you very much. Please take care."

She had brought forty dollars in fifty-cent coins wrapped in a white handkerchief. I must have counted it more than a hundred times. I would count it crying, and I would count it while I prayed. God miraculously had given me forty dollars. I then realized that God would take care of the rest. That afternoon, I went to the bank manager and said, "Mr. Manager, God has given us a house, and we are now able to move. We will be moving the day after tomorrow. Please, come then."

"Mr. Park, I have children myself. Evicting you, I feel like I am standing in the way of a young man's success. I feel very terrible. I would like to become a public official someday. Mr. Park, please do not have a low opinion of me." He then went to the safe and counted out some money.

"Mr. Park, please accept this as an expression of my good will."

I was thankful. "Thank you very much!" I said and took it. He asked me to have a cup of tea with him, but I couldn't wait to count how much he had given me. As soon as I turned the corner, I counted it. "Ah! Ten dollars!" Ten dollars was a lot of money. I still hadn't prepared the entire 80 dollars, but I could only continue to praise God. How thankful I was to see that God was working for me.

Folks, ever since I began ministering, since then, many people have tempted me, telling me to come to their church, and they would give me a higher salary. I received guidance from God because I was His servant. I was assured that, from heaven, all my needs would be met. I do not wish to receive compensation for this week's conference because God watches over everything in my life.

I still needed thirty dollars. I had only two days left, but I was not worried. After a while, I received a phone call. It was a friend.

"Hey, I heard you were going through some hard times. As a friend, I have been unable to help you, and I feel bad about it. I just started my business and things are a little tight. I do have twenty dollars I can let you have if it'll help. If you can pay it back fine, if not, that's okay, too."

I received help from someone so unexpectedly. I went to his house and borrowed the twenty dollars. I was still $10 short. I gathered all the brothers, who were working and witnessing with me, and told them to give me all the money they had. We emptied all our pockets, counting every last penny. The total came out to about eight dollars. Through this and that, we eventually pulled together the eighty dollars that we needed. The day had finally come. On April 19, 1970, we moved in, as the rain drizzled down. I will never forget that day. I asked all the brothers and sisters to help with the move, while I spent the day witnessing. I was preaching the gospel to a certain family, but they were worried for me, saying, "It's raining."

"It's okay. Even Jesus got wet when it rained," I replied.

As I was coming home, I began to think, "Lord. When You were in this world, You didn't even have a roof over Your head. You lived without having a change of clothes. On a rainy day, where did You take shelter? How did You get through the cold winters? In the wilderness, everyone else would go home after listening to the Word, but when it became dark, You had nowhere to go. You went up to the mountain and prayed. Lord, You suffered like that, when You lived in this world. Who is this pitiful servant, that You have prepared such a fine shelter for me?"

Tears rolled down my face. I could not hold them back. Jesus never left me; not even for a little while, starting from the day I received forgiveness of sin. Whether there were hardships or good times, He was always there, taking care of me and protecting me.

"God, thank You for using such a pitiful and worthless person like me." While leading conferences, I often cry in my heart, "Thank You, God."

Many people have raised their hands each night and have come forward to receive forgiveness of sin. After the service, the pastors would come together and talk about things that had happened at the conference. We would then have prayer meetings. As we looked at the fellowship cards, we could see that this person or that person had received forgiveness of sin, and our hearts became thankful.

Jesus is with you if you have received forgiveness of sin and are truly born again. You are no longer alone. Jesus will hold you, crossing the river of death. I believe that until we get to that land beyond, He will never let go of your hand.

My great-grandmother passed away this past spring. My hometown is Seonsan, Kyungbuk Province, and because my father and older brother had already passed away, I became the chief mourner.

The funeral was on a Tuesday. Coincidently, I had to lead a conference, beginning that evening. I went down to the countryside from Seoul. Almost nothing had been prepared, so we had to stay up all night long. On Tuesday, we finished the burial and met with all our relatives. By the time I returned to Seoul, it was already 6 p.m. I was barely able to have some dinner before I had to lead the service. That was a very busy and tiring week.

After finishing the conference, on Saturday I thought I should take a break. However, we had our scheduled ministers' Bible study, and I had some families to visit, so I still could not rest. When I laid down, at around seven o'clock that evening, my stomach began to hurt. It got worse, and by 10 o'clock, I could not bear it. I told my wife to call the church to send a car for me.

By 1 o'clock in the morning, I had to be hospitalized. I had been out of my mind the entire day. I thought, "I'm going to die now." That was the first time in my life that I had that thought. There were no specialists available since it was early in the morning. It felt like I was going to die, but the interns kept asking me about the symptoms. After I would answer, another intern would come and ask me the same questions. I repeated myself half-a-dozen times. I was hurting so much and my mind was fading in and out. I decided that the next time I came to the hospital, "I would bring a recorder with me." The doctor came and took an X-ray. He told me that my intestines had become completely twisted and stuck together. He then put a tube in my nose and began to remove water from my body. It was very painful.

As I was being wheeled out of the emergency room, I thought about the Lord. "The church will be fine because Minister Kim is there. My two children have received forgiveness of sin, and as long as my wife walks with the Lord, they will be fine." I thought about many different things, but there was nothing for me to put in order. I felt, "It would be good if I could live just 10 more years." On the other hand, I felt that even if I do live 10 more years when I'm about to die then, I would probably feel again, "If I could live just 10 more years." When I thought about confronting death, I felt peace in my heart.

"When I leave this world, the loving Lord will welcome me. There are so many things I want to say to the Lord when I stand before Him. Lord, why didn't You help me then? I will ask Him about this and that."

Thinking, I began to cry. In 1962, I received forgiveness of sin. Since that time, many people have come to me and many have left. The Lord, however, has never left me. There were times when, I did well before God, and there were times when I did wrong before Him, but the Lord was always with me and has never abandoned me. I thought about how I would grasp the Lord's hand and cross the river of death into the eternal land and live with Him forever. I thought about my family. "Lord, when I die, I hope You will protect my wife and children better than when I was here." I had so much peace. I felt, "Yes, it's a blessing to have received forgiveness of sin."

The doctor said that I had to have surgery and moved me into the surgical ward. The surgeon said to me, "If more than 24 hours pass after the intestines become clogged, the person dies.

In some rare cases, however, people's intestines untangle themselves within two hours. Even though you're in pain, why not wait a little longer? Let me know when you release some gas."

The next day was Sunday, and my church members came to the hospital after service. They were there for a while and then left for the evening service. Right then, I released some gas. I was very thankful for that. How valuable and precious it was to feel that but whether I am in pain, sad, or suffering, I am never alone. I will not be alone, even when I cross the river of death. Therefore, I live moment to moment, waiting for that final day.

The image of Samson in Judges chapter 15, verse 13 is of him tightly bound by two new cords. Let's read verse 14 together:

And when he came unto Lehi, the Philistines shouted against him: and the Spirit of the LORD came mightily upon him, and the cords that were upon his arms became as flax that was burnt with fire, and his bands loosed from off his hands.

There are many people who say, "Pastor, I'm busy, can you just tell me how to receive forgiveness of sin?" Even though they raise their hand and come forward to receive forgiveness of sin, when ministers and pastors talk to them about the Bible, they say, "Okay, okay. Just tell me how to receive forgiveness of sin." They do not understand that we can't talk about redemption just like that.

When we talk to people about forgiveness of sin, they come to understand it in their mind, but there are many who still have sin in their heart. That person's heart is not yet freed from sin. When the Holy Spirit works on them, they are freed from the chain of sin in their heart. If the Holy Spirit does not work, they may know in theory that Jesus cleansed them of their sins, but in their heart, they don't have faith that their sins have been taken care of. As a result, they feel unresolved. Samson was bound tightly with the cords, but when the Spirit of the Lord came mightily upon him, the cords became like flax, burnt with fire, and fell off of him.

No matter what sin it is that binds you, it loosens when the Holy Spirit comes upon you. That's what salvation is. Because they don't understand this, most people think they have received salvation because they know that Jesus has washed their sins clean. Some people think they will receive forgiveness of sin if they just say a prayer of acceptance. It is different from that. Our hearts must be freed from sin if we are to receive salvation and become born again. Your heart must be freed from sin.

Just as Samson was bound tightly with new cords, most people today are bound by the guilt of sin or by fear. The loosening of those cords can be accomplished only through the power of the Holy Spirit of God. When this conference was ahead of us, we fasted and had prayer meetings, asking the Holy Spirit of God to work here. We prepared many things for this conference. I hope that those among you, who have received forgiveness of sin, will continue to pray for me.

Those of you who have not received forgiveness of sin, we'll leave you alone because even if you pray, God does not hear you. Those of you who have received forgiveness of sin, please pray that God will allow Pastor Park to be filled with the Holy Spirit and that, wherever he goes, he will help many souls become freed from sin.

Let's read on and see what happens after we receive forgiveness of sin. Verse 14, says,

And when he came unto Lehi, the Philistines shouted against him: and the Spirit of the LORD came mightily upon him, and the cords that were upon his arms became as flax that was burnt with fire, and his bands loosed from off his hands. (Judges 15:14)

No matter how thick the cords may be, they are powerless when they are burnt. They will become loose, even if you only breathe on them.

Verse 15 reads,

And he found a new jawbone of an ass, and put forth his hand, and took it, and slew a thousand men therewith. (Judges 15:15)

You gain new strength when you are freed from sin. When you read the Word, the Word comes to you in a different way. The way you pray for changes, and no matter what you do, good things just happen. Before, you thought, "I need to witness," but now, if you open your mouth, great works arise and one thousand men die. If the Lord is with you, then this sort of thing happens. Samson killed one thousand men and afterward became thirsty. He was about to be captured when he called out to God. After that point, God caused the water to spring forth.

Why, then, did Samson have his eyes plucked out? And

how did the powerful Samson get caught by the Philistines and wind up strapped to a grinding wheel in prison? He could not do everything with only his own strength. He needed a guide. The difference between David and Samson was that, while David was not as strong as Samson, he always had a leader next to him. One day, when David sinned with Uriah's wife, Nathan, the prophet of God, appeared to David and chastised him ruthlessly. Although David was a king, he knew how to obey the true servant of God. Samson, however, believed in only his own strength and did not look for a spiritual leader to guide him.

Some people today think, "Now that I'm saved, I can manage my spiritual life on my own." These people go about and do as they like. They wander, not knowing where to go. They have the same directionless spiritual life because they do not have a leader. If Samson had had a leader, a true servant of God would have said, "Samson! Wake up! Repent! What are you doing? Delilah, you treacherous woman! How dare you come upon a servant of God! Get out!" when Samson fell in love with Delilah. That's how he would have spoken to her. If the servant of God had been there, he could have saved Samson. Although Samson was a powerful person, he did not have a leader to guide him. People who have received forgiveness of sin need shepherds. Why? Because they are sheep, not shepherds.

Since I have been conducting my ministry in Seoul, I have met many church members. They have all distrusted their pastors in the same way. It pained my heart, whenever I heard it.

Sometimes, when I meet with public officials and speak

with them, they say, "Pastor, I know you are not like other pastors, but..." When I hear that, it breaks my heart. I want to say, "Please don't talk like that. Of course, there are some pastors who are, as you say, but pastors are servants of God." They would then reply, "Well, how can we tell who the true pastors are?" There have been many times when I have been at a complete loss for words. But you must look for the true shepherd. Jesus said, "Beware of false prophets," in Matthew chapter 7.

How, then, are the true servants of God different from the false prophets? Jesus also said, "which come to you in sheep's clothing, but inwardly they are ravening wolves." These "wolves," are false prophets who are wearing "sheep's" clothing, but how can we distinguish that? We cannot know, but the Lord has taught us something. The wolves may come wearing sheep's clothing, but they cannot produce sheep. That is why Jesus said, "By their fruits ye shall know them." That's why You must select your churches well. You must manage your spiritual life under a true servant of God.

There are many servants of God in Busan. We don't know if there might be one false prophet in every one thousand or one in every ten thousand. How can you tell them apart? You must look at their fruits. You must distinguish according to their fruits by seeing whether people have received from them forgiveness of sin and through them have become born again. If you think that your pastor is a true servant of God, he may still make mistakes because he is human, but you must trust and put all of your heart upon him. Then he can support you and chastise you when you go down a wrong path. When we do well, we don't need shepherds. We need ministers when we are going in the wrong direction. Do not look upon others, according to your feelings, thinking they are true servants of God when you are feeling good, and that they are false prophets when you are feeling bad.

Don't distinguish a true shepherd by thinking, "Well, he is a gentleman and well educated." That is not how you do it. In fact, Jesus told us not to do that. Through the words of God, when you see that the pastor of your church is a true servant of God, by clearly seeing that forgiveness of sin and becoming born again arise through him, then you must give yourselves up to him completely and trust him. Then you can live a spiritual life. People who do not trust ministers cannot live a spiritual life. Even though you may not have faith, when you believe that he is a true servant of God, you must trust him. Even though your ministers may disappoint you or scold you when he gives a sermon, don't think, "He is picking on me." I hope that you will think, "That's what I need. That's why he is saying that." I hope that's how you will take it.

First, however, you must see whether he is a truly born again servant of God. You must see whether he is a person who has received forgiveness of sin and has the Holy Spirit; or whether he is a person who graduated from seminary, knowing everything in his ministry as knowledge. When you distinguish a person as a false prophet, according to the words of the Bible, you must turn away from him coldly. When you see that he is a true servant of God, you must support and pray for him all the way, and work together with him. The Bible, not the word of man, should become the standard by which you live.

While winding down this conference, many feelings cross my heart. I don't know how you will live after you receive forgiveness of sin, but I pray for this conference: "God, there are many people who are in pain because they don't know how to receive forgiveness of sin. We need many workers for them. Allow many people to receive forgiveness of sin and power through this conference. I hope that many new workers will come forth for you. We need workers to go to China, Brazil, and Africa and to risk their lives to go into Islamic countries of the Middle East with this gospel. We need workers to go to prosperous countries, like Japan, that are full of sin. God, we hope that every person who is saved and has received forgiveness of sin becomes nourished under your precious servants. Don't allow them to fall into the world, get married, enjoy this life, die and simply waste their lives like the rest of the world. Allow them to cry and be lashed for the gospel of God. Allow them to starve for Jesus, go through sorrow, conflict, and suffering, and become people who are even closer to the Lord. Allow us to go to that eternal land, holding onto one another, sharing our testimonies."

Those of you who have received forgiveness of sin during this conference, I truly want to see you working for the Lord.

For one year, I'd like to send you "Good News", which is published every month by our mission. I hope that the Lord works inside of you and leads you, step by step. When you are in hardship, and when you are suffering, don't go through it by yourself. The Lord, who was with me after I received forgiveness of sin, is the Lord who has been with me in everything for the past 25 years. I have the sincere expectation that the Lord will walk with you in all that you do.

In delivering the sermons for this conference, I am sad because I feel as though I've delivered only one third of what I had prepared. If God allows, I want to come back and stand before the citizens of Busan again. Folks, please pray for me. I will not be able to forget the faces of you who have been born again during this conference. I don't know why, but my heart is drawn to you. I've gone all over the country conducting many conferences, but this was the first time I have trembled, standing at the podium. I've given sermons in front of many people, but this time I was very nervous.

I cannot stay with you continually, but I hope that you will live a blessed spiritual life within the Holy Spirit. I hope that the salvation you have received here will become stronger and more settled, and you will become precious people of faith; people whose faith will not be shaken, no matter where you go. That is my hope for you. With this, I will end my morning sermon. Thank you.

9

Cain and Abel

What Do You Bring
Before God?

Cain brought of the fruit of the ground an offering unto the LORD. Cain put all his heart unto the offering. However, God never accepts the fruit of the ground by effort or labor of man. On the contrary, the firstlings of the flock symbolize Jesus Christ. Therefore, God had respect unto Abel and to his offering.

9

Cain and Abel

Folks, how are you this evening? I thank God, who has allowed us to carry out this amazing conference. As the pastor who presided said, I give thanks to Isabelle Women's High School for providing us with this precious hall. Because our conference is special, and people are so taken by what they hear that they don't go home until after 11 o'clock, the elder who manages this building must be very tired. I extend my sincere thanks to him for cooperating with us.

I'd also like to thank you for not complaining about the long hours. In addition, I'd like to thank the pastors who supervised and labored on behalf of this conference, and I especially want to thank and glorify God, who gave us the precious grace to be born again in the gospel.

This, then, is our last sermon. I will now read in the Old Testament, Genesis chapter 4, from verse 1 to 7. If you have found it, I will read.

And Adam knew Eve his wife; and she conceived, and bare Cain, and said, I have gotten a man from the LORD. And she again bare his brother Abel. And Abel was a keeper of sheep, but Cain was a tiller of the ground. And in process of time it came to pass, that Cain brought of the fruit of the ground an offering unto the LORD. And Abel, he also brought of the firstlings of his flock and of the fat thereof. And the LORD had respect unto Abel and to his offering: But unto Cain and to his offering he had not respect. And Cain was very wroth, and his countenance fell. And the LORD said unto Cain, Why art thou wroth? and why is thy countenance fallen? If thou doest well, shalt thou not be accepted? and if thou doest not well, sin lieth at the door. And unto thee shall be his desire, and thou shalt rule over him.

There are so many things I'd like to tell you this evening, in this, our last meeting, that I don't know where to begin. Early tomorrow morning, I will be on the train to Seoul. I don't think that my heart can easily leave Busan.

Late last night, I spoke with several brothers and sisters, who had received forgiveness of sin through this conference. People who had gone to church for a long time, but had suffered and struggled all alone inside of sin, attended this conference and received forgiveness of sin. When I heard their testimony, of how they received the Lord into their heart, I cannot express in words how my heart glowed. Yesterday evening, I heard testimonies from four people. I know that those four are not the only ones who have such testimonies.

I believe that through this conference He has come unto you to free you from sin because God loves you.

This evening, I'd like to give you a testimony about how my father came to believe in Jesus. My mother passed away on August 14, 1950, immediately after the beginning of the Korean War. We were five brothers and sisters, and our father loved us deeply. My father could have remarried because he was young, and there were even rumors to that effect, but he saw how much heartbreak and sorrow a friend of his had gone through, living under a stepmother. He made up his mind not to remarry, and in hardship raised his five children.

Now we are all grown up, married, and have families of our own. At that time I was leading a small church. My father needed to believe in Jesus, receive forgiveness of sin, and go to heaven, but he refused to listen to the Word. This made my wife and I very uncomfortable in our hearts. When my father came to the countryside, at times he'd bring us a sack of rice, and sometimes he would bring us money because we were living so poorly. Whenever we could, my wife and I would ask my father to believe in Jesus. My father would say, "Kids, don't be like that. I will believe. You believe in Jesus. Why wouldn't I believe in Jesus? I will believe starting this fall."

That's how he answered. Father had many friends in his hometown. When his friends had their 60th birthday parties, or if their children got married, he'd go to their parties, sit around the table, drink, and have pleasant conversations with them. Father enjoyed that very much. A friend of his was turning 60 in the fall, and he thought that it would be impolite to his friend, if he could not drink at the party because he believed in Jesus. That's why he said that this fall he'd believe in Jesus. I couldn't force him to believe, when he said he didn't yet want to believe in Jesus. All I could do was to wait.

Fall would pass and winter would come.

"Father, now believe in Jesus."

"I will definitely start believing next spring."

"Oh, come, now! Why?"

"My friend's son is getting married in the spring, and I can't do that to my friend. After my friend's son gets married, I will believe in Jesus." That's how he postponed it. Finally, 10 years had passed. My father had become old. He was living with my elder brother. One time, my elder brother had to go to Japan on business. Although it was uncomfortable, my father stayed at our house. At that time, he had a bad case of gastric ulcer, and although he did not have a check-up, he was diagnosed as having something close to cancer. The doctor in charge did not recommend surgery. Since my father had already passed seventy, the doctor said we should avoid the surgery and find out a different way to treat him. I knew that my father could not live for long.

"If, as a pastor, I cannot lead my own father to heaven, where can I go and confidently tell others to believe in Jesus?" That thought came to me and I became desperate. One day, I prayed and went to my father. "Father," I said. "Believe in Jesus."

"I believe. Don't worry, I believe." That's what he would always say, but that day, I was not going to just back off so easily.

"Father, you can't go on like this. Our lives are so empty." I was about to start speaking, when my father became angry.

"You, Ock Soo, you, how dare you speak to your father that way!"

I had never before seen my father so angry with me. Strangely, I saw once again that Satan strongly forges resistance when this gospel of life is trying to enter in. It is like that with everyone. When I go out to conduct conferences, some people say that they hate Pastor Park so much and that they want to kill him, for no apparent reason. The Word is right, but they feel insecure. There are a lot of people like that. I don't know why. Then one day, I started to see people's hearts break down before the Word, and many people became born again. Satan opposes when people are about to hear the gospel and become born again. Anyway, my father became extremely upset that day, and I could not say anything else to him. I had to leave. I was so frustrated and troubled that it was unbearable.

At that time, in Daegu, every Monday afternoon, pastors and ministers would come over, and I would teach the Bible. That day was a Monday, so many pastors had come over. As I came out from my father's room, looking downcast, they said, "Oh, Pastor Park, are you not well? Did something bad happen?" They were worried about me.

"Oh, it's nothing like that. The doctor says that my father does not have much time to live. I was asking him to believe in Jesus, and he scolded me. I really hate Satan, who has taken hold of my father's heart." The pastors asked, "Pastor Park, what should we do?"

"Let's pray."

That afternoon, we passed up Bible study, and about 10 pastors and ministers gathered and prayed for my father. The next day, at about the same time we had been praying the day before, my father called out, "Hey, is Ock Soo out there?"

"Yes, Father, I am right here."

"Come in here. My stomach is hurting, and even when I need to go to the bathroom, I am unable. Do you have any medicine?"

I told my wife to go to the pharmacy and buy an enema. My wife was about to go out, when, all of sudden, my father sat up and vomited blood. There was bleeding in his intestines, and the black blood that had accumulated had come out. We were completely stunned. "Ah, now my father is going to pass away," I thought. My wife was crying and did not know what to do. My father closed his mouth and was very quiet. I guess he felt, "Ah, now I will die." We cleaned up the blood with towels and put our father down on fresh blankets.

"Father, how do you feel?" I asked.

"I am okay."

"Honey, bring me a tape recorder," I said to my wife. "Father, elder brother is not here, so if there is something you want to say, please go ahead and say it. We will record it."

"Oh, so you're going to record?"

"Yes."

"Good. There are some things that I've been wanting to say. Let me say them now, before I die."

The tape was 30 minutes on each side, and my father spoke for about an hour. Mentioning something, he said,

"I am very sorry about this to all of you. I was disappointed in you about this and that." And then he said, "When I die, you children do not fight with one another over the little wealth that I have. And finally, when I die, when you bury me, bury me next to your mother. There is a person who will handle my body. I helped him very much during my lifetime, so if you ask him to touch up my dead body, he will not say no."

Father said everything in his heart about the funeral. When the tape was about to end, he finished giving his will. Then I asked him, "Father, when you pass away, we will do the funeral for you exactly as you have said. That will do for your body, but where will your spirit go?"

"I want to go to heaven, but what virtue do I have? What merit do I have? It's too late for me now."

I have never felt as thankful as I was then that our salvation is not by our actions or our good deeds, but by the life of Jesus. I was also very thankful that I was a pastor and could clearly tell anyone about receiving forgiveness of sin and going to heaven. That day, I told my father that heaven is not a place we go to by our deeds. No matter how much God tells us to come to heaven, because we humans do not have the strength, and because we are weak, we become tired and faint as we try. I told him that Jesus came and did all the work for us. For two hours, I told him that we are able to go to heaven through the good deeds of Jesus. I talked to him about how our sins passed over to Jesus, how the blood of Jesus cleansed us from our sins, and how we were saved from sin. Father revealed his true heart. Before that, he'd only say, "Kids, they have good medicine over there. They have good doctors over there." That's how he always thought. And then he would always teach us, saying, "Why are you so stupid? This is how you are supposed to do that."

My father, who had always indulged in worldly ambitions, seemed to have released all those ambitions that had piled in his heart, as he thought of himself standing before death. My father had never gone to church. He came to church only because his son was a pastor, and because my quarters were attached to the chapel. Not once did he come on his own. But that day, Father rejected all the ambitions and doubts that had enveloped his life, and listened to the Word with a pure heart. After a couple of hours, the light upon my father's face began to change.

"I believe. I do believe!" mumbled my father. "Jesus. Thank You. The cross, the cross. Jesus, thank You for taking away all of my sins and for taking care of them on the cross. In a little while, I'll go to Your land. Father, please accept me."

By that time, the brothers and sisters had come in because they knew that my father was about to pass away. As my father closed his eyes and began to pray, their eyes filled with tears. It seemed as if my father would not live long, so we got an ambulance and took him to his hometown. He woke up the next day and said, "Kids, I slept so peacefully yesterday. Won't you sing me some hymns? Pray and sing me some hymns."

My father's heart changed completely. Whoever opens their heart and accepts the gospel of forgiveness of sin can receive forgiveness of sin and become born again if he listens with an open heart. Unfortunately, most people today do not listen with an open heart. That really saddens me.

It seemed as though when he was in his hometown, my father was getting better, so I returned to Daegu. My wife stayed behind to care for him, and one day, my wife called, telling me to come quickly. I went as quickly as I could. I could see that my father was only a few hours away from dying. Many people were there, and Father told me to bring together all of his friends. His friends came. They held my father's hand and cried with grief.

He said, "I can go to heaven because of the Jesus that my second son, Ock Soo, believes in. I'm going ahead, and I'll save some places for you, so you guys believe in the Jesus that Ock Soo believes in. He will tell you about Him and you come along later."

Then he called my cousins over and said, "You guys listen. My throat is dry, and I'm very tired. It's difficult for me to speak, but because you're my nephews, I am speaking to you. When your father died, he died like this. This is how your uncle died. How do you want to die when you die? Believe in the Jesus Ock Soo believes in. Not believing in Jesus doesn't mean you will or will not live well. Don't always think of only money, but believe in Jesus."

He spoke those words and went to sleep. He slept snoring loudly, and the next morning, in his sleep, he was called by our God and went over to the eternal land. The day of his funeral, I put on my funeral suit, went out to the backyard, knelt down and prayed tearfully. The tears flowing from my eyes had two meanings.

One meaning was that I had been such a bad son to my father. After Mother passed away early, he raised five children alone, selflessly sacrificing himself. I wanted to serve that Father by fulfilling my filial duties, but he passed away while I was in the midst of hardship, so I cried tears of apology for not being a better son. The other meaning was thankfulness to God who had saved my father. Folks, my father never went to church, and he never once read the Bible, but when I saw him change, after hearing the gospel, I was so thankful in my heart. I often think about my father.

"Father, I'll go to where you are soon. God, thank You for saving my father."

Folks, why do so many people not know about this simple and easy gospel? There are great pastors, brilliant religious leaders and many famous theologians. They have a lot of knowledge, they are good at helping the poor, volunteering, making offerings and witnessing. However, they only know on the outside, the fact, "My sins have been washed clean through the blood of Jesus Christ," which is the core. Many of them have not been freed from sin. How frustrated God must be, to have such an unworthy person as me stand up here preaching the Word?

As I came here, and saw Busan this time, Busan is not an exception. It is the same as other cities. I have met many people here, people who suffer, go to the mountains to pray, struggle, and do all kinds of strange things, out of sin. But they continue to suffer from sin because they don't know how to have their sins washed clean through the gospel.

I would like to ask the pastors who are here. What do you testify on the podium? Although you say that your sermons can move people, if you cannot save one soul from his conscience, then that sermon is not from God. For those of you who are pastors! If you cannot preach the Word of God to those souls that have been left to you, to have them freed from sin, what will become of them?

How will you bear the responsibility for those souls before God? I hope that the pastors attending here this evening will listen to this. You need to cry out the blood of the cross of Jesus Christ; how that blood can flow into our souls and cleanse us of our sins. Don't just preach this in theory. You must free souls from sin. The theology that you have learned cannot save souls. The effort you put into your church members does not lead them to salvation. They must be born again, through the blood of Jesus Christ that is in the Word of God.

Pastors, ministers, and if there are those who are studying theology to become ministers here this evening, I want you to listen. You bear the responsibility for your flock. You must know what you should testify to your flock. You may be a pastor, but you also may not be born again. If that is your case, then this evening, you must put aside your reputation and say, "I'm a sinner. I know the gospel in theory, but I'm a sinner. I cannot properly testify to souls how to be freed from sin because I, myself, am not freed from sin. Please save me."

You need to seek Him and kneel down before God.

Many powerful servants of God have done this throughout history. Martin Luther did this, and so did John Wesley. They were famous servants of God, but at some point, they came to know that they were not freed from sin. They knew intellectually that on the cross Jesus had washed away their sin, but they realized that their hearts were not freed from sin. There, their hearts broke and crumbled. After they became born again, they were able to minister powerfully. They were able to minister without using worldly ways. We know that the power of the Holy Spirit of God worked in their ministry.

This afternoon, I went to West Busan for an inaugural service. Several cars were to go there together, and because I'd been there once already, my car took the lead. I was able to show the way to the five cars that were following me, and we arrived at West Busan Church safely. How was that so? It was because I had been there before. People who have the experience of having been born again can teach and guide other people to be born again.

Folks, our duty is great. If you have received forgiveness of sin, I hope that you will stop being only a religious person and become a living Christian. I hope that you will become a person who walks with Jesus. I agonized deep in sin, but in 1962, after the day I was freed from sin, I lost the meaning of working for anything else. How can I testify the precious gospel to even just one soul? I had only that heart and amazingly, God opened a path before me, and I was able to do this precious work. Not only with my father, but when I preached the gospel afterward, people realized the gospel and received forgiveness of sin. I saw people change, after receiving forgiveness of sin. Hallelujah! This is a gift that God has freely given unto us.

Let's now talk about Genesis chapter 4. In Genesis chapter 4, it talks about Cain and Abel. We all know this story well. I'm sure you have heard sermons about it a number of times. Adam's elder son, Cain, was very healthy. I think he was very good in every way. After Adam had Cain, Adam said, "Great, the Lord has given me a son," and he was very proud. After having Abel, however, I think Adam was disappointed. It's because the word Abel comes from the root word, "Hebel," which means breath. On a cold morning, if you say "Hooo," you will see your breath coming out of your mouth, right? It means that the person disappears, in vain, like his breath, so the meaning of Abel's name is something in the order of, "emptiness."

In the past, in Korea, when children were born they did not report the birth immediately. Only after 100 days, or a year, would pass, and sometimes, even after several years, would they finally report the birth. In those days, health care was not good, so the infant mortality rate was high. If you recorded a child, who may die, on the family register, when that child died, your heart would be broken, so people delayed reporting. Some children were actually 10 years old, but according to the family register, they were only six years old. There were a lot of cases like that, when we were growing up. It's not like that any longer, of course, but I'm sure people of my age, or even older, understand.

After Adam had Abel, I think he must have thought, "Hmm, will he grow to adulthood?" Adam wasn't even sure whether Abel would live, so he didn't even name him, saying, "Emptiness. Vanity. How vain." Maybe he was saying that, and that's why he started to call him, "Abel, Abel." Compared to Cain, who was so strong and healthy, Abel must have been very weak. It doesn't say that in the Bible, but I think that's how it was. Because Cain was strong, he did the difficult work of digging the ground with wooden sticks, turning it over and sowing the seed. Abel was so skinny, he would take his sheep around and feed them grass. I think he would be trembling in the sun, and when it became evening, he would bring the flock home. That's why his name was "Emptiness."

It seemed he would die soon, but he did not die. He lived. The boys both grew up. After some time, Cain gave the fruits of the ground as an offering to the Lord, and Abel gave the firstlings of the flock and of the fat thereof. The Lord respected Abel and his offering, but He did not respect Cain and his offering. After I read the story, I had the heart, "Gee, why would God do that?" No matter what offering Cain had made, I don't think I would have done that. This is what I would have said, if I were God.

"Hey Cain, get over here."

"What, God, what's wrong?"

"You good-for-nothing, what kind of an offering is that? You call this an offering? Okay, this is your first time so I'll let you off, but if you give another offering like this, next time, I will not accept it. Do a better job next time. Now, go!"

The God of the Old Testament is a very cold God. He turned the offering away without even looking at it, and Cain became angry.

Folks, most people think, as they live spiritual life, that God's heart is the same as theirs, but that is not true. In Isaiah chapter 55, verse 8, it says,

For my thoughts are not your thoughts, neither are your ways my ways. . .

Our thoughts are different from God's thoughts. Do you know why God wrote this story in Genesis chapter 4?

"You may give service, but if you give it in that manner, I will not even look at it. But if you make your offering this way, I shall accept even you." He wrote this in the Bible to teach us that. Do you think He wrote this because He had nothing else to write?

Even today, many people give service before God with all their diligence and with all of their heart, but in their own way. Most people think that the heart of God is the same as their own heart and think, "I heard that even demons listen to you when you beg. Why wouldn't God listen?" They comfort themselves, thinking, "Since I gave service, I'm sure God received it." But He does not even look at certain offerings, and He happily accepts others. Why does He accept certain kinds of offerings and reject others? The reason is simple. He accepts offerings that are like Abel's, and He does not accept offerings that are like Cain's. If you give offerings that are like Cain's, then God does not accept them. However, if you give offerings like Abel, He will accept them. From time to time, when I ask people, "Why did God accept the offering of Abel and reject the offering of Cain?"

Most people say, "It's because Abel gave his offering with diligence, but Cain put no heart into his offering." I can tell what kind of faith they have, when I ask them this question.

A certain man gathered some sons of various government ministers who were in an elementary school and asked them, "What does your father do?" One child answered, "Honk! Honk! Out of my way please!"

"Oh, your father must be the Minister of Transportation!" Another child answered, "Old MacDonald had a farm, E-I-E-I-O."

"Your father must be the Minister of Agriculture and Fisheries!" Another child sang, "This is the way we go to school. Go to school, go to school. This is the way we go to school, early in the morning."

"Oh, your father must be the Minister of Education." This is just a funny story, but it tells how the man could figure out who their fathers were. We can tell a person's heart by listening to his answers to questions. People, who think, "I never work hard enough," in believing God, think that God accepted Abel, and God refused Cain because Abel gave the offering with all of his heart and Cain lacked devotion. People who think, "My problem is that I commit too many sins," think that, although Cain gave an offering, God did not accept it because Cain had sinned. They also think that God accepted Abel because he had not sinned.

However, those explanations are only assumptions. There's no support in the Bible for any of it. The Bible does not say that Cain gave the offering without any diligence, nor does it say that Abel gave his offering with all his heart. Folks, we should not interpret the Bible however we want to. Who do we leave the interpretation of the Bible up to? Do you leave it up to Pastor Ock Soo Park? If you do, you shouldn't. You must leave the interpretation of the Bible up to the Bible. The difference between the offering of Abel and the offering of Cain is not diligence, effort, labor, or zeal. The Bible has described the offerings in an interesting way. Don't just skim over the Bible.

Seek ye out of the book of the LORD, and read: no one of these shall fail, none shall want her mate. . .

That's what it says in Isaiah chapter 34, verse 16. Folks, if you read carefully the words of Genesis chapter 4, verse 3, it says,

. . . Cain brought of the fruit of the ground an offering unto the LORD.

On the other hand, what was the offering Abel gave? We can discover something a bit awkward in this. If it described the offering of Cain as the fruits of the ground, it should have described Abel's offering as simply animals. But if it describes Abel's offering as, "the firstlings of the flock and the fat thereof," then the Bible should describe Cain's offering, not as the fruit of the ground. For example, "He brought cabbages, pumpkins and carrots," and specifically record the names of the things he gave from "the fruit of the ground." The Bible consciously states that one offering was, "the firstlings of the flock and the fat thereof," and the other as the "fruit of the ground." We need to pay attention to this.

God took the dust of the earth and made flesh when He created humans. When our bodies or carnal things are expressed in the Bible, they are often described as dust or the earth. In Ecclesiastes chapter 12, verse 6, it says, "Or ever the silver cord be loosed, or the golden bowl be broken, or the pitcher be broken at the fountain, or the wheel broken at the cistern." This is talking about our bodies. In 2 Corinthians chapter 4, verse 7, it says, "For our light affliction, which is but for a moment, worketh for us a far more exceeding and eternal weight of glory;" which is also talking about our bodies. Thus, "the fruit of the ground" represents what comes forth from us humans; what comes from our bodies. In other words, those things that come from our flesh, from our effort, as humans and from our worldly thoughts. God does not accept the efforts of humans, or anything that may come from humans, no matter what it may be.

On the contrary, why did God accept Abel's offering? The firstlings of the flock, the lamb, represents the first Son of God, Jesus Christ. The fat thereof represents the Holy Spirit. It means that Abel came forth to God relying on Jesus and the Holy Spirit. There are two ways for us to make an offering to God. One is to make the offering through our effort and labor. The other is to make the offering by relying on Jesus Christ. God does not accept the things of the flesh, no matter how beautiful or good they may be.

Because God accepts all things that come through Jesus Christ, not only did He accept Abel's offering, but He accepted Abel as well. On the other hand, not only did God not accept the offering of Cain, but He did not accept Cain either. In Genesis chapter 4 verse 4, we read, "And Abel, he also brought of the firstlings of his flock and of the fat thereof. And the LORD had respect unto Abel and to his offering:"

It says that God accepted Abel along with his offering, and in verse 5, it says that God had no respect unto Cain and his offering. Because God could not accept Cain's offering, He did not accept Cain. And because He accepted the offering of Abel, He was able to accept Abel along with it.

Folks, these are words that greatly shock our spiritual lives today. Most people think that God's heart is like their own, so they think that God will accept them if they try hard and do this or that. God will only see things that do not come forth from Jesus Christ as fake and unworthy, and will reject them, no matter how beautiful and good they may appear, or how precious they are. Those who worship God must do it in spirit and in truth. Jesus must come within us for us to worship in spirit and in truth. For Jesus to come within us, we must receive forgiveness of sin and become born again.

Because most people do not know a lot about the Bible, we see that they live a spiritual life according to their own thoughts. They think that God will accept them, if they do things with zeal, speak in tongues and prophesy. Even in speaking in tongues, there is speaking in tongues that comes from God, but there is speaking in tongues that comes from Satan. There is also zeal that comes from God and zeal that comes from Satan. And in the same way, there is labor that comes from God, and labor that comes from Satan.

Cain made his offering. Cain gave his heart to God. Nevertheless, God could not accept the fruit of the ground that comes from man. Thus, you must receive forgiveness of sin, and you must receive Jesus in your heart, for you to go forth to God through Jesus Christ. Then God can accept you.

Today, many people fall into despair and become disappointed when they try to do something with all their zeal, but fail because they do not know this precious secret. Over the years, I have been to many prisons and have preached the gospel. Amazingly, 70 percent of the criminals are people who once went to church. They were church goers who believed in God. How, then, did they end up in prison? God left them alone to become corrupt because God could not accept their faith.

Folks, why does your heart wallow in despair and disappointment? God cannot accept your prayer, worship, and offerings, unless your sins are washed clean and you receive Jesus into your heart. Some people worship with their emotions, with their feelings, and with burning passion, but God is saying, "I can't accept that." I am telling you, you must truly be born again. Today, we need servants of God who will deliver to others this truth of becoming born again.

Long ago, the Egyptian king, the Pharaoh, had a dream. It was a dream that decided whether the people of Egypt would live or die. There was no one among the many wizards and wise men of Pharaoh who could interpret the dream. They were knowledgeable in dealing with issues such as controlling the floods of the Nile, political problems, or military problems, but they could not interpret the dream. Likewise, today, many people talk about a good religion of relieving the poor, or helping others, since they cannot talk about what they truly need to know, which is how to be born again, and how to receive forgiveness of sin; there are many people wandering around, helpless and in pain.

Loving folks! I hope that you will open your eyes. Open your heart and accept the Word of God. Your eyes must be open toward this precious secret of God and toward the will of God. If you receive forgiveness of sin and become born again by welcoming Jesus Christ into your heart, then you will be a child of God. So even if you pray walking down the street, God hears your prayers. If you're born again, God will accept your life. The Holy Spirit will lead you, but if you are not born again, there is nothing God can accept from you. There are so many people who are deceived into thinking that vain faith is good faith.

That is why we must put aside all things and receive forgiveness of sin through the true gospel, be born again, and have our hearts freed from sin. Also, we must meet the true servant of God. Then I believe your faith will not suffer. It will grow strong and bold. The firstlings of the flock and the fat thereof that Abel gave represents Jesus Christ. God accepts only His Son, Jesus Christ.

Folks, suppose I were to beat up a minister simply because I am stronger than him. The pastors around me try to stop me, saying, "Gee, Pastor, how can you beat him up like that? Don't do that." I beat him up to such an extent that I knock out one or two of his teeth and his cheeks are all swollen. The people around me counsel me, "Please reconcile."

"Okay," I say. "Shall we reconcile? Minister, I am sorry. Let's be friends. Let's just say this never happened." So we shake hands and reconcile. That's easy for me to say, but then are we truly reconciled? I may be at peace because I just beat him up, but the minister will not be at peace.

"How can a pastor beat someone up? He'll pay for this."

"C'mon, Minister. Let's forget about this."

"Alright pastor, I'll do that."

But Minister Choi does not feel reconciled. True reconciliation is not through words. It must be accomplished in the heart. It has to be resolved in the hearts of everyone to have true reconciliation. Even if I apologize to Minister Choi a hundred times, it cannot be true reconciliation unless it is entirely resolved in his heart. True reconciliation depends on whether the hearts are open to it.

"God, I hope that you will forgive me of my sins. I believe in you. Amen." That is not how sin is taken care of.

"Jesus, come into my heart, please. I open my heart, and accept Jesus. Come in, come in." That does not work either. The problem of the barrier between God and us must be taken care of. Then reconciliation can take place and everything can be at peace.

"Jesus was crucified for my sins, and my sins are washed clean." You may know all of that, but if your heart is not resolved, then true reconciliation between God and you will not happen. There is a wall blocking you from God. Through this conference you may have heard all the words of forgiveness of sin. However, you need to be checked one more time, whether your heart is freed from sin.

Suppose I am lecturing at a university about philosophy, mathematics, or English and you are students, listening to my lecture. Whether I steal or murder, I can still give the lecture. Then you would say, "That professor is a horrible person, but he is a good professor," and you would accept my teaching. But folks, as a pastor, not as a professor lecturing on mathematics or English, it will not work, if I give a sermon and you say, "That horrible man!" Why? Because knowledge enters the mind, but faith enters the heart. The heart may say, "He's a horrible person. He's a thief. He should be struck dead by lightning and die," but the lesson, "A + B = C," can still be accepted. Because faith enters the heart, if you say, "That Pastor is a fraud," his words may enter your mind, but not your heart. Spiritual life cannot be lived through learning. It is not an intellectual endeavor. It must enter through the heart. That is what forgiveness of sin is and that is what salvation is. You must meet a true servant of God, if you are to live a proper spiritual life: not a pastor who speaks about great philosophies, emphasizing morals and the law, but servants of God, who speak about how your sins can be forgiven, so your heart can be freed from sin. Only that kind of a servant can connect you with God. I meet servants of God like these from time to time. I hope that many such pastors will emerge from here in Busan. At each church, pastors should not only speak about forgiveness of sin, but souls, who actually receive forgiveness of sin, rejoicing tearfully, should continually be added to the church.

Loving folks, God coldly refused Cain's offering. Unless you, too, are born again through Jesus, God says in the Old Testament, Isaiah chapter 1, that He will not accept you.

> *To what purpose is the multitude of your sacrifices unto me? . . . When ye come to appear before me, who hath required this at your hand, to tread my courts? Bring no more vain oblations . . . your hands are full of blood.*

It says that your hands are full of blood and have been dirtied with sin. God is telling us to pray and make an offering to God, only after we've been washed clean.

Folks, let's worship according to the Word of God, not according to your heart or how you feel, and do not make offerings as you want. I hope you will give gifts and make offerings according to the Word of God.

Loving folks, not long from now, we will have to stand before Jesus. Some people will stand there in joy. Others will stand there in fear.

There is something I would like to say to those of you who have received forgiveness of sin this week. First, your redemption is not through your effort or deeds. It has nothing to do with your deeds. It has nothing to do with how well you obey the Word of God, how well you pray, how well you witness, or how well you make offerings. Forgiveness of sin is connected only with the blood of the cross of Jesus Christ. Satan knows that we are humans, full of blemishes and imperfections. He fixes us to our actions and saps us of our strength. If you do something wrong, he may deceive you, saying, "How can you say that you are saved, when you are doing such terrible things? Have you really received forgiveness of sin? No, you are not born again." Each time, reply, "Get behind me Satan. I am not saved because I am great. I am saved through the blood of Jesus." When Jesus saved you, He did not save you because you were sinless. He delivered you, knowing that you had fallen into sin. Thus, your salvation does not derive from your deeds.

Let's look at another verse in the Bible. Let's read together Ephesians in the New Testament, chapter 3, verse 12.

In whom we have boldness and access with confidence by the faith of him.

That's what it says, doesn't it? No? Okay, then, let's read it again. "In whom we have boldness and access with confidence by not only us believing in Him, but also living perfectly according to our conscience."

Is this right? No. You coming forth to God has absolutely nothing to do with your actions. If you are attached to your deeds when you go out to God, you cannot go to Him. At times you do well, but often you do ill. At times you are good, but often you are evil. If you are thinking of your deeds, you can never go forth to God. There is only one way for you to go out to God, and that is by believing in the blood of Jesus Christ.

"Father God, please do not look upon me, accept me having looked upon Jesus."

You can go out to God with confidence like this anytime. Even though you may lack because Jesus is perfect, you must rely completely on Jesus.

Secondly, if you have received forgiveness of sin, you are a child of God. It's not as if the world acknowledges you because you are a child of God, but there is no need for you to shrink away just because you are not acknowledged.

Once upon a time, there lived a Prime Minister. You may be saying that Pastor Park only knows about Prime Ministers, so that's all he ever talks about. This Prime Minister, too, did not have any children. Finally, late in his life he had a child. It was a daughter. He had been very lonely because he had no children, so he was very pleased to have this daughter. She was very lovely, as she was growing up. Anyway, this Prime Minister was completely taken by his daughter. She was very smart and good at playing the Kayagum, a Korean musical instrument. She was also talented at writing poetry. In the past, women used to get married early. These days, a lot of people turn 20 or 30 and still have not married, but back then, people tried to get their children married as adolescents. Requests were coming in, asking for the hand of the Prime Minister's daughter. Because she was the only daughter in the family, there were many proposals for her. Finally, she became engaged to the youngest son of the sheriff of a village in the Kyungsang Province. On her wedding day, the Prime Minister's daughter cried, unable to forget her father's love.

In those days, they had the extended family system. The sheriff's son had five brothers, all married, and everyone in the family lived together. The Prime Minister's daughter became the youngest daughter in-law.

One day, it was her father-in-law's birthday. Because he was the town sheriff, all the in-laws and relatives were called over for a big party. All the in-laws were invited, and were on their way there. The father of the first daughter-in-law came, and the fathers of the second, third, and fourth daughters-in-law were coming. They were all people of high position, so their arrival was a major event. They would enter the village with their soldiers and flags waving and trumpets blowing. That was how the first in-laws came, and the second in-laws, and so on. Now the party had started, but the Prime Minister was nowhere to be seen. After his daughter had married into this family, she missed her father so much, but back then, they had no phones or taxis like today. She had waited so long for her father, and now he would finally come. Her sisters-in-law were all happy and excited to have their own fathers come, but the Prime Minister still did not come.

When the party was about to end, they received a message saying that the Prime Minister was coming. When they all went out, the Prime Minister was indeed coming, but he was coming on a very small pony, and with no servants. The daughter was very happy to see him and did not know what to do. If it were today, she would have run to him saying, "Daddy!" and clung to him. But since this was long ago, she couldn't do that. Working so hard, she had lost all her heart, looking at her father through the corner of her eye. Even though she was seeing him for the first time in a long time, she could not speak to him freely about what had been going on. Eventually, the party ended, and she had to say goodbye.

Then things began to happen. The four sisters-in-law said, "Your father is a Prime Minister, but did you see the way he was dressed? He looked so shabby." They began to despise and insult the youngest daughter-in-law. She was already struggling with her painful and difficult married life, and it became harder for her to bear. Nevertheless, you can't say that to your husband the way you do today, so it all built up inside of her. She would complain on the inside, "Why did my father come like that today?" Then she comforted herself saying, "Oh, well. He'll come differently next time."

Then there was another party and, once again, all the relatives came. Other people came with their flags waving; soldiers in front of them, with trumpets, making a grand entrance, but once again, this Prime Minister came late and was riding a little pony. The daughter felt resentful toward her father. She said to her father, who was leaving after the party, "I have one request, Father."

"What is it?"

"Father, next time you come, I hope that you come with a lot of people and make a grand entrance."

The Prime Minister said, "Okay, fine."

Then he left. All he said was, "Okay, fine," nothing else, but the Prime Minister's daughter said, "We'll see now. My father is the Prime Minister. If he wants to make a grand entrance, do you think it would be anything like that of the other daughters-in-law's fathers?" One year passed by slowly, and as the day of the party drew closer, the youngest daughter-in-law of the sheriff was waiting for her father to come. Time passed quietly and quickly. The day of the feast finally arrived. From a few days before, the other relatives began to arrive.

Like before, they came with their flags waving, trumpets and flutes blowing, and many soldiers ahead of them, and the whole village became very noisy. The horses were coming into the streets, but the Prime Minister still had not arrived. It was the day of the party, and rain was drizzling down, but the Prime Minister had not arrived. Still the daughter comforted herself, saying, "I asked this favor of my father, and my father loves me. There is no way that he would not do that for me. I guess he's late because he's preparing a huge, grand entrance."

Now the sun was setting, and somebody yelled out, "The Prime Minister is coming!" When she looked afar, the father, for whom she had waited so long, was coming on a tiny, galloping pony just like before. This time because of the rain, he looked pathetic, like a wet dog. The daughter all of a sudden became dizzy and fainted. Her shocked sisters-in-law immediately took her to the back room, and laid her down. The Prime Minister entered the main floor of the room, wiped his wet face with a handkerchief, and talked about this and that. Of course, he was most curious about his daughter. As he was speaking with the relatives, he was thinking to himself, "When will she come out? When will she come out?" But the daughter did not come out.

"Ahem!" He cleared his throat and the atmosphere changed.

"Did something bad happen? Did something upset her? Her own father is here. Why has she not come out? Ah! Last year, when I was leaving, there was a favor she asked of me, but why did she tell me to make such a grand entrance when I came?" Then, he saw that all the other relatives had come wearing fancy, nicely decorated clothes.

"Ahem!" He cleared his throat again. Everyone became quiet, as if a chill were cast upon them.

"You may be sitting here in the living room with me like this, but according to the law, you are not allowed to do this." When he spoke, all the relatives and in-laws, who were sitting there in the living room, began to crawl slowly out into the yard, with their heads down, and began to kneel. In addition, it began to shower, as if the heavens were saying, "Now is the time." This old man, who had come on a small pony, was the only one sitting in the living room. When the people of the village saw that all these so-called elders had their heads bowed, lying on their stomachs in the yard, they began to gossip with one another. Now a small light went on in the kitchen. The other daughters-in-law, who used to despise the youngest daughter-in-law, what could they dare do now, in front of the Prime Minister?

"Oh, no. We're in big trouble. Where is our youngest sister-in-law? Where is she?"

"I heard that she's lying down somewhere because she is sick."

"Really? Let's go to her." All the daughters-in-law went to see their sister-in-law, as she was lying there sick.

"Hey, are you really sick? Go, fetch her some honey water." They were busy massaging and rubbing her and the room became very noisy.

"You should have rested earlier. Gee, I think we made you work too hard. Oh, a person like you, who grew up so preciously." Now the Prime Minister's daughter had no idea what was going on because her sisters-in-law, who always used to pick on her, became so concerned. She felt bad that she was lying down and said, "No, sisters. It's okay."

She opened the door and went out, and saw what was going on. Of course, although she could not express it openly, she could not hide her joy of victory. Inside, she had the smile of complacency. How could she have laughed out loud, "Hahaha?" She acted as if she didn't know, went to the kitchen and turned on the light and tried to work. One sister-in-law came to her and said, "You know, my father has bronchitis, and he gets a cold whenever the weather is bad. How can we leave him in the rain like that?" Saying that, she was about to cry. Another sister-in-law came and said, "You know, my father always suffers terribly from neuralgia."

"Sisters, don't worry. I'll speak to my father."

"Ah, that would be great. That would be just wonderful, if you could do that."

So the Prime Minister's daughter combed her hair, neatly tucked in her clothes, and went out to her father. She gave a big bow and said, "Father, it must have been a difficult trip, coming all the way here. How is Mother doing?"

"Oh, yes. She is doing well." When the Prime Minister saw that his daughter came out, he thought, "Yes, she is satisfied." Then now he knew what his daughter would say, did he not?

"Now you may go. Although I am your father, you must still mind your manners."

"Oh, Father. . . . Oh, Father."

"I told you to go."

"No, what I'm saying is. . . . Father, the fathers of my sisters-in-law are getting soaked in the rain." Only then did the Prime Minister look out into the yard. "Oh, are you all still getting soaked? Then why don't you come in?"

"Yes, your honor." And they all went inside, out of the rain.

That's how it is when you are the daughter of a Prime Minister, but we are the children of God, who created the universe. Do not complain or blame the world because the world does not acknowledge you. Do you know what happens, if just one word comes from our Father's lips? Folks, Pastor Park looks short, and he looks unimportant. Indeed, I may look like this, but do you know what? I'm a prince! A prince! I'm a son of God, His servant. How can you compare me to a daughter of an insignificant Prime Minister? I've freely become the son of God. The world does not acknowledge this. Folks, neither the mayor of Busan, nor the police commissioner came and welcomed me when I came to Busan. Because of that, would I go to City Hall and say to the mayor, "Hey, the servant of God is here! Why didn't you welcome me?" They would call the mental institution right away, so I couldn't say or do anything about it.

Folks, the world may not acknowledge us, but we don't need to shy away because of that. We have received forgiveness of sin and have been born again, through the blood of Jesus Christ, the Son of God. We are the children of God. Hallelujah! So what, if we are poor? If we suffer pain, are despised by others, or are beaten, so what if we are cursed at? Our Father would see it and allow it up to a certain point, but if it became too severe, He would say one word.

"By law you are not allowed to do that!" Do you know what happens if He says this? It doesn't matter whether outside its raining or snowing.

How blessed we are! How did we ever become the servants of God and the sons of God? That's how it is when we live in this world, but do you know what it will be like later, when we go to that land beyond? I cannot tell you every detail about it. Even if I were to tell you, you could not understand. Rather, you would say that I am crazy. The Lord gave us an amazing blessing. I praise the Lord. Because Jesus loves us, He shed His blood and died for us and suffered for us.

"Wider than the ocean.
Higher than the sky.
Deeper than the sea.
The love of my Lord.
I am his child.
Though I may be dirty.
The Lord said,
He would love me always."

Folks! Even though we may not have a fancy home on this earth and even though we may be poor on this earth, we are not the people of this earth. All of our treasures are in that land. People who have received forgiveness of sin can freely enter there.

Loving citizens of Busan! I hope that you receive forgiveness of sin through the blood of Jesus Christ and live a born again life through Him. I'm thankful to Him that, although it has been short, God has given me this chance to speak with you. I feel so much sadness in my heart. It feels as though we have just begun, but it's already time for us to end! Folks, I may be leaving Busan, but God will not leave those of you who have received forgiveness of sin this week. He will be with you forever. I hope that you take all of your matters up with the Lord.

Let's quietly bow our heads and close our eyes. I am ending my sermon a little early, in case there is anyone among you who still has not had your spiritual problems resolved. If there is anyone among you who still has doubt in your heart, or aspects you do not understand, I hope you will have individual fellowship with the servants of God.

Who Is the Gracias Choir?

FIRST PRIZE
14th International Choir
Competition Marktoberdorf
GERMANY 2015

GRAND PRIZE
Riva del Garda International
Choral Competition
ITALY 2014

FIRST PRIZE
Montreux
Choral Festival
SWITZERLAND 2014

The Gracias Choir was founded for the purpose of delivering the hope, love, and heart of God to the world. Every member has given their selves to this dream and they have become a choir led by the heart of God. This has taken them to world famous venues as well as remote parts of the world, where they have performed and touched the lives of presidents, kings, and people of all nations. The Gracias Christmas Cantata, Gracias Easter Cantata, their countless annual performances, and the many music schools the Gracias Choir has established around the world, testify to how Gracias Choir truly is a gift of God that finds new ways of spreading the light and pure joy to everyone they meet.

To make a donation, visit us at
christmascantata.us or call **347-468-6084.**

 Follow the Gracias Choir
on Instagram @gracias_choir

Preaching the Gospel to the Ends of the Earth

GOOD NEWS MISSION

The Good News Mission has been faithfully preaching the gospel of the eternal remission of sins since 1962. It has grown to include over 1,200 churches in over 100 countries. The Good News Mission is very active in leading people to become freed from the heavy burdens of sin that lead people to darkness. It has led them to live new lives of righteousness through Jesus Christ. From evangelizing to young children to national leaders, the Good News Mission has always been on the front lines of spreading the message of the gospel. The Good News Mission holds Bible Crusades in major cities across the world, holds student camps for youths, offers volunteer mission programs, holds Gracias Easter and Christmas Cantatas, and so much more. Many people wandering in sin have found salvation through the Good News Mission. Today, it continues to bring the gospel to the uttermost parts of the world.

CLF
MAHANAIM BIBLE TRAINING CENTER
EXECUTIVE PROGRAM

The Religious Reformation and the Great Awakening movements began with pastors realizing the Gospel's true message of eternal salvation as they studied and returned to the Bible, the Word of God. As the Word filled their hearts, it led them beyond denominations and traditions to deliver the true Gospel all over the world. The CLF Executive Program is igniting a new Great Awakening through an intense, month-long program of studying the Bible, the living Word of God. Join the many pastors returning to the true message of the Gospel and learning the faith to only rely on God. Come and join the CLF Executive Program, and be a part of the work of God that is changing the world through the Gospel!

📅 **Education period** 1 month

✉ **Contact** Philemon Yoo (678) 770-8822
info@clfusa.org
www.clfusa.org

CLF
CHRISTIAN LEADERS FELLOWSHIP

Publications by the Author

How I Became Free from Sin

The best-selling book that touched the lives of millions of people around the world! Romans 3:24 says, "Being justified freely by his grace through the redemption that is in Christ Jesus." Unlock the secret of the forgiveness of sin, and how Jesus made you completely righteous.

Repentance and Faith

Many people believe that repentance is confessing their sins and asking for forgiveness. But because they sin again and again, their hearts are never freed from sin. This book will guide you, step by step, to true Biblical repentance. Never be unsure about repentance again!

Out from Despair

Many people are trapped in sin, although they have always gone to church. The life of being dragged by sin, temptation, despair, condemnation will come to an end. Pastor Park will teach you how to believe in Jesus, where you will be able to overcome all things.

Lectures on the Offerings of Leviticus

Jesus Christ was the final offering for man's sins, but so many people still believe they are sinners because they don't know what Jesus's sacrifice accomplished. This amazing 4-book series reveals never-before-seen insight into the Burnt Offering, Meat Offering, Peace Offering, and Sin Offering in the book of Leviticus. You will discover how God washed, sanctified, and justified us forever!

Navigating the Heart

Instead of living according to their own will, people are dragged by another force. They think, "I shouldn't do this," but are powerless against what is dragging their hearts. After they have fallen into these wrongful things, they don't know how to get out. Pastor Park teaches us about the world of the heart, and how to fill your heart and life with hope and joy.

The Heart Store: A Place Where Hearts Are Sold

What if there was a store where people could come, browse, and purchase any happy heart wanted, whenever they needed to? Pastor Ock Park reveals how to resolve the issues in your heart, and how to live a secure and happy life through receiving a new heart.

Standing on the Field of the Heart

Pastor Ock Soo Park discovered the solution to people's problems and development takes place in one's heart. In this book will teach you to see the world of the heart, and just to plant hope, love, and thankfulness in the field of your heart.

The Amazing Heart Journey

The wisdom of the Bible and world of the heart put in colorful pictures for children to read and change! This delightful and easy to read book will keep your children's attention, and the words of wisdom from Pastor Park will lead their hearts.

WHO IS
PASTOR OCK SOO PARK?

Former President Boni Yayi, Benin

Former President Fernando Lugo, Paraguay

President Edgar Lungu, Zambia

Pastor Ock Soo Park has been preaching the gospel of the forgiveness of sins around the world for the last 57 years. He is the founder of the Good News Mission, which has over 1,200 churches in 100 countries. He has authored 78 books on spiritual life, and five books on mind education. Countless souls have returned to Jesus Christ through his work, and his books have impacted millions of people worldwide. He has also done extensive work for the youth, through the International Youth Fellowship (IYF), delivering to them the heart of God revealed in the Bible. He has also founded the Christian Leaders Fellowship (CLF), which is bringing together Christian leaders of different denominations and backgrounds to unite in spreading the gospel of Jesus Christ.

Pastor Ock Soo Park, preaching to 100,000 people at the Nelson Mandela Stadium in Uganda, at the annual Passover Service

Individual & Family
COUNSELING

We listen to your heart here

We provide counseling on issues such as:

- substance abuse
- parent-child relationship
- domestic violence
- youth issues

Keep in touch with us
We look forward to hearing from you.
1. 888.466.9846

🏛 Church Directory (North America)

Good News New York Church
718-878-4246
300 Nassau Rd, Huntington, NY 11743

Good News Manhattan Church
212-695-1294
2152 3rd Ave, New York, NY 10035

Good News Bronx Church
646-898-9961
685 Morris Park Ave 2nd Fl, Bronx, NY 10462

Good News Brooklyn NY Church
917-526-7498
765 43rd St 1st FL, Brooklyn, NY 11232

Good News Flushing Chinese Church
631-535-1169
134-24 Cherry Ave, Flushing, NY 11355

Good News Atlanta Church
678-473-1594
11000 Rogers Circle, Johns Creek, GA 30097

Good News Atlanta Spanish Church
470-257-6208
2635 Fairlane Drive, 2nd FL, Doraville, GA 30340

Good News Philadelphia Church
215-379-0501
305 Township Line Road, Elkins Park, PA 19027

Good News Chicago Church
847-329-0237
4825 W Jarlath St, Lincolnwood, IL 60712

Good News Washington Church
703-973-7975
7461 Miramar Dr, Manassas, VA 20109

Good News Memphis Church
901-646-0055
764 Chatwood Cove, Memphis, TN 38122

Good News Minneapolis Church
612-367-7774
3000 West Broadway Ave, Minneapolis, MN 55411

Good News Orlando Church
407-900-3442
301 S Oak Ave, Sanford, FL 32771

Good News New Jersey Church
201-857-2516
1075 Queen Anne Road, Teaneck, NJ 07666

Good News Detroit Church
248-608-1409
1181 Harding Ave, Rochester Hills, MI 48307

Good News Indianapolis Church
317-537-7103
383 S Emerson Ave, Indianapolis, IN 46219

Good News Miami Church
954-667-7753
331 NW 65th Way, Hollywood, FL 33024

Good News New Orleans Church
504-602-9930
3720 Saratoga Dr, Metairie, LA 70002

Good News Jacksonville Church
904-646-7885
3850 Beach Blvd, Jacksonville, FL 32207

Good News Boston Church
617-606-3433
180 Blue Hill Ave. #3, Roxbury, MA 02119

Good News Fort Wayne Church
260-444-4918
3316 S Calhoun St, Fort Wayne, IN 46807

Good News Central Church
213-386-0097
3183 Wilshire Blvd, Ste 196 P, LA, CA 90010

Good News Tacoma Church
253-582-3599
10103 South Tacoma Way, Lakewood, WA 98499

Good News Albuquerque Church
3001 Cuervo Dr NE, Albuquerque, NM 87110

Good News Dallas First Church
972-272-4724
1149 N Plano Rd, Garland, TX 75042

Good News San Jose Church
619-559-6287
1548 Curtner Ave, San Jose, CA 95128

Good News San Jose Spanish Church
408-784-0163
1710 Moorpark Ave, San Jose, CA 95128

Good News Las Vegas Church
702-248-0572
2880 Red Rock St, Las Vegas, NV 89146

Good News Salt Lake Church
385-482-0566
829 N Sir Patrick Dr, Salt Lake City, UT 84116

Good News O.C. Church
213-422-8908
3330 W Lincoln Ave, Anaheim, CA 92801

Good News Anchorage Church
907-258-9987
1020 W Fireweed Lane, Anchorage, AK 99503

Good News El Paso Church
3817 Edgar Park Ave, El Paso, TX 79904

Good News Portland Church
503-884-9085
6225 SW Dale Ave, Beaverton, OR 97008

Good News San Antonio Church
210-993-9417
405 Walton Ave, San Antonio, TX 78225

Good News Denver Church
720-319-8067
12640 E Bates Circle, Aurora CO 80014

Good News Kansas Church
816-384-1633
7900 Jarboe St, Kansas City, MO 64114

Good News Hawaii Church
808-223-9681
1219 Keeaumoku St, Suite 400, Honolulu, HI 96814

Good News Houston Church
346-202-4433
2516 Wavell St, Houston, TX 77088

Good News Phoenix Church
575-224-6372
5239 N 17th Ave, Phoenix, AZ 85015

Good News Sacramento Church
916-996-4655
3501 Bradshaw Rd #115, Sacramento, CA 95827

Good News Oklahoma Church
405-535-9553
5801 S Pennsylvania Ave, Oklahoma City, OK 73119

Good News Springfield Church
417-413-1307
3000 N Grant Ave, Springfield, MO 65803

CANADA & CARIBBEAN

Good News Vancouver Church
1-778-608-4230
66-8740 Maple Grove Crescent,
Burnaby, BC V5A 4G5

Good News Ottawa Church
1-819-776-0087
132 Rue Brodeur, Gatineau, QC J8Y 2R2, Canada

Good News Toronto Church
1-416-321-2004
70 Mcgriskin Rd, Toronto, ON M1S 5C5, Canada

Good News Winnipeg Church
1-647-685-6691
1030 Lansdowne Ave, Winnipeg,
MB R2X 1S3, Canada

Good News Jamaica Church
1-876-759-9688
63B Deanery Road, Kingston 3, Jamaica W.I.

Good News Dominican Republic Church
1-809-350-1429
Calle 26 #2, Valle Verde 1, Santiago,
La Republica Dominicana

Good News Haiti Church
509-70-8253-2511
Rue Jeremie #22 Delmas 33, Port-au-Prince, Haiti